ENHANCING ASSESSMENT IN HIGHER EDUCATION

ENHANCING ASSESSMENT IN HIGHER EDUCATION

Putting Psychometrics to Work

Edited by

Tammie Cumming and

M. David Miller

Foreword by Michael J. Kolen

Copublished in association with

ASSOCIATION FOR INSTITUTIONAL RESEARCH
Data and Decisions for Higher Education

Association
of American
Colleges and
Universities

Sty/us

STERLING, VIRGINIA

Sty/us

Published by Stylus Publishing, LLC.
22883 Quicksilver Drive
Sterling, Virginia 20166-2102

Library of Congress Cataloging-in-Publication Data

Names: Cumming, Tammie, 1965- editor. |
Miller, M. David, editor.
Title: Enhancing assessment in higher education : putting
psychometrics to work / edited by Tammie Cumming & M. David
Miller.
Description: Sterling, Virginia : Stylus Publishing, 2017. |
Includes bibliographical references.
Identifiers: LCCN 2017007192 (print) |
LCCN 2017034320 (ebook) |
ISBN 9781620363690 (Library networkable e-edition) |
ISBN 9781620363706 (Consumer e-edition) |
ISBN 9781620363676 (cloth : alk. paper)
Subjects: LCSH: College students--Rating of. |
Educational tests and measurements--Psychological aspects. |
Psychometrics.
Classification: LCC LB2368 (ebook) |
LCC LB2368 .E65 2017 (print) |
DDC 378.1/662--dc23
LC record available at https://lccn.loc.gov/2017007192

13-digit ISBN: 978-1-62036-367-6 (cloth)
13-digit ISBN: 978-1-62036-369-0 (library networkable e-edition)
13-digit ISBN: 978-1-62036-370-6 (consumer e-edition)

Printed in the United States of America

All first editions printed on acid-free paper
that meets the American National Standards Institute
Z39-48 Standard.

Bulk Purchases

Quantity discounts are available for use in workshops and for
staff development.
Call 1-800-232-0223

First Edition, 2017

10   9   8   7   6   5   4   3   2   1

Association
of American
Colleges and
Universities

About AAC&U

AAC&U is the leading national association concerned with the quality, vitality, and public standing of undergraduate liberal education. Its members are committed to extending the advantages of a liberal education to all students, regardless of academic specialization or intended career. Founded in 1915, AAC&U now comprises nearly 1,400 member institutions—including accredited public and private colleges, community colleges, research universities, and comprehensive universities of every type and size.

AAC&U functions as a catalyst and facilitator, forging links among presidents, administrators, and faculty members who are engaged in institutional and curricular planning. Its mission is to reinforce the collective commitment to liberal education and inclusive excellence at both the national and local levels, and to help individual institutions keep the quality of student learning at the core of their work as they evolve to meet new economic and social challenges.

Information about AAC&U membership, programs, and publications can be found at www.aacu.org

ASSOCIATION FOR INSTITUTIONAL RESEARCH
Data and Decisions for Higher Education

The Association for Institutional Research

The Association for Institutional Research (AIR) is the world's largest association of higher education professionals working in institutional research, assessment, planning, and related postsecondary education fields. The organization provides educational resources, best practices and professional development opportunities for more than 4,000 members. Its primary purpose is to support members in the process of collecting, analyzing, and converting data into information that supports decision-making in higher education.

The field of institutional research (IR) is over 50 years old and is embedded in nearly every college and university in the United States and many others around the world. Often working behind the scenes, IR professionals support campus leaders and policy makers in wise planning, programming, and fiscal decision-making covering a broad range of institutional responsibilities. These areas can include research support to senior academic leaders, admissions, financial aid, curriculum, enrollment management, staffing, student life, finance, facilities, athletics, alumni relations, and many others. In addition to providing the data-informed foundation for good decision-making, institutional researchers use the data they collect for governmental reporting and to benchmark their results against similar institutions.

In short, most of the important decisions made on campuses regarding an institution's most vital programs and responsibilities are based on analytics produced by IR professionals. AIR makes sure these professionals are fully equipped to perform their jobs at the highest levels.

For further information, see the following:

Website: www.airweb.org

Telephone: 850-385-4155

E-mail: air@airweb.org

This assessment volume is dedicated to Dr. Earl James "Jim" Maxey

(1935–2016)

"Never give up."

Thank you for your wisdom, guidance, and brilliant contribution to education—and, most importantly, to the many people whose lives you have touched.

CONTENTS

PART THREE: CASE STUDY APPLICATIONS

FOREWORD

This book, *Enhancing Assessment in Higher Education: Putting Psychometrics to Work*, considers the assessment of student learning outcomes in higher education. As Peter Ewell and Tammie Cumming state in chapter 1, the emphasis is on using assessment data "to provide information that will enable faculty, administrators, and student affairs professionals to increase student learning by making changes in policies, curricula, and other institutional programs" (p. 20, this volume). Thus, the emphasis is on using data to make program-based decisions rather than decisions about individual students. These decisions can involve program evaluation, accreditation, and accountability.

I met Tammie Cumming when she was a doctoral student in the educational measurement and statistics program at the University of Iowa. In addition to her graduate training, her significant and varied professional activities include working at ACT, Inc. as a program manager and as director of the Office of Assessment and Institutional Research at the City University of New York–New York City College of Technology. Cumming's training and experience provides her the rare combination of being well versed both in assessing student learning outcomes and in evaluating the psychometric soundness of assessments. I am familiar with M. David Miller's work through his presentations at conferences and his substantial publication record. His career has focused on developing methodology and evaluating the soundness of assessments. Clearly, Cumming and Miller form a very knowledgeable editorial team.

The chapter authors include individuals with substantial experience in developing sound assessments, as well as those who have spent years implementing assessments of student learning outcomes in colleges. With so much practical and technical knowledge involved, it is no surprise that the editors and authors have produced an excellent book on educational assessment in higher education.

Michael J. Kolen
Professor of Educational Measurement and Statistics
The University of Iowa
August 2016

Testing and accountability are now pervasive throughout public and private education from prekindergarten through graduate education. Testing in the K–12 environment can be traced back to the middle of the nineteenth century, and psychometrics, or the science of measurement, can be traced back to early writings of Sir Francis Galton and his student Karl Pearson in the early twentieth century. Thus, there has been a long-established and growing history of assessment, accountability, and psychometrics in the K–12 environment. Assessment and accountability did not experience the same growth in higher education until the latter half of the twentieth century. Nevertheless, assessment and accountability now pervade all levels of the American educational system.

Whereas assessment and accountability are widespread in higher education, psychometrics is a fairly recent issue in higher education receiving attention during the last 30 years (dating back to the First National Conference on Assessment in Higher Education in 1985). However, the importance of having psychometrically sound or quality assessments for accountability has become a high priority for accrediting agencies.

Currently, the Council for Higher Education Accreditation holds eligibility standards for degree-granting institutions or programs through the following regional agencies (see Figure P.1):

- Middle States Commission on Higher Education (MSCHE)
- New England Association of Schools and Colleges (NEASC)
- Higher Learning Commission (HLC)
- Southern Association of Colleges and Schools Commission on Colleges (SACSCOC)
- Western Association of Schools and Colleges (WASC)

The Council for Regional Accrediting Commissions, an umbrella group of all regional higher education accreditors, also includes the Northwest Commission on Colleges and Universities (NWCCU). Each of these regional accrediting agencies maintains rigorous standards for assessment practices.

The intent of this book is to bring together the higher education assessment literature with the psychometric literature. That is, the book focuses on

Figure P.1. Regional accreditation organizations.

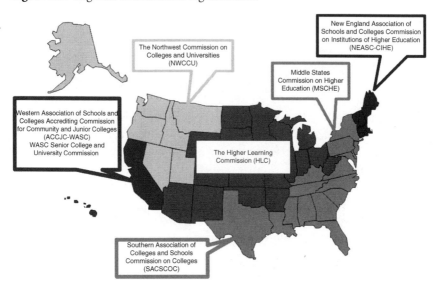

how to practice sound assessment in higher education. The book is divided into the following three parts: overview, assessment in higher education, and case studies. The first six chapters (the first two parts) alternate chapters written by experts in assessment in higher education and experts in psychometrics. The remaining three chapters are applications of assessment practices in three higher education institutions.

Part one provides an overview of assessment in higher education and an overview of psychometric principles. In chapter 1, Ewell and Cumming focus on the history and conceptual basis of assessment in higher education. This chapter also establishes the terminology for many of the assessment terms used throughout the book. In chapter 2, Harris provides the foundation for *validity*, *reliability*, and *fairness* as defined in the *Standards for Educational and Psychological Testing* (AERA, APA, & NCME, 2014). The professional test standards are the latest consensus of the technical standards for testing as defined by the American Educational Research Association (AERA), the American Psychological Association (APA), and the National Council on Measurement in Education (NCME). The first edition of the professional standards was published by APA in 1954 and is also referred to as the *Standards* throughout this text.

Part two emphasizes assessment and psychometric practices in higher education. Accreditation usually distinguishes assessments that are direct measures of student learning from those that are not (indirect). The direct assessments are typically some form of achievement measures that are specifically designed to measure program effectiveness as specified by student learning outcomes (SLOs). Indirect assessments include a wide variety of assessments that measure program effectiveness other than those defined by SLOs. Thus, indirect assessments might include attitudes, beliefs, grade point averages, attendance, or other measures. In chapter 3, Rhodes and Bergeron provide definitions and examples of *direct assessments*. In chapter 4, Twing and O'Malley provide psychometric methods for examining the quality of direct assessments. In chapter 5, Nelson Laird and BrckaLorenz provide definitions and examples of *indirect assessments*. In chapter 6, Miller and Poggio provide psychometric methods for examining the quality of indirect assessments.

Part three includes three chapters that are case studies of assessment practices at three institutions. In chapter 7, Cumming, Deiner, and August describe assessment practices as implemented at City University of New York–New York City College of Technology. In chapters 8 and 9, Wehlburg and Brophy describe assessment practices at Texas Christian University and the University of Florida, respectively.

The language used to describe assessment and psychometrics has varied across authors and over time in the literature. To assist readers, we have provided a glossary of the terminology used in this book. However, even within this book, select chapters have specified and used slightly different definitions. For example, Wehlburg describes specific definitions that have been adopted at Texas Christian University, and Twing and O'Malley point to some disagreements in the literature about how to define *validity*.

Reference

American Educational Research Association, American Psychological Association, & National Council on Measurement in Education. (2014). *Standards for educational and psychological testing*. Washington, DC: American Educational Research Association.

ACKNOWLEDGMENTS

This volume has been a collaborative effort among the contributing chapter authors and the editors of this book. The editors wish to thank each of the contributing authors for their time and dedication to helping faculty and administrators understand the value of educational measurement, psychometrics, and assessment. We are delighted to include the contributions of experts within the fields of educational measurement and higher education assessment.

The editors also acknowledge the faculty and staff with whom we have had rich discussions about improving education through assessment activities, especially those at ABET, ACT, the Association of American Colleges & Universities, City University of New York–New York City College of Technology, Harvard University, Indiana University, National Center for Higher Education Management Systems, Pearson, Texas Christian University, University of Florida, and the University of Iowa.

We also wish to thank our editorial staff at Stylus Publishing. David Brightman offered valuable suggestions.

Finally, most of all, we appreciate the enduring encouragement we received from John, Alex, Matthew, and Anne.

PART ONE

OVERVIEW

HISTORY AND CONCEPTUAL BASIS OF ASSESSMENT IN HIGHER EDUCATION

Peter T. Ewell, National Center for Higher Education Management Systems

Tammie Cumming, City University of New York–New York City College of Technology

I n introducing the volume, this chapter has two main purposes. Its first purpose is to offer a brief historical and analytical review of major events and forces influencing the evolution of assessment from 1985 to date including demands for curricular and pedagogical reform, shifting patterns of accountability, and changes in instructional delivery. At the same time, it examines significant methodological and conceptual issues that have arisen in assessment's short history in such realms as epistemology, assessment design, psychometric properties, politics, and the use of assessment information. Its second purpose is to briefly review key concepts, terms, and approaches that characterize the current practice of assessment. Some of these, to be sure, have historical roots and have evolved a good deal since they were introduced decades ago. But all are robust components of student learning outcomes assessment as practiced today.

The Evolution of Assessment in Higher Education

Assessment of student learning has evolved throughout the years. In this chapter, we explore the historical basis for modern assessment techniques and usage in higher education and accreditation.

Some Intellectual Forbearers

The intellectual roots of assessment as a distinct collection of concepts and methods for gathering evidence extend well before its emergence as a recognizable movement. Some of its most visible forbearers are about undergraduate learning and the student experience in college. Others helped ground its conscious orientation toward action and improvement. Methods and techniques drawn from these established traditions decisively influenced the language and methods of early assessment practitioners and continue to do so today. In parallel, each of these traditions left its distinctive methodological footprint affecting how evidence of student learning is gathered and how it is handled in analysis. The historical discussion in this chapter updates Ewell (2002) and develops additional methodological implications.

Student Learning in College

This research tradition examines collegiate learning as a particular application of educational and developmental psychology. As such, its primary objective is discipline-based hypothesis testing and theory building, though its authors have often drawn implications for practice. Some of this work dates back to the 1930s and 1940s (e.g., Learned & Wood, 1938), and much of it focused on single colleges enrolling 18- to 21-year-old students in traditional residential environments. General maturation and attitudinal development was thus as much an area of interest as cognitive gain (e.g., Chickering, 1969). By the end of the 1960s there was a large enough body of work in this area for Feldman and Newcomb (1969) to synthesize its findings, updated some two decades later by Pascarella and Terenzini in 1991 and again in 2005. On the verge of assessment's emergence in the late 1970s, a trio of volumes was especially influential: Astin's (1977) *Four Critical Years* established the idea of "value added" and promoted the use of longitudinal studies to examine net effects; Bowen's (1977) *Investment in Learning* helped establish a public policy context for assessment by emphasizing the societal returns on investment associated with higher education; and Pace's (1979) *Measuring the Outcomes of College* emphasized the role of college environments and student behaviors, providing the conceptual roots of the National Survey of Student Engagement (NSSE). The contributions of this research tradition to assessment were both theoretical and methodological. Among the most prominent were basic taxonomies of outcomes; models of student growth and development; and tools for research like cognitive examinations, longitudinal and cross-sectional surveys, and quasi-experimental designs.

Retention and Student Behavior

Closely related to research on college student learning, a distinct literature on retention emerged in the late 1960s and the 1970s and had very specific impacts on assessment practice. First, it quickly organized itself around a powerful theoretical model—Tinto's (1975) notion of academic and social integration—which proved equally useful in guiding applied research on student learning. Second, the phenomenon of student attrition constituted an ideal proving ground for new methodologies involving longitudinal study designs, specially configured surveys, and multivariate analytical techniques that were later adopted by many assessment practitioners. Third and perhaps decisively, retention scholarship was *action* research: Although theoretically grounded and methodologically sophisticated, its object was always informed intervention (e.g., Lenning, Beal, & Sauer, 1980). Together, these features yielded an excellent model of applied research that, consciously or unconsciously, many assessment practitioners worked to emulate.

Evaluation and "Scientific" Management

The 1960s and 1970s also saw the rise of program evaluation as an action research tradition. Occasioned by the many large-scale federal programs launched at that time, program evaluation first relied almost entirely on quantitative methods. It was also related to a wider movement toward "scientific" management that quickly found applications in higher education in the form of strategic planning, program review, and budgeting. The kind of "systems thinking" embedded in this tradition demanded explicit attention to student outcomes (e.g., Enthoven, 1970) in order to provide a needed "output variable" for cost–benefit studies and investigations of social return on investment. This tradition also yielded one of the most extensive taxonomies of collegiate outcomes ever produced (Lenning, Lee, Micek, & Service, 1977). Literature drawn from program evaluation further provided assessment with a ready-made set of models and vocabularies (e.g., Light, Singer, & Willett, 1990). Somewhat later, program evaluation began to embrace more qualitative methods (e.g., Guba & Lincoln, 1981). These more "authentic" approaches, which emphasized holistic examination of organizational situations and often employed open-ended interviewing and participant observation, also provided an early language for assessment for those skeptical of overly empirical methodologies.

Mastery Learning

The mastery and competency-based learning movement began in elementary and secondary education, but quickly found postsecondary applications in adult and professional education by the mid-1960s. Because mastery-based designs for learning are entirely based on agreed-upon outcomes, assessing and certifying individual student achievement was always paramount. A related development was the assessment of prior learning (Whitaker, 1989). Corporate assessment centers, meanwhile, were developing ways to examine and certify complex higher order abilities by observing group and individual performances on authentic tasks (Thornton & Byham, 1982). Collectively, these traditions provided the conceptual foundation for "alternative" institutions like Empire State; Evergreen State; Regents College; Antioch College; the School for New Learning at DePaul; and, by far the most influential, Alverno College (Alverno College Faculty, 1979). They also yielded a cadre of early assessment practitioners, skilled in evaluating student portfolios and other authentic evidence of student attainment. Two contributions were especially important for the early assessment movement. First, mastery methods posed an effective alternative to the prominent (and politically popular) "testing and measurement" paradigm that had its roots in K–12 accountability programs. Second, they could boast a track record that proved that assessment in higher education was not just a popular "theory"; it could actually be done.

These four practice traditions and their associated literatures are quite different and only a few in the early 1980s were reading all of them. More significantly, their values and methodological traditions are frequently contradictory, revealing conceptual tensions that have fueled assessment discussions ever since. One is a clash of guiding metaphor between quantitative "scientific" investigation and qualitative "developmental" observation. Others address how assessment is positioned in the teaching–learning process: The "evaluation" and "measurement" traditions, for example, consciously divorce the process of investigating student attainment from the act of instruction in the name of objectivity; "mastery" traditions, in contrast, consider the two inseparable. A final distinction concerns the predominant object of assessment—whether its principal purpose is to examine *overall* program/institutional effectiveness or to certify what a *particular* student knows and can do. As any examination of early assessment citations will show, all four traditions helped shape language and practice in the early 1980s. What is surprising in retrospect is that such disparate scholarly and methodological traditions would come together after more than 30 years as a recognized and reasonably well-integrated amalgam of theory and practice.

Birth of a Movement

Although no one has officially dated the birth of the "assessment movement" in higher education, it is probably safe to propose the First National Conference on Assessment in Higher Education held in Columbia, South Carolina, in the fall of 1985. Cosponsored by the National Institute of Education (NIE) and the American Association for Higher Education (AAHE), the origins of this conference vividly illustrate the conflicting political and intellectual traditions that have been with the field ever since. The proximate stimulus for the conference was a report called *Involvement in Learning* (NIE, 1984). Three main recommendations formed its centerpiece, strongly informed by research in the student learning tradition. In brief, they were that higher levels of student achievement could be promoted by establishing high expectations for students, by involving students in active learning environments, and by providing students with prompt and useful feedback. But the report also observed that colleges and universities as institutions could learn from feedback on their own performances and that appropriate research tools were now available for them to do so.

This observation might have been overlooked were it not consistent with other voices. The first set of voices came from within the academy and focused on curriculum reform, especially in general education. Symbolized by other prominent reports like *Integrity in the College Curriculum* (Association of American Colleges & Universities, 1985) and *To Reclaim a Legacy* (Bennett, 1984), this group's central argument was the need for coherent curricular experiences that could best be shaped by ongoing monitoring of student learning and development. From the outset in these discussions, the assessment of learning was presented as a form of scholarship. Faculties ought to be willing to engage in assessment as an integral part of their everyday work. A concomitant enlightened, but unexamined, assumption was that the tools of social science and educational measurement, deployed appropriately, could be adapted by all disciplines to further this process of ongoing inquiry and improvement.

The second set of voices arose simultaneously outside the academy, consisting largely of state-based calls for greater accountability. In part, these calls were a byproduct of the far more visible attention then being paid to K–12 education, symbolized by the U.S. Department of Education's (1983) report *A Nation at Risk*. In part, it stemmed from a renewed activism by governors and legislatures, based on their growing recognition that postsecondary education was a powerful engine for economic and workforce development. Both themes were apparent in yet another national report, revealingly titled *Time for Results* (National Governors Association, 1986). As it was being issued, states like Colorado and South Carolina adopted assessment mandates requiring public colleges and universities to examine learning outcomes and report what they found. By 1987, when the first stocktaking of this growing policy trend occurred (Boyer, Ewell, Finney, & Mingle, 1987), about a dozen states had similar mandates. By 1989, this number had grown to more than half the states (Ewell, Finney, & Lenth, 1990).

Given this history, the motives of those attending the first national assessment conference were understandably mixed. Many were there under the banner of *Involvement in Learning* (NIE, 1984), seeking reasonable and valid ways to gather information to improve curriculum and pedagogy. At least as many (and probably more) were there in response to a brand new mandate. Clear to all were the facts that they had few available tools, only a spotty literature of practice, and virtually no common intellectual foundation on which to build. Filling these yawning gaps between 1985 and 1988 was a first and urgent task. In beginning this task, practitioners faced the following challenges.

Definitions

The first immediate challenge was that the term *assessment* meant different things to different people. Initially, at least three meanings and their associated traditions of use had to be sorted out. The first and most established had its roots in the mastery-learning tradition, where *assessment* referred to the processes used to determine an individual's mastery of complex abilities, generally through observed performance (e.g., Alverno College Faculty, 1979). Adherents of this tradition emphasized development over time and continuous feedback on individual performance—symbolized by the etymological roots of the word *assessment* in the Latin, *ad + sedere*, "to sit beside" (Loacker, Cromwell, & O'Brien, 1986). A second, far different meaning emerged from K–12 practice, where the term described large-scale testing programs like the federally funded National Assessment of Educational Progress (NAEP) and a growing array of state-based K–12 examination programs. The primary object of such large-scale assessment was not to examine individual learning but rather to benchmark school and district performance in the name of accountability. Its central tools were standardized examinations founded on well-established psychometric principles, designed to produce summary performance statistics quickly and efficiently. Yet a third tradition of use defined *assessment* as a special kind of program evaluation, whose purpose was to gather evidence to improve curricula and pedagogy. Like large-scale assessment, this tradition focused on determining aggregate rather than individual performance and employed a range of methods including examinations, portfolios and student work samples, surveys of student and alumni experiences, and direct observations of student and faculty behaviors. An emphasis on improvement, moreover, meant that assessment was as much about using the resulting information as about psychometric standards.

All three definitions raised explicitly the dichotomy of purpose apparent from the outset: accountability versus improvement. Other differences addressed methods and units of analysis—essentially whether quantitative or qualitative methods would predominate and whether attention would be directed largely toward aggregate or individual performance. Clarifying such distinctions in the form of taxonomies helped sharpen initial discussions about the meaning of assessment (Terenzini, 1989). The taxonomies also helped further a terminological consensus centered on the use of multiple methods for program improvement. The *Standards for Educational and*

Psychological Testing (AERA, APA, & NCME, 2014; subsequently referred to as the *Standards*), the gold standard in educational measurement, notes that assessment is sometimes distinct from testing and refers to a broader process that integrates assessment information with information from other sources or it can consist of a single procedure in which a sample of examinee behavior is obtained and scored in a standardized manner.

Instruments

The second challenge faced by early assessment practitioners was to quickly identify credible and useful ways to gather evidence of student learning. Virtually all available instruments were designed to do something else. Ranging from admissions tests like the ACT college readiness assessment and the Graduate Record Examinations, through professional registry and licensure examinations, to examinations designed to award equivalent credit, none of the available testing alternatives were really appropriate for program evaluation. Their content only approximated the domain of any given institution's curriculum and the results they produced usually provided insufficient detail to support improvement. But this did not prevent large numbers of institutions—especially those facing state mandates—from deploying them.

In the period from 1986 until 1989, the major testing organizations quickly filled the instrument gap with a range of new purpose-built, group-level examinations aimed at program evaluation—all based on existing prototypes. Among the most prominent were the ACT Collegiate Assessment of Academic Proficiency (CAAP), the Educational Testing Service (ETS) Proficiency Profile (formerly known as the Academic Profile), and a range of ETS Major Field Achievement Tests (MFAT). Student surveys provided another readily available set of data-gathering tools, especially when they contained items on self-reported gain. Although many institutions designed and administered their own surveys, published instruments were readily available including the CIRP Freshman Survey and follow-up surveys, the College Student Experiences Questionnaire (CSEQ), and a range of questionnaires produced by organizations like ACT and National Center for Higher Education Management Systems.

The principal appeal of off-the-shelf tests and surveys was their ready availability—a property enhanced when the first comprehensive catalogues of available instruments appeared (Smith, Bradley, & Draper, 1994). Faced with a mandate demanding immediate results, most institutions felt they had little choice but to use such instruments, at least in the short term. But there were also growing doubts about the wisdom of this approach (Heffernan, Hutchings, & Marchese, 1988), stimulating work on more authentic, faculty-made assessment approaches in the coming years.

Implementation

The third challenge faced by early assessment practitioners was lack of institution-level experience about how to carry out such an initiative. One concern here was cost and, as a result, some of the first how-to publications addressed financial issues (Ewell & Jones, 1986). Others considered the organizational questions involved in establishing an assessment program (Ewell, 1988). But absent real exemplars, the guidance provided by such publications was at best rudimentary. Enormous early reliance was therefore placed on the lessons that could be learned from the few documented cases available. Three such early adopters had considerable influence. The first was Alverno College, whose abilities-based curriculum designed around performance assessments of every student was both inspiring and daunting (Alverno College Faculty, 1979). The second was Northeast Missouri (now Truman) State University, which since 1973 had employed a range of nationally normed examinations to help establish the "integrity" of its degrees (McClain, 1984). The third was the University of Tennessee–Knoxville, which under the stimulus of Tennessee's performance funding scheme became the first major public university to develop a comprehensive multimethod system of program assessment (Banta, 1985). These three cases were very different and provided a wide range of potential models.

In the late 1980s, a second wave of documented cases emerged, including (among others) James Madison University, Kean College, Kings College, Ball State University, Miami-Dade Community College, and Sinclair Community College—many of which were responding to new state mandates. To a field hungry for concrete information, these examples were extremely welcome. More subtly, they helped define a standard approach to implementing a campus-level program, which was widely imitated.

This founding period thus generated some enduring lines for assessment's later development. One addressed concept development and building a coherent language. The purpose here was largely to stake out the territory—although much of this early literature was, frankly, hortatory, intended to persuade institutions to get started. A second line of work concerned tools and techniques. A third strand comprised case studies of implementation, supplemented by a growing body of work addressing practical matters like organizational structures and faculty involvement. Finally, accountability remained a distinct topic for comment and investigation, looking primarily at state policy, but shifting later toward accreditation.

Into the Mainstream

By 1990, predictions that assessment would quickly go away seemed illusory. Most states had assessment mandates, although these varied in both substance and the vigor with which they were enforced. Accrediting bodies, meanwhile, had grown in influence, in many cases replacing states as the primary external stimulus for institutional interest in assessment (Ewell, 1993). Reflecting this shift, more and more private institutions established assessment programs. These external stimuli were largely responsible for a steady upward trend in the number of institutions reporting involvement with assessment. For example, in 1987 some 55% of institutions claimed they had established an assessment program on ACE's annual *Campus Trends* survey. By 1993, this proportion had risen to 98% (although the survey also suggested that most such efforts were only just getting started). Clearly, at least for administrators, assessment was now in the mainstream. But "entering the mainstream" meant more than just widespread reported use. It also implied consolidation of assessment's position as a distinct and recognizable practice.

An Emerging Modal Type

As institutions scrambled to "implement assessment," it was probably inevitable that they evolved similar approaches. And despite repeated admonitions to ground assessment in each institution's distinctive mission and student clientele, they approached the task of implementation in very similar ways. As an initial step, most formed committees to plan and oversee the work. Following widespread recommendations about the importance of faculty involvement, most comprised faculty drawn from multiple disciplines. But partly because the pressure to implement was so great, assessment committees rarely became a permanent feature of governance or of academic administration.

The clear starting task of these committees, moreover, was to develop an assessment plan. Often, such a product was explicitly required by an accreditor or state authority. Equally often, it was recommended by a consultant or by the burgeoning how-to literature of practice (e.g., Nichols, 1989). The resulting plans thus often had a somewhat formulaic quality. Most, for example, included (a) an initial statement of principles, (b) a list of stated learning goals for general education and for each academic program, (c) a charge to departments to find or develop a suitable assessment method (frequently accompanied by a list of methods to be considered), and (d) a schedule for data collection and reporting. Implementing such plans, in turn, often involved the use of specially funded pilot efforts by volunteer departments. Keeping track of implementation and reporting, moreover, often demanded use of a tabular or matrix format (Banta, 1996) and this, too, became a widespread feature of the standard approach. Methods, meanwhile, were healthily varied, including available standardized examinations, faculty-made tests, surveys and focus groups, and (increasingly, as the decade progressed) portfolios and work samples.

A Literature of Practice

In assessment's early days, practices and experiences were recorded in a fugitive literature of working papers, loosely organized readings in *New Directions* sourcebooks, and conference presentations. But by the early 1990s, the foundations of a recognizable published literature could be discerned. Some of these works were by established scholars who summarized findings and provided methodological advice (Astin, 1991; Pace, 1990). Others tried to document assessment approaches in terms that practitioner audiences could readily understand (Erwin, 1991; Ewell, 1991). Still others continued the process of documenting institutional cases—of which there were now many—in standard or summary form (Banta & Associates, 1993).

The establishment of the movement's own publication, *Assessment Update*, in 1989 was also an important milestone—providing relevant commentary on methods, emerging policies, and institutional practices. As its editorial board envisioned, its contents were short, practical, and topical—providing the field with a single place to turn for ideas and examples. *Assessment Update*'s existence also provided an important alternative to established educational research journals for faculty-practitioners who wanted to publish. This supplemented the already-established role of *Change* magazine, which provided an early venue for assessment authors and continued to regularly print assessment-related essays (DeZure, 2000). Through its Assessment Forum, moreover, AAHE issued a range of publications, building first upon conference presentations and continuing in a set of resource guides (AAHE, 1997). In strong contrast to the 15 previous years, assessment practitioners in 2000 had a significant body of literature to guide their efforts that included systematic guides to method and implementation (e.g., Palomba & Banta, 1999), well-documented examples of campus practice (Banta, Lund, Black, & Oblander, 1996), and comprehensive treatises integrating assessment with the broader transformation of teaching and learning (e.g., Mentkowski & Associates, 2000).

Scholarly Gatherings and Support

Initiated on a regular annual cycle in 1987, the AAHE Assessment Forum was by 1989 *the* conference for practitioners, providing a regular gathering place for scholarly presentation and exchange. Sessions developed for the forum required formal documentation and often ended up as publications. The forum also maintained professional networks, promoted sharing of ideas, and provided needed moral support and encouragement. The latter was especially important in assessment's early years because there were few practitioners and they were isolated on individual campuses. Other conferences arose at the state level including (among others) the South Carolina Higher Education Assessment (SCHEA) Network, the Washington Assessment Group (WAG), and the Virginia Assessment Group (VAG)—often directly supported by state higher education agencies. Some of these state-level groups published regular newsletters updating members on state policy initiatives and allowing campuses to showcase their programs. When the AAHE Assessment Forum ceased with the demise of its parent organization, its place was soon taken by the Assessment Institute in Indianapolis, with attendance figures topping 1,500. This gathering was joined by other important conferences at North Carolina State University; Texas A&M; and California State University, Long Beach by 2010.

A "Semi-Profession"

Although assessment remained largely a part-time activity, entering the mainstream also meant a rise in the number of permanent positions with assessment as a principal assignment. Position titles like assessment coordinator, with formal job descriptions, are now commonplace, usually located in academic affairs or merged with institutional research. The creation of such positions was in large measure a result of external pressure to put recognizable campus programs in place so that accreditors could notice them. Certainly such roles helped build badly needed local capacity and infrastructure.

Early conversations, meanwhile, considered the advisability of creating a national professional organization for assessment similar to the Council for Adult and Experiential Learning (CAEL). A strong consensus emerged to maintain assessment as an "amateur" activity—undertaken by faculty themselves for the purpose of improving their own practice. Avoiding excessive professionalization was important because it promoted later linkages with the scholarship of teaching. But large and growing numbers of individuals on college and university campuses, often without conscious choice, have nevertheless adopted careers identified primarily with assessment as a distinguishable field.

For assessment as a whole, one clear result of this evolution today is an established community of practice that in some ways resembles an academic discipline. Among its earmarks are an identifiable and growing body of scholarship; a well-recognized conference circuit; and a number of subdisciplines, each with its own literature and leading personalities. Those doing assessment, moreover, have evolved a remarkably varied and sophisticated set of tools and approaches and an effective semiprofessional infrastructure to support what they do. These are significant achievements—far beyond what numerous early observers expected.

Why Didn't Assessment Go Away?

In assessment's first decade, the question "When will it go away?" was frequently posed. This was largely because the movement was diagnosed by many as a typical "management fad," like Total Quality Management (TQM) or Management by Objectives (MBO), that would quickly run its course (Birnbaum, 2000). Yet assessment has shown remarkable staying power and has undoubtedly attained a measure of permanence, at least in the form of a visible infrastructure. Several factors appear responsible for this phenomenon. Probably the most important is that external stakeholders will not let the matter drop. State interest remains strong, fueled by demand-driven needs to improve "learning productivity" and by burgeoning state efforts to implement standards-based education in K–12 education (Ewell, 1997). Accreditation organizations, meanwhile, have grown increasingly vigorous in their demands that institutions examine learning outcomes, though they are also allowing institutions more flexibility in how they proceed (Eaton, 2001). Market forces and the media are not only more powerful but also far more performance conscious and data hungry than they were three decades ago. Assessment has thus become an unavoidable condition of doing business: Institutions can no more abandon assessment than they can do without a development office.

The last 20 years have also seen a revolution in undergraduate instruction. In part, this results from technology. In part, it reflects the impact of multiple other "movements" including writing across the curriculum, learning communities, problem-based learning, and service-learning. Together, these forces are fundamentally altering the shape and content of undergraduate study. These changes are sustaining assessment in at least two ways. Most immediately, new instructional approaches are forced to demonstrate their relative effectiveness precisely because they are new. Assessment activities are therefore frequently undertaken as an integral part of their implementation. More subtly, the very nature of these new approaches shifts the focus of attention from teaching to learning. In some cases, for instance, direct determination of mastery is integral to curricular design (O'Banion, 1997). In others, common rubrics for judging performance are required to ensure coherence in the absence of a more visible curricular structure (Walvoord & Anderson, 1998). Assessment has thus been sustained in part because it has become a necessary condition for undertaking meaningful undergraduate reform—just as the authors of *Involvement in Learning* foresaw.

Defining the Territory

Although familiar elements of the academic landscape like *teaching*, *courses*, and *degrees* have evolved some reasonably common meanings through continuing use, distinctions among such concepts as *outcomes*, *learning*, *assessment*, and *effectiveness* remain relatively underdeveloped. But discussing learning outcomes sensibly requires an approach that can appropriately distinguish

(a) different levels of analysis, (b) different kinds of "results" of an academic experience, and (c) different perspectives or viewpoints. One way to begin to make sense of this topic conceptually, therefore, is to think systematically about each component of the core concern of student learning outcomes. Doing so first requires discussion of what is meant by an *outcome* and how this is different from other dimensions of activity. Second, it demands distinctions among units of analysis—at minimum, individual students and aggregations of students grouped by characteristic, academic program, or institution. Third, it requires one to distinguish learning from other kinds of "good effects" that students may experience as a result of participating in a postsecondary experience. Fourth, it necessitates explicit consideration of how we know whether (and to what degree) any of these results has occurred, and to what causes we can attribute them. A brief tour of the terminology associated with assessment is provided next, organized around two categories—attributes of collegiate results and attributes of assessment approaches and evidence (key terms are noted in italics).

Attributes of College Results

The definitions that follow are merely the central tendencies of a large and diffuse literature that has evolved over many years. Readers should be aware that some of these terms are defined differently by different authors and some remain contested. But they are nevertheless reasonably consensual across a wide body of practice within the learning outcomes tradition. A glossary is also provided within this volume.

"Outcomes" Versus "Outputs"

Although an *outcome* in current academic usage is clearly the result of institutional and student activities and investments, there is a fair degree of conceptual consensus that not all results are properly considered outcomes. Numbers of graduates, numbers of teaching hours generated, or instances of service or research products are clearly results of what an institution of higher education does. But they are more commonly defined as *outputs* of higher education. An output is the result of program participation that specifies types, levels, and targets of service and is often measured as a count. Other dimensions of institutional or program performance like *efficiency* or *productivity* are equally the results of what an institution does, and assessing them may be important for evaluative purposes. But they are not the same thing as outputs. This latter kind of performance constitutes the central conceptual foundation of what has come to be called *institutional effectiveness*, which examines the extent to which an institution as a whole attains the performance goals that it establishes for itself. Although outputs and performance are predominantly institution-level concepts, outcomes are only visible at the institutional level by aggregating what happens to individual students. An *outcome*, therefore, can be most broadly defined as something that happens to an individual student (hopefully for the better) as a result of her or his attendance at an institution of higher education and/or participation in a particular course of study. Outcomes are usually measured with a test or an assessment.

Learning as a Special Kind of Outcome

Similarly, relevant and valuable outcomes are not confined to learning because students can benefit from their engagement in postsecondary study in many other ways. Additional *behavioral outcomes* that may result include employment and increased career mobility, enhanced incomes and lifestyles, the opportunity to enroll in more advanced educational studies, or simply a more fulfilled and reflective life. Presumably these are related to learning in some way, and evidence that students have obtained such benefits is often used by institutions as a proxy for instructional effectiveness. But the learning outcomes literature emphasizes that such subsequent experiences should not be confused with actual mastery of what has been taught. Although equally an outcome and frequently examined by institutions, student *satisfaction* with the university experience should also not be confused with learning. Certainly, satisfaction is important—especially if it is related to *motivation* and *persistence* (and therefore continued opportunity to learn). *Student learning outcomes*, then, are properly defined in terms of the particular levels of knowledge, skills, and abilities that a student has attained at the end (or as a result) of her or his engagement in a particular set of teaching/learning experiences.

Learning as "Attainment"

When *learning* is defined in terms of the levels of *attainment* achieved, it requires learning outcomes to be described in very specific terms. Although institutions, disciplines, and professions vary considerably in the ways (and the extent to which) learning outcomes are described, several broad categories are usually distinguished. *Knowledge* or *cognitive outcomes* generally refer to particular areas of disciplinary or professional content that students can recall, explain, relate, and appropriately deploy. *Skills outcomes* generally refer to the learned capacity to do something—for example, think critically, communicate effectively, collaborate productively with colleagues, or perform particular technical procedures—as either an end in itself or a prerequisite for further development. *Attitudinal* or *affective outcomes*, in turn, usually involve changes in beliefs or the development of certain values—for example, empathy, ethical behavior, self-respect, or respect for others. Learned *abilities* or *proficiencies* typically involve the integration of knowledge, skills, and attitudes in complex ways that require multiple elements of learning. Examples include leadership, teamwork, effective problem-solving, and reflective practice. All such taxonomies require institutions or programs to define *learning goals* or *learning objectives* from the outset as guides for instruction and as benchmarks for judging individual student attainment. Expressed in terms of *competencies*, moreover, such goals describe not only what is to be learned but also the specific levels of performance that students are expected to demonstrate. *Certification* or *mastery*, in turn, implies that these specific levels have actually been attained, generally indicated by a credential or award of some kind. Finally, the relationship among these various outcomes is frequently portrayed through a *qualifications framework*—for example, the Lumina Degree Qualifications Profile (DQP).

"Learning" as Development

In many cases, assessment addresses student learning not just in terms of attainment, but in terms of *growth* or *enhancement*. This construction not only emphasizes the unique contribution of the educational program to current levels of student attainment but also requires some knowledge of what levels of attainment characterized a given student before enrollment. *Value added*, *"before–after,"* and *net effects* are terms frequently used to describe such longitudinal ways of looking at development. This perspective, of course, need not be confined to student learning. For example, many educational programs base their claims of effectiveness on things like enhanced income, changes in career, or even increased satisfaction. From the standpoint of quality assurance, both attainment and development may be important. Certification of specific levels of knowledge, skill, or ability for a given program completer—for example, in the form of a licensure examination—is thus intended to guarantee that the certified individual is able to perform competently under a variety of circumstances. Evidence of this kind is claimed as especially important for employers seeking to hire such individuals or the clients who seek their services. Evidence about value added or net effects, in contrast, will be especially important elements of quality for prospective students who are looking for institutions or programs that will benefit them the most, or for policymakers and the public who seek maximum payoff for the resources that they have invested.

But the classic approach to assessing learning gain—testing students on entry, then retesting them at exit—poses perplexing conceptual issues and formidable methodological problems. Conceptually, it can be argued, a pretest is simply silly because students have not yet been exposed to the subject being tested (Warren, 1984). The terminology of *value added*, moreover, suggests a mechanistic view of education in which students are viewed as products and learning merely additive. Actually determining growth, meanwhile, entails multiplicative sources of measurement error and can sometimes lead to real misinterpretation of underlying phenomena (Baird, 1988; Banta, Lambert, Pike, Schmidhammer, & Schneider, 1987; Hanson, 1988). Because classic test-retest is so difficult to implement in practice, a frequently used alternative is an analytical model based on multivariate statistical controls. Here, a given student's actual performance on an assessment is compared to a "predicted" performance estimated from scores obtained on other assessments (e.g., admissions tests) and additional demographic descriptors.

Attributes of Assessment Approaches and Evidence

Most assessment work involves the collection and use of aggregated information about student abilities (either in absolute or value-added terms). But assessment methods are also used to certify individual students for the award of credentials or credits. Both of these can be examined from the point of view of attainment against established standards (*criterion-referenced assessment*) or from the standpoint of how the performance of an individual or group compares to others' (*norm-referenced assessment*). The term *evaluation* also commonly refers to evidence-gathering processes that are designed to examine program- or institution-level effectiveness. But the object of evaluation usually extends beyond learning outcomes to examine a much wider domain of institutional performance. Finally, all of these applications can be undertaken from a *formative* standpoint (i.e., to advise or improve performance) or from a *summative* standpoint (i.e., to judge performance for a decision or the record).

Validity and Reliability

All assessment measures are in some way flawed and contain an error term that may be known or unknown. In general, the greater the error, the less precise—and therefore less useful—the measure. But the level of precision needed depends on the circumstances in which the measure is applied. Measures are *reliable* when they yield the same results consistently over time or across settings. Assessment measures need to be founded on reliable measurement procedures, but they also need to be designed to operate under less-than-ideal measurement conditions. Uses or interpretations of measures are established as *valid*, in turn, when they yield results that faithfully represent or describe the property or properties that the assessment is intended to measure within a specific context. Note that a measure can be used for multiple purposes. Consequently, validity is a property of the use or interpretation rather than the assessment or test. Historically, four types of validity were generally considered. *Construct validity* is present when the assessment accurately addresses the ability that it is supposed to address. *Content validity* is present if all the elements of the ability (or domains) are examined and in the proper balance. *Predictive validity* is present if results of the assessment enable confident predictions to be made about future test taker behavior when deploying the ability in question. *Face validity*, although not considered a form of validity in the measurement literature despite the name, is present if the assessment looks like it measures what it is supposed to measure to most observers. More recently, the meaning of *validity* has evolved in high-stakes situations such as accountability and has come to embrace the appropriateness of the evolving uses and interpretations, which is frequently termed *consequential validity* (Messick, 1988).

The latest revisions to the *Standards* reflect the current consensus that validity is a unitary concept that should be established with multiple sources of evidence. The different types of validity evidence are considered under the broad term of *construct validity* to include *content, response process, structure, relations to other measures,* and *consequences* (AERA, APA, & NCME, 2014). This is further discussed in chapters 4 and 6 of this volume.

Types of Assessment Approaches

Assessment approaches and instruments like the ones addressed in this volume are of many kinds and there is no generally accepted taxonomy that embraces them all. Among the most common, however, are the following. *Standardized examinations* typically address cross-cutting attributes such as communications skills, quantitative reasoning, and critical thinking or specific disciplinary content areas. They are "standardized" because their construction allows valid comparisons to be made across performances occurring in different settings (e.g., institution, program). Standardized examinations, in turn, are typically *forced choice* in which a single response set is provided for each item, only one of which is correct. More rarely, they contain *constructed response tasks*, which require the respondent to write essays or short answers of some kind that must be physically scored. Evaluating these requires use of a *rubric* or *scoring guide*, which is typically a matrix of attributes of the work to be scored and a range of scores to be assigned (generally of four to five points for each). Rubrics or scoring guides can also be applied to other pieces of student work (or *artifacts*) such as essays, performances (e.g., a musical performance or medical procedure), oral reports, exhibits, and so on that are generated as special assignments or in regular coursework. Sometimes such artifacts are assembled in a *portfolio* that contains multiple examples drawn at the end of a student's academic career or at different points within it to show growth.

Evidence and Outcomes

Differences in concept and terminology are also apparent when describing the informational results of an assessment. Here, terms like *measurement* and *indicator* are frequently used, implying that legitimate assessment should yield only quantitative results. Measurements, however, are only a special kind of *evidence*, which has come to predominate as the descriptive term for assessment results in quality assurance contexts. Evidence can embrace the results of both quantitative and qualitative approaches to gathering information, both of which can be useful in examining learning. At the same time, the term *evidence* suggests both the context of making and supporting a case and the need to engage in consistent investigations that use multiple sources of information in a mutually reinforcing fashion. But to count as evidence of student learning outcomes, the information collected and presented must go beyond self-reports provided by students and graduates through such means as surveys and interviews or employment placements to include the direct examination of student work or performance.

This brief tour of the territory of student outcomes assessment can only scratch the surface of the myriad terms and techniques that this volume covers. By providing an overview of concepts and terminology, though, it may help readers link these elements around a coherent whole.

Conclusion: A Prime Directive

This volume is intended to provide comprehensive and detailed coverage of tools and approaches to assessing student learning outcomes in higher education. As readers peruse this rich body of material, it is important to continually bear in mind the overriding purpose of assessment: Provide information that will enable faculty, administrators, and student affairs professionals to increase student learning by making changes in policies, curricula, and other institutional programs, and to ensure these changes are actualized through pedagogy and student experience. This is less a method than a mind-set, and it has several relevant dimensions.

First, the animating motives for assessment should reside within institutions and programs themselves. Far too much assessment in higher education is undertaken at the behest of government bodies and accreditors instead of arising from a genuine interest and concern on the part of institutions and their faculties about what is happening to their students (Kuh et al., 2015). Although accountability is important and the tools and techniques addressed in this volume can help institutions and programs discharge this responsibility appropriately, assessment should not be approached with accountability as its sole purpose. This, in turn, implies that the stance of an assessment should be proactive rather than reactive: The questions that it seeks to answer should be generated by members of an academic community itself, not some outside body.

Second, assessment should always be characterized by a commitment to go wherever the evidence suggests with respect to drawing conclusions or taking action. This may seem obvious, but all too often, expressed conclusions are affected by preconceived notions about how students are experiencing a teaching–learning situation or how faculty members want or expect them to behave. A familiar example is the widespread surprise that greeted NSSE results reporting that most students spend only about half as much time studying and preparing for class than faculty expect (NSSE, 2000).

Third, those practicing assessment in whatever form should bear in mind a number of admonitions about how to proceed, which counteract some of the many myths that the field has encountered over its 30 or more years of evolution. Ironically, these are best expressed as negatives—things that assessment should emphatically not be about. They are as follows:

- *Not "measuring everything that moves."* In part stimulated by accreditors, it is a common misperception that assessment is about gathering as much data as possible about as many things as possible. This can be a recipe for frustration. Rather, the limited assessment energy that an institution or a researcher can devote to the topic should be carefully allocated to questions that are carefully focused, directed toward matters that are considered important, and that will result in genuine improvement.

- *Not just "checking up after the fact."* Assessment is indeed about outcomes, so concentrating attention on end results is appropriate. But if outcomes data are all that are collected, assessors have no information about what caused or occasioned the results obtained, and therefore have no information about how to intervene or improve. Data about educational processes and student experiences should therefore always accompany information about educational outcomes so that causal inferences about what is responsible for the latter can be made.

- *Not searching for "final" answers.* Like the results of any research, conclusions suggested by assessment are always provisional; they may be overturned by later inquiry, and they need to be consistently revisited and tested in the light of newer evidence. More important, the questions raised by each successive cycle of inquiry are at least as important as their results because they sometimes suggest new lines of research and data collection that had not been considered before.

- *Not always being as precise as possible.* Certainly assessment is a science and, as such, its practitioners should strive for accuracy and precision insofar as this is possible. But the real admonition is to be as precise as necessary, given the question being asked and the level of precision required to take action in response. The well-known aphorism about inappropriate method, "measure it with a micrometer, mark it with chalk, and cut it with an axe" captures the difficulty nicely (quoted in Coduto, 2001). Appropriate levels of precision will thus vary by circumstance including how much information is needed to make a particular decision and the urgency of the action to be taken.
- *Not ever expecting to be done.* Finally, assessment should not, under any circumstances, be regarded as a closed enterprise that ends with definitive answers. The process is never entirely finished; rather, assessment is an important part of a continuous improvement cycle (see Figure 1.1). As previously discussed, each answer begets new questions to be pursued, and the resulting spiral of inquiry continues to generate new insights and associated actions. Although this can seem frustrating, it is a fundamental property of scholarship. And scholarship, after all, is what the practice of assessment should model and embody.

Although the topical coverage of this volume is both comprehensive and detailed regarding theory and technique, readers must never forget that the

Figure 1.1. Continuous improvement cycle.

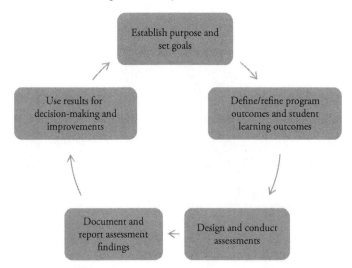

foundational values of assessment lie in action and improvement. As assessment techniques evolve, every assessment approach is a means to an end, and each end is different. Returning to the basic question to be answered or pedagogical problem to be addressed is always a basic prerequisite to effective assessment.

References

Alverno College Faculty. (1979). *Assessment at Alverno College.* Milwaukee, WI: Alverno.

American Association of Higher Education. (1997). *Learning through assessment: A resource guide for higher education.* Washington, DC: Author.

American Educational Research Association, American Psychological Association, & National Council on Measurement in Education. (2014). *Standards for educational and psychological testing.* Washington, DC: Author.

Association of American Colleges & Universities. (1985). *Integrity in the college curriculum: A report to the academic community.* Washington, DC: Author.

Astin, A. W. (1977). *Four critical years.* San Francisco, CA: Jossey-Bass.

Astin, A. W. (1991). The changing American college student: Implications for educational policy and practice. *Higher Education, 22*(2), 129–143.

Baird, L. L. (1988). Value added: Using student gains as yardsticks of learning. In C. Adelman (Ed.), *Performance and judgment: Essays on principles and practice in the assessment of college student learning* (pp. 205–216). Washington, DC: U.S. Government Printing Office.

Banta, T. W. (1985). Use of outcomes information at the University of Tennessee, Knoxville. In P. T. Ewell (Ed.), *Assessing educational outcomes: New directions for institutional research #47* (pp. 19–32). San Francisco, CA: Jossey-Bass.

Banta, T. W. (1996). The power of a matrix. *Assessment Update, 8*(4), 3–13.

Banta, T. W., & Associates. (1993). *Making a difference: Outcomes of a decade of assessment in higher education.* San Francisco, CA: Jossey-Bass.

Banta, T. W., Lambert, E. W., Pike, G. R., Schmidhammer, J. L., & Schneider, J. A. (1987). Estimated score gain on the ACT COMP exam: Valid tool for institutional assessment? *Research in Higher Education, 27,* 195–217.

Banta, T. W., Lund, J. P., Black, K. E., & Oblander, F. W. (1996). *Assessment in practice.* San Francisco, CA: Jossey-Bass.

Bennett, W. J. (1984). *To reclaim a legacy: A report on the humanities in higher education.* Washington, DC: National Endowment for the Humanities.

Birnbaum, R. (2000). *Management fads in higher education: Where they come from, what they do, why they fail.* San Francisco, CA: Jossey-Bass.

Bowen, H. R. (1977). *Investment in learning.* San Francisco, CA: Jossey-Bass.

Boyer, C. M., Ewell, P. T., Finney, J. E., & Mingle, J. R. (1987, March). Assessment and outcomes measurement: A view from the states. *AAHE Bulletin,* 8–12.

Chickering, A. W. (1969). *Education and identity.* San Francisco, CA: Jossey-Bass.

Coduto, D. P. (2001). *Foundation design: Principles and practices* (2nd ed.). Upper Saddle River, NJ: Prentice-Hall.

DeZure, D. (Ed.). (2000). *Learning from change: Landmarks in teaching and learning in higher education from Change Magazine 1969–1999.* Washington, DC: American Association of Higher Education.

Eaton, J. S. (2001). Regional accreditation reform: Who is served? *Change: The Magazine of Higher Learning, 33*(2), 38–45.

Enthoven, A. C. (1970). Measures of the outputs of higher education: Some practical suggestions for their development and use. In G. B. Lawrence, G. Weathersby, & V. W. Patterson (Eds.), *Outputs of higher education: Their identification, measurement, and evaluation* (pp. 51–58). Boulder, CO: Western Interstate Commission for Higher Education.

Erwin, T. D. (1991). *Assessing student learning and development.* San Francisco, CA: Jossey-Bass.

Ewell, P. T. (1988). Implementing assessment: Some organizational issues. In T. W. Banta (Ed.), *Implementing outcomes assessment: Promise and perils, new directions for institutional research #59* (pp. 15–28). San Francisco, CA: Jossey-Bass.

Ewell, P. T. (1991). To capture the ineffable: New forms of assessment in higher education. *Review of Research in Education, 17,* 75–126. Washington, DC: American Educational Research Association.

Ewell, P. T. (1993). The role of states and accreditors in shaping assessment practice. In T. W. Banta & Associates (Eds.), *Making a difference: Outcomes of a decade of assessment in higher education* (pp. 339–356). San Francisco, CA: Jossey-Bass.

Ewell, P. T. (1997). Accountability and assessment in a second decade: New looks or same old story? In AAHE, *Assessing impact: Evidence and action. Presentations from the AAHE Conference on Assessment & Quality* (pp. 7–22). Washington, DC: Author.

Ewell, P. T. (2002). An emerging scholarship: A brief history of assessment. In T. W. Banta & Associates (Eds.), *Building a scholarship of assessment* (pp. 3–25). San Francisco, CA: Jossey-Bass.

Ewell, P. T., Finney, J. E., & Lenth, C. (1990). Filling in the mosaic: The emerging pattern of state-based assessment. *AAHE Bulletin, 42,* 3–7.

Ewell, P. T., & Jones, D. P. (1986). The costs of assessment. In C. Adelman (Ed.), *Assessment in American higher education* (pp. 33–46). Washington, DC: U.S. Government Printing Office.

Feldman, K. A., & Newcomb, T. M. (1969). *The impact of college on students.* San Francisco, CA: Jossey-Bass.

Guba, E. G., & Lincoln, Y. S. (1981). *Effective evaluation: Improving the usefulness of evaluation results through responsive and naturalistic approaches.* San Francisco, CA: Jossey-Bass.

Hanson, G. R. (1988). Critical issues in the assessment of value added in education. *New Directions for Institutional Research*, No. 59 (Implementing Outcomes Assessment: Promise and Perils), *15*(3), 53–67.

Heffernan, J. M., Hutchings, P., & Marchese, T. J. (1988). *Standardized tests and the purposes of assessment.* Washington, DC: American Association of Higher Education.

Kuh, G. D., Ikenberry, S. O., Jankowski, N. A., Cain, T. R., Ewell, P. T., Hutchings, P., & Kinzie, J. (2015). *Using evidence of student learning to improve higher education.* San Francisco, CA: Jossey-Bass.

Learned, W. S., & Wood, B. D. (1938). *The student and his knowledge.* New York, NY: Carnegie Foundation for the Advancement of Teaching.

Lenning, O. T., Beal, P. E., & Sauer, K. (1980). *Retention and attrition: Evidence for action and research.* Boulder, CO: National Center for Higher Education Management Systems.

Lenning, O. T., Lee, Y. S., Micek, S. S., & Service, A. L. (1977). *A structure for the outcomes and outcomes-related concepts.* Boulder, CO: National Center for Higher Education Management Systems.

Light, R. J., Singer, J. D., & Willett, J. B. (1990). *By design: Planning research on higher education.* Cambridge, MA: Harvard University Press.

Loacker, G., Cromwell, L., & O'Brien, K. (1986). Assessment in higher education: To serve the learner. In C. Adelman (ed.), *Assessment in American higher education: Issues and contexts* (pp. 47–62). Washington, DC: Office of Educational Research and Improvement, U.S. Department of Education.

McClain, C. J. (1984). *In pursuit of degrees with integrity: A value-added approach to undergraduate assessment.* Washington, DC: American Association of State Colleges and Universities.

Mentkowski, M., & Associates. (2000). *Learning that lasts: Integrating learning, development, and performance in college and beyond.* San Francisco, CA: Jossey-Bass.

Messick, S. (1988). *Meaning and values in test validation: The science and ethics of assessment.* Princeton, NJ: Educational Testing Service.

National Governors Association. (1986). *Time for results.* Washington, DC: Author.

National Institute of Education, Study Group on the Conditions of Excellence in American Higher Education. (1984). *Involvement in learning: Realizing the potential of American higher education.* Washington, DC: U.S. Government Printing Office.

National Survey of Student Engagement. (2000). *The NSSE 2000 report: National benchmarks of effective educational practice.* Bloomington: National Survey of Student Engagement, Indiana University.

Nichols, J. O. (1989). *Institutional effectiveness and outcomes assessment implementation on campus: A practitioner's handbook.* New York, NY: Agathon Press.

O'Banion, T. (1997). *A learning college for the 21st century.* Washington, DC: American Council on Education, Oryx Press.

Pace, C. R. (1979). *Measuring the outcomes of college.* San Francisco, CA: Jossey-Bass.

Pace, C. R. (1990). *The undergraduates: A report of their activities and progress in the 1980s.* Los Angeles: Center for the Study of Evaluation, University of California.

Palomba, C. A., & Banta, T. W. (1999). *Assessment essentials.* San Francisco, CA: Jossey-Bass.

Pascarella, E. T., & Terenzini, P. T. (1991). *How college affects students.* San Francisco, CA: Jossey-Bass.

Pascarella, E. T., & Terenzini, P. T. (2005). *How college affects students, volume 2: A third decade of research.* San Francisco, CA: Jossey-Bass.

Smith, M. K., Bradley, J. L., & Draper, G. F. (1994). *Annotated reference catalog of assessment instruments, catalogs A–G.* Knoxville: Assessment Resource Center, University of Tennessee–Knoxville.

Terenzini, P. T. (1989). Assessment with open eyes: Pitfalls in studying student outcomes. *The Journal of Higher Education, 60,* 644–664.

Thornton, G. C., & Byham, W. C. (1982). *Assessment centers and managerial performance.* New York, NY: Academic Press.

Tinto, V. (1975, Winter). Dropout from higher education: A theoretical synthesis of recent research. *Review of Educational Research, 45,* 89–125.

U.S. Department of Education, National Commission on Excellence in Education. (1983). *A nation at risk: The imperative for educational reform.* Washington, DC: U.S. Government Printing Office.

Walvoord, B. E., & Anderson, V. J. (1998). *Effective grading: A tool for learning and assessment.* San Francisco, CA: Jossey-Bass.

Warren, J. (1984). The blind alley of value added. *AAHE Bulletin, 37*(1), 10–13.

Whitaker, U. (1989). *Assessing learning: Standards, principles, and procedures.* Chicago, IL: Council on Adult and Experiential Learning.

2

THEORY AND PRINCIPLES OF EDUCATIONAL MEASUREMENT

Deborah J. Harris, ACT, Inc.

Higher education professionals typically make use of a variety of assessments, from standardized tests used as a piece of information in the admissions and placement process, to classroom assessments used to assign course grades to students at the end of a semester. There are a wide variety of assessment types, from multiple-choice tests, to projects, to collections of work or portfolios, to surveys and observation checklists. Regardless of the type of assessment, they are given to inform some decision.

If the results of an assessment, such as the scores from a test, are not going to be used to inform some action, there is little point in administering the assessment. If no differential decisions are made, the data add nothing to the decision process, and again, there seems little gain in administering the assessment. The decisions themselves can range from obtaining an estimate of the current level of knowledge from a student or group of students to know where to start instruction, to assessing knowledge of the contents of a chapter in an introductory psychology course, to determining if a program of study has the anticipated outcomes for students who enroll and complete it. Regardless of the magnitude of the decision or the scope of individuals it impacts, to be an effective part of the decision-making process, the assessment needs to have two basic characteristics: validity and reliability.

Reliability in measurement refers to consistency in scores; validity refers to the support provided for any interpretations of uses of the assessment data accurately measuring what they are intended to represent. With extremely rare exceptions, it is not possible to look at an item or a question and determine if it belongs to an assessment that will lead to good decisions based on reliable and valid test scores. The context of the decision, and therefore what you intend the scores to represent, is of utmost importance, and a test that leads to reliable and valid test scores for one purpose may be completely inappropriate for a different purpose. It is the particular use of data (test scores, inventory score, personality type, etc.), and not the data itself, that is considered when evaluating validity.

If, for example, you are interested in developing or using an assessment intended to aid in the evaluation of a mathematics program, you might recognize that a science item, or a request to submit a tape of a student playing a clarinet, might not be relevant, but it is highly likely that a single math item could not be so easily judged. An item that in isolation appears to measure higher order thinking on the part of the examinee may turn out to be rote recall if the same item was used as an example in the textbook and may even measure less than that if the assessment is one in which students are allowed access to their textbook during the examination/administration.

Even looking at the entire assessment in and of itself is not sufficient. A test consisting of a series of math problems may be appropriate for assessing prerequisite skills for placement into a series of course modules but not have adequate (representative) coverage to serve as a final exam in a different course. In order to evaluate whether an assessment will lead to reliable and valid data to facilitate the desired decision, the user needs to consider the type of evidence he or she is trying to ascertain. In the previous example of wishing to evaluate a mathematics program, the first step would be to closely examine the outcomes one was looking for, the curriculum the program was intended to cover, and the stated objectives of the program. The next step would be to evaluate the items on the assessment to determine if they were aligned with those objectives and whether the overall coverage was appropriate, neither including extraneous material nor leaving out important content.

The items, individually and as a whole, would also need to elicit the skills one was desirous of observing at the end of the program. The administration conditions and the scoring of the assessment would also need to be considered. Data would need to be collected to demonstrate that reliability and validity for the intended use of the assessment scores was indeed present and appropriate for the intended decisions. There is no universal requirement around the level required for reliability or validity: The use and stakes help dictate what is appropriate. The level of rigor for a classroom test would likely be less than that needed for an assessment to determine if the desired outcomes from an entire program of study were achieved.

In the same way that there is no fixed value of a reliability or validity coefficient to use as a criterion, it also needs to be kept in mind that reliability and validity are not static and need to be constantly monitored. An assessment that is adequate for program evaluation at one point in time may not be at a later point in time if, for example, the curriculum evolves, or the test items become compromised, or the characteristics of students enrolling in the program change over time. Changing the prerequisites for enrolling in a program can also change the benefits, or likely outcomes, attributable to the program. If, for example, performing a particular skill is now required to enter a program of study, students completing the program would be able to demonstrate that skill, but it would not be appropriate to use exhibition of that skill as an outcome to determine the effectiveness of the program. In addition to all the issues around specifying the decisions one wishes to make, and evaluating assessments to ensure the resulting data interpretations align with the decision context, it also needs to be kept in mind that regardless of how reliable or valid assessment data appear to be in a particular context, information in addition to assessment data should be taken into consideration in informing a decision. A particular program of study may indeed lead to some desirable outcome but may be prohibitively expensive or require decades of student time to complete and therefore not be practical to implement for other reasons. If the majority of a class scores below chance on a multiple-choice final exam, it may be because the students really do not know the required material, but it could also be the course objectives were confusing or poorly executed.

Examination of data in addition to test scores, such as attendance on the part of both the students and the instructor, may help in interpreting the test scores and assigning semester grades. Assessment data are one important piece of information to inform many decisions in the higher education arena, but it is only one piece. To assist practitioners in maximizing the value of assessment data, the *Standards* (American Educational Research Association [AERA], the American Psychological Association [APA], and the National Council for Measurement in Education [NCME], 2014) offers guidance.

The *Standards*

The *Standards* provides a framework for discussing validity and reliability and is intended to guide practitioners in best practices in the development and use of assessments (see, e.g., Wise & Plake, 2015). The *Standards* was sponsored by three leading organizations in the development and application of assessments and in interpreting assessment data (the AERA, APA, and NCME), and the individual chapters were written by teams of assessment professionals with expertise in the appropriate area and were reviewed numerous times by members of all three organizations, with the end result being a document that guides test developers and users in the current best practices of the industry. Several versions of the *Standards* have been developed over the years, with new editions commissioned when it is thought the field has changed sufficiently to require new guidelines, including new developments in testing practice, new legislation affecting assessment, availability of new assessment tools such as the prevalence of iPads or other school-issued devices to students, new threats from a test security perspective, changes in testing populations such as increasing need for translated or transadapted tests, or when assessment data are used to inform new decisions that were previously viewed as outside its purview.

Adherence to the *Standards* is not a legal requirement in the sense that it is not illegal to, for example, fail to follow one or more particular standards. However, many recommendations in the *Standards* are written with an eye to requirements that laws, statutes, and judicial decisions do impose, such as the Americans with Disabilities Act (see AERA, APA, & NCME, 2014). Not all standards are relevant to each assessment context or event, nor are all standards equally important in different contexts. The *Standards* is intended "to promote sound testing practices and to provide a basis for evaluating the quality of these practices" (AERA, APA, & NCME, 2014, p. 1). Those individuals and organizations involved in developing, administering, interpreting, and using the results of assessments should be familiar with and do their best to adhere to the recommendations in the *Standards*.

The three foundational chapters of the *Standards* deal with validity, reliability and precision of scores in general, and fairness. The chapter on validity provides an overarching or general standard, as well as 25 specific standards. The reliability chapter provides one overarching standard, and 20 additional, more specific standards. The final foundational chapter deals with fairness in testing. The *Standards* views fairness as a validity issue, intended to protect those taking and using assessments. The fairness chapter also has one overarching standard followed by 20 more specific standards.

Validity is typically regarded as the most important property of an assessment, though it is actually a function of score use. On the surface, it is easy for most people to understand that to assess statistics knowledge at the completion of an entry-level statistics course an assessment consisting of dates and events that occurred in American history would not be appropriate. But it is probably more difficult to assess if the questions are actually assessing statistics or some other trait, such as whether the context of a problem requires background information irrelevant to the statistical equation allegedly being assessed. A problem intending to assess the student's ability to compute an average might be presented in a sports context where knowing there are three outs per team in an inning of baseball is necessary to correctly solve the problem, or the vocabulary might be such that reading ability is also being (indirectly) assessed. Poorer readers might then be earning lower scores not because they do not know the statistical content, but because they are having difficulty understanding the questions due to reading load. Poorly written questions that make it difficult to understand what is being asked, or questions that provide clues to the correct answers to those who have not mastered the material, also make it problematic to interpret the resulting scores as indicators of mastery of the subject matter.

In addition to inappropriate individual questions, the overall test or assessment needs to be considered. The test needs to support the purpose in giving the assessment. If it is to assess knowledge in a course, the coverage of material on the test needs to be appropriate to the content of the course. This does not mean every single fact or equation mentioned in the book or the class needs to be covered; rather, a sampling that is representative of the course content would be sufficient. Note that if the intent of the test is to assess only material covered since a previous test, only covering that material is appropriate. If the test is intended to cover material from throughout the semester, some coverage of material from earlier sections of the course is appropriate. Including material that was not covered in class, meaning it was not included in the course objectives, would not be appropriate in a test designed to measure the course content. However, seeing if material learned in the course can be applied in a novel context likely is appropriate, such as when a test question asks a student to apply a formula in a setting not explicitly covered in the textbook, assuming that being able to generalize the use of the formula was one of the course objectives.

The administration and scoring of the test also need to be considered in determining if the test scores are really a measure of what one intends them to be. Is the mechanism to record responses so novel or complex it prevents students from accurately demonstrating knowledge they actually have? Is the test too long for the time needed for competent students to complete? Are responses being graded on neatness where the scores are intended to represent only accuracy? And so on.

A test that provides scores that validly indicate the amount of basic statistics concepts a student knows may be an invalid measure of some other trait, such as general mathematical knowledge. Prior to starting construction of a test, one needs to decide how one wishes to use the assessment scores. This may not be as obvious as it appears at first. Deciding one wants to create a final for a statistics course begs the question of what the test score is supposed to indicate. Open book tests may indicate, in part, how familiar the student is with the text. Open note tests may partially indicate how good a student's notes are. Reusing examples worked in class on an exam may result in scores that include memorization skills or class attendance as a component of the score. Including new problems on an exam may indicate if a student can apply concepts to novel problems. Is it important to know if the students can explain why they are doing an operation or is it only important that they know which operation to do and can execute it correctly? Knowing what the resulting scores are supposed to indicate influences the development of the assessment in terms of what content appears on the test and the type of items that are used (problems where students produce the correct answer, problems where they select the correct answer, problems where they look at a solution and indicate the errors present). How important is speed of work as a component in demonstrating knowledge or completing a task? What aids are permitted (notes, textbook, calculator, ability to search the Internet)? What are the test conditions: Is it a take-home test, a group activity, a proctored exam? Many additional decisions need to be made, but all these decisions should be informed by the intended use of the assessment scores.

To continue the example, for a score to be useful as an indicator of the statistics knowledge a student has after completing a course, the score should be consistent. This means a score should not include a large component of random error or variance that is not due to the construct one is trying to measure. This consistency in scores is influenced by many of the components affecting validity, such as whether a test is speeded or if students have adequate time to complete it, whether the items are well written, or whether the items are of appropriate coverage and difficulty level for the intended score use. Various reliability formulas are used to compute score consistency. Some of these formulas require only one administration of a test, some require two administrations of either the same or an equivalent form of the test, and some consider raters if the test requires a student to generate (as opposed to select) a response. (See chapter 6 of this volume for more information on types of reliability and how to compute reliability coefficients.)

Fairness is a basic concept of assessment that is more difficult to articulate than either validity or reliability, but the intent of the *Standards* chapter is that all those taking and using assessments are treated equitably. This refers to all aspects of the assessment process, from considering fairness in the purpose of testing, constructing test items and instruments, and interpreting and using test scores. According to the *Standards*, fairness is a validity issue and needs consideration throughout the assessment process.

There are many interlocking pieces involved in developing an assessment, regardless of the stakes of the assessment. The magnitude of the decisions, or impact, based on the resulting assessment data may influence the resources brought to bear on each aspect. The *Standards* provides a set of comprehensive guidelines covering aspects of assessment from the initial assessment design and development, through administration and subsequent interpretation and reporting of assessment results. Although there are differences in the resources available to a classroom instructor making a chapter quiz for her students and a group of professors trying to develop a common assessment to support an accreditation review, the same basic steps are followed in deciding what to assess, developing the assessment, administering and scoring the assessment, and making decisions based on the assessment results. Reading through the *Standards* provides guidance at all levels on best practices to follow, regardless of the particular situation.

Validity

The first foundational chapter of the Standards focuses on validity. Validity is best viewed as a property associated with assessment use, and not the assessment itself. A multiple-choice test built around a chapter in a textbook may be a fine choice for assessing a unit in a college class but have inadequate coverage as an evaluation tool for a college program of study, or even the course in its entirety. Validation consists of accumulating evidence to support a use or an interpretation of assessment results and encompasses all aspects of assessment including the content of the instrument itself, the administration conditions, the scoring process, and the way results are reported. The full magnitude of how researchers have defined and categorized *validity*; how it has been conceptualized; how various types of evidence have been compiled, consolidated, and evaluated; and common pitfalls in validity arguments are well beyond the scope of this chapter. (The interested reader is referred to Kane, 2006a, 2006b; Lissitz and Samuelsen, 2007; Markus and Borsboom, 2013; and Messick, 1989, among others, for a deeper dive into validity issues than this chapter can provide.) However, although the implementation can be very complex, the articulation can be quite simple: Do you have evidence that your assessment results (scores) are appropriate for the interpretation you are making based on them?

For example, suppose you are interested in developing an assessment to show students are benefiting from a particular course of study. The wrong approach is to convene a panel of professors to start writing items. The preferred approach is to thoughtfully consider what *benefiting* means in this context. Does it mean students know more content after coursework than before? Does it mean students who complete the course of study can reason in a way similar to that of professionals in that field? Or that they are sought after for jobs in the field? The goal is to define a measureable outcome. Once one knows what outcome he or she wants to achieve, one needs to determine what would provide evidence of that outcome. For example, consider a scenario where a desired outcome of a course of study is to create lifelong readers. It is not practical to literally assess lifelong readers, which would involve following participants for their lifetime and determining if indeed they remained *lifelong readers*, however that was defined. Perhaps an acceptable substitute would be graduates who read more than some benchmark five years after they completed the program or who respond on a survey that they spend three or more hours a week reading. The issue here is not that everyone needs to define a desired objective in the same way. Rather, one defines the learning outcomes one wishes to achieve and clearly articulates them in a way that is feasible and practical to measure. Then the assessment needs to be aligned with those outcomes to help ensure the scores can be interpreted appropriately (in this example, as an indicator of whether the graduate is a lifelong reader). A traditional test is not the only way to assess an outcome, and in many cases, it may be clumsy or ineffective. But there are also many situations where an assessment is appropriate and an effective evaluation tool.

Relevant questions in building an assessment include considerations of what factors influence a score. In the earlier example of the effectiveness of a program of study, an assessment that students do well on if they have completed the course of study and do not do well on if they have not completed the course is not the intent. Basically, this would just be an indication of whether a student completed the course of study, and registration or attendance data could indicate that more efficiently. Instead, the goal is to articulate what particular outcomes should happen as a result of effective participation and administration of the program, such as increased knowledge in the subject area or a change in behavior. The goal is to define the desired outcomes of the program of study, such as increased skill in interpreting graphical data, and then create an assessment around those outcomes. The assessment could then be administered to students who did and did not complete the course of study, and it could be determined if those who complete the course of study score higher on the desired outcomes (in this example, were students who completed the course better at answering questions on interpreting data from graphs than students who did not complete the course?).

The *Standards* discusses evidence based on different types of data. In university settings, content-related evidence is generally important, as there is typically a component of mastery of knowledge in some area. Validity evidence can be based on test content: Do the tasks or items on the assessment align with the stated goals? For example, if the goals are to assess mastery of a biology course: Does the content of the test provide balanced coverage of the course curriculum, not overemphasizing or underemphasizing subjects in ways that are not representative? Evidence can also be accumulated through relationships to other assessments. For example, scores from a Spanish 101 test that correlate well with other assessments of Spanish mastery and correlate poorly with assessments of general reasoning or test wiseness provide support for the assessment scores to be a measure of Spanish mastery and not an assessment of Spanish mastery confounded with other constructs. Practically, it is unlikely that a test will be a completely pure assessment of any single trait, or that the resources exist to rule out the influence of every other construct, such as reading ability, background information, general intelligence factor, or speed of work. However, likely confounding attributes, such as reading ability or familiarity of the testing conditions (e.g., novel item type, testing on an unfamiliar device, or speededness), should be considered and ruled out as factors contributing substantially to the assessment scores (presuming, of course, these are not components of constructs and outcomes one is intending to measure). It is highly unlikely that any assessment will include everything everyone thinks should be included and nothing any of them think is unnecessary. In general, one is looking for evidence to support one interpretation and to rule out others; for example, if one wishes to know if a particular course of study is successful in instilling certain knowledge, ways of thinking, the ability to apply concepts to novel situations, and so on in students who complete the course. Once an assessment has been identified or constructed that can measure these outcomes, the assessment may be administered in two different approaches. The first approach is administering the assessment to students at the beginning and end of completing the course of study. The second approach is to administer the assessment to students who are alike in other ways but some have completed the course and some have not. The specifics vary by the context, but if the assessment can measure the desired outcomes, the assessment results can be used as one component in evaluating the program. This chapter focuses on assessments, but additional factors, such as cost, undesirable outcomes if any, and students in large numbers switching majors after completing the course, must also be considered.

Other types of data used to validate use of assessment scores include looking at what variables help predict the assessment scores and what variables the assessment scores help predict. Scores on a placement exam might logically predict subsequent course grades. Scores on an end-of-course exam might be predicted by performance on chapter quizzes. The validity chapter in the *Standards* provides a broad discussion of the different types of validity evidence commonly used. The chapter also provides a discussion on integrating the validity evidence, cementing the notion that validity is not a dichotomy—that one has it or not—but, instead, is a matter of degree: Does a preponderance of evidence support a specific use of the assessment scores, and, given the context, is the evidence that has been examined sufficient? Some types of evidence are easier to gather than others, but may be more or less relevant to the particular context. Where the decisions are high stakes and not easy to reverse, care must be taken not only to collect evidence but also to collect the appropriate types of evidence. For a classroom quiz where scores will be used to determine whether to go on to the next section of a unit or spend another day reviewing the current section, the effort put into validating the score use may be relatively low: If scores are low and one stays on the current section in the next class period and students seem to need that review given their questions and comments during the class period, that would appear to be sufficient validation. If students' questions and comments indicate they do not need the review, the quiz scores may not have been valid for that purpose, but one can move on to new material during the class period. However, if the stakes are high and the decision is not easy to reverse, such as discontinuing a program of study because the desired outcomes do not seem to be occurring, determining if a set of scores are valid for that purpose should be a much more stringent process.

The validity chapter of the *Standards* starts with an introduction that provides a broad discussion on different types of evidence that can be gathered to support a particular test use, then provides an overall general standard that serves as a guiding principle of the *Standards'* view of validity, and parses the remaining 25 specific standards into three clusters. The first cluster is called "Establishing Intended Uses and Interpretations", and it sets forth the need for specifying intended score use(s) and the importance of validating each score use. The second cluster, "Issues Regarding Samples and Settings Used in Validation", discusses data used in validation research. The final section, "Specific Forms of Validity Evidence", lists six types of evidence that could be used to validate a use of scores, from evidence based on the content of an assessment being matched to the domain of knowledge about which one is seeking to draw inferences to evidence based on the consequences of score use. The most relevant types of evidence, as well as the magnitude and rigor of that evidence, depend on the situation. Content-oriented evidence consisting of a description of the domains covered on an assessment and the relationship of the individual items and those domains may be sufficient for a classroom test, whereas a placement test used to determine the correct math course sequence for a student might require evidence regarding relationships with criteria such as a meta-analysis of studies using the test and the associated course grade outcomes. It is unlikely that university professionals would have the resources to comprehensively validate all assessments used on a campus, nor would it be practical. However, the *Standards* provides good guidance and principles around assessments and the use of scores, and reading through the validity chapter will make users more aware of issues in the assessments they author and administer, and what should be considered when using test scores.

Reliability

The second foundational chapter of the *Standards* focuses on reliability or the precision of assessments. If one is making a decision based on the results of a test score, one would like to be confident that the data used for basing the decision are accurate. In the measurement literature, this means the data are reliable. Reliability can be computed and interpreted in several ways, based on how it is conceptualized. For example, for a score earned on an assessment, reliability can be thought of as consistency across the same test questions on different occasions or administrations, or different test questions over the same content domain. *Reliability* can be defined from multiple sources of inconsistency. In higher education, the sources of inconsistency may include different items within or between forms, scoring inconsistencies, or inconsistencies over time. The inconsistencies can also occur at the student, classroom, or institution level. However, not all changes in scores are considered an issue of reliability. For example, when instruction occurs, changes in scores between the pretest and posttest would be in part attributed to instruction and not just reliability.

Some methods of computing reliability assume that a single set of questions is administered over and over. Other reliability estimates include the consideration of different sources of error such as different sets of questions, different occasions, and different raters. Chapters 4 and 6 in this volume address the different types of reliability coefficients and how to compute them. In this chapter, we are concerned with reliability as a concept to inform the construction of assessments and administration conditions, and to inform the interpretation of scores. Greater consistency in scores indicates higher precision of scores.

Different types of consistency also exist, sometimes referred to as norm referenced and criterion referenced. *Norm-referenced* consistency typically refers to rank ordering students, and the consistency desired is that students preserve their rankings. *Criterion-referenced* consistency typically refers to the amount of material that is mastered, independent of how other students score or rank, or the consistency around a cut score. This could mean achieving the score needed for placement into a particular course, or an accountability measure where achieving "meets expectations" is what is important in a given context, and the consistency with which a student scores above or below the cut-score is what matters.

Because validity refers to the appropriateness of scores for the use one intends, reliability becomes a factor in validity. If scores are highly inconsistent, basing a decision on them is more like rolling a pair of dice than making an informed judgment. Consider a writing assessment used to place incoming students into different levels of a composition course. If the score an examinee received depends largely on who rates his or her paper, the score is not likely to be effective in assigning students to classes because based on the same essay a student would be placed in one class if Rater A scored her paper and another class if Rater B scored her paper. The paper itself did not change, but the score did. This would be an indication of inconsistency, or low reliability. To improve the consistency, one could have all graders rate all essays and use an average or sum score across raters. In this way, each paper would be scored by both "hard" and "easy" graders and the effect of different raters would disappear as all raters would rate all papers. Obviously this is practical only in certain settings. Other ways to address rater differences are to improve the training process, teaching raters what aspects of an essay to pay attention to and which to ignore, and monitoring them throughout the rating process, perhaps by having them score some percentage of papers in common to be sure they are staying consistent in scoring.

Reliability is a necessary component for valid assessment data use. If the data are not consistent, there is too much random variability in linking the scores or assessment data to outcomes. Think of trying to predict someone's weight when all one knows is his or her height. Now imagine that height is being measured using a tape measure made of elastic. The elastic can be saggy or pulled very tight. If it is very saggy, one's height will appear taller, whereas if it is pulled very tight, one's height will appear shorter. Because of the inconsistency in how height is being measured, the ability to estimate, or predict, weight from height is lessened as a result of the uncertainty that shows up in the measurement or assessment of height. The same is true for test scores. The more uncertainty in an assessment, the more variability in using it to predict an outcome. This prediction is not due to the fact that people differ (i.e., people of the same height may vary widely in weight), but because we can't be sure if a person with a height recorded as 5 feet 6 inches is really 5 feet 6 inches tall, or 5 feet tall or 6 feet tall.

The computation of reliability coefficients is dependent on the particular sample of examinees it is computed on, as well as the conditions of the administration and the formula computed and other factors. (The interested reader is referred to Feldt & Brennan, 1989; Haertel, 2006; and Thompson, 2003, among others, for more information about reliability and precision in assessment, and the pivotal role they play in the validity of test score use.) In general, longer assessments are typically more reliable, as well as instruments with more objective scoring, such as multiple-choice tests. However, the context and appropriateness needs to be considered. More items can actually lower reliability if inappropriate items are added, or if so many items are added that the examinee does not have time to answer them or is so fatigued he or she ends up making careless errors. The spread of scores of the group of examinees can also influence the magnitude of the reliability coefficients, not because the assessment changes, but because of the way reliability coefficients are computed, which often includes the variance of the examinees. In general, more heterogeneity within a sample of examinees results in a higher reliability coefficient. Thus, increasing the variability of scores within the same population of college students should increase the magnitude of the reliability estimate.

The *Standards* chapter on reliability and precision provides a single over-arching standard and 20 more specific standards, organized in 8 clusters, which deal with more specific themes, like standard errors of measurement and the reliability of aggregate information or the average test scores for groups of students. The overall standard specifies the need of reliability evidence for "each intended score use" to be considered (AERA, APA, & NCME, 2014, p. 42). Assessments are rarely applied for a single use. Scores that may be reliable for one purpose may not be for another. For example, a very short test might be sufficiently accurate for a pretest to see whether a student has been exposed to certain content, but not sufficient for determining how much of the content the student actually knows. As with validity, the higher the stakes of the decisions and the more difficult they are to reverse, the more important it is to have highly reliable scores. For example, if you do not know French, you may consistently score low on any set of questions in French—whether they are math or reading or science questions. If you take a test again after learning French, your score may be an indication of how well you know French but may also be confounded by the fact that you do not know some particular math content that shows up in the questions. If you received reading questions, you may score well consistently, and this may be interpreted as evidence you know French, whereas if you receive questions with that particular math content, your scores may be inconsistent depending on whether you receive geometry questions or not. (There are also validity issues here, in that you need to determine what you wish to assess: French knowledge or one's ability to function in a university math class taught in French.)

A university professional would look for different types of reliability evidence depending on the type and use of assessment. For an essay test scored by college faculty, one would be interested in interrater consistency, or how much agreement there is between raters when local educators are trained on a scoring rubric. To use an assessment before and after a treatment, alternate forms of reliability would be important to rule out different sets of questions as a confounding factor in difference scores.

Fairness

The third of the foundational chapters is on fairness, which the *Standards* views as a validity issue that "requires attention throughout all stages of test development and use" (AERA, APA, & NCME, 2014, p. 49). This means that fairness is not viewed as something added on at the end of an assessment, but instead permeates throughout the entire process, from deciding what use one wishes to make of the test scores, to developing the assessment's specifications, writing the items, assembling items into an assessment form, administering the assessment, scoring responses, and interpreting the scores of the assessment. This process of considering fairness to all examinees throughout the assessment process is sometimes referred to as *universal design*, an approach to test design seeking to maximize accessibility for all examinees.

The essence of the concept of fairness is that the use of the assessment scores is consistent and appropriate across examinees, meaning that the construct being represented by the assessment scores is equivalent across examinees. A student lacking manual dexterity to fill in bubbles on an answer document needs to be provided with an alternate way of recording responses, as scanning his or her answer document would probably not be an accurate indication of biology knowledge. Higher education institutions typically have offices dedicated to dealing with disabilities, cultural differences, and other aspects of fairness and should be able to provide local guidelines to assist those developing, administering, and interpreting the results of assessments, to ensure test score results can be used and compared appropriately.

Fairness covers wide-reaching aspects of assessment, including the absence of bias or construct-irrelevant bias for all examinees; access or exposure to the constructs being assessed; and the validity of the score use, implying scores from all individuals represent the same constructs and are equally appropriate to inform the decisions being made. These aspects are not always obvious to evaluate and need to be considered in light of the constructs one wishes to measure. For example, does one wish a score on a math test to predict only math ability, or math ability in English? This would inform whether it would be appropriate to translate an assessment into another language for a student limited in English proficiency. For all students, a test intended to measure math should not lead to scores where math ability is confounded with reading ability. The fairness standards are to ensure examinees are provided an equitable opportunity to perform in a manner that results in an accurate estimate of their ability or achievement on the construct of interest, and to make certain the estimate is not influenced by other irrelevant examinee characteristics or confounded with other factors.

Fairness does not mean all examinees score the same, or all subgroups score high. For example, students who choose not to attend classes may score lower than students who do attend classes. The intent is to ensure that the assessment scores accurately reflect the students' standing on the intended construct, regardless of whether they learn material inside or outside of class or do not learn material at all.

The specific standards in this chapter of the *Standards* are grouped into four clusters. The first cluster covers fairness issues in test design, development, and scoring. The second cluster refers to the interpretation of score uses, whereas the third cluster relates to using accommodations to remove barriers that could potentially interfere with the assessment of the intended construct. The fourth cluster refers to preventing inappropriate score interpretations. In evaluating the fairness aspect of using an assessment, university professionals should look for research dealing with what types of accommodations or accessibility factors have been found to remove construct-irrelevant barriers without changing the fundamental construct being assessed. In addition, documentation showing the assessment was developed under universal design principles as well as score information on multiple subgroups is important.

Incorporating Reliability and Validity Into Higher Education Assessments

The question of how much validity or reliability evidence is necessary for a particular use of test scores is really unanswerable. One can sometimes estimate consequences; for example, one could estimate the rate at which a student is incorrectly placed in a remedial course, or erroneously placed in the standard course. Often the different types of decision errors have different consequences, but there may not be universal agreement on which error is worse: sending a student through a course he does not need, which is a waste of resources (time, expense, etc.), or putting a student in a course for which he or she is not prepared (e.g., failing a course or additional stress). The composition of the anticipated examinee population is also a consideration: Placing students in a particular course when 98% of the students are anticipated to be placed in it is very different from selecting from a population where 40% of the students would be appropriately placed in the course. The use of the assessment scores, and the consequences of the decisions and wrong decisions, need to be kept constantly in mind when selecting an assessment.

In selecting or developing a test, one must consider the purpose of the test and how the assessment scores will be used. The assessment design, from content to item types to administration conditions and scoring rules, should be aligned with this purpose. There are different ways to determine what is appropriate coverage on a test; the amount of time spent on a topic and the number of pages in the text are options but are not without flaw. For example, a book may spend many pages in early chapters on teaching a way of thinking or on the building blocks for more complex material, which means once a student is able to apply this way of thinking in later chapters, less time is needed on the later topics. Assessment content should be aligned with course or program objectives. Other sources of evidence of validity could include correlations of the multiple assessments or components of the assessments within a class that point to the common goals of the instruction or learning outcomes.

In addition to trying to build in reliability and validity, at least for the primary score use(s), there is a need to examine the data from the tests once the tests have been administered. From a reliability perspective, the running of different reliability formulas is relatively straightforward (see chapters 4 and 6 in this volume). In interpreting the numerical values of the index, one needs to keep in mind that in addition to the actual items on the tests, the test administration conditions (whether the test is too speeded, or the directions are too confusing) as well as the homogeneity of the students on whom data are gathered all impact the magnitude of the reliability coefficients. If the value obtained seems too low for a particular use (a judgment call), possible solutions are generally suggested by the detailed data. For example, looking at the number of items students omit or the amount of time they spend on items (latencies are typically gathered in online testing) may suggest if the time limits are appropriate for the test. Looking at the distribution of scores may provide insight into how homogeneous the group of examinees are; if all the scores are bunched together, the reliability index may appear artificially low. Item analysis—looking at the percentage of students who select each option on a multiple-choice assessment, or who make the same errors in responding to a constructed-response item— can also provide valuable information, such as which items or options seem confusing to students and which items might need to have a reexamination of a key, given that the higher ability students tend to be missing the item and the lower ability students seem to be getting it correct.

Following up on the outcomes of decisions also informs the evaluation of validity, particularly in areas that are less well defined than a single course's content. Consider, for example, a college desires to foster "good citizens" and develops an assessment to determine whether or not students need to enroll in a citizenship program. The students' score on the assessment at the end of their junior year determines whether a student should attend the citizenship program to become a good citizen. Examining students who did and did not attend the program could inform whether the decision was appropriate. For example, if a definition of *good citizen* is adopted that includes voting in elections, one would like to determine that students not assigned to the program voted at the acceptable criterion (say, 80% of elections) both before and after they were administered the assessment, whereas students assigned to the program voted at the desired higher level after completing the program. Many of the constructs or traits we are interested in assessing are complex, and the data we use to examine the decisions we make may be indirect, including self-reporting.

Looking at an assessment's reliability is typically more direct than evaluating the validity for a particular score use. An instructor would have an opportunity to observe students in class and evaluate how they answer questions, their reactions in class, and so on, which may provide confirming information on whether a student understands or grasps material. If students who do well in class also do well on an item or the assessment as a whole, and students who demonstrate a lack of understanding in class do poorly, that would seem to provide support for the test assessing knowledge of the course material. More formal methods of evaluating validity typically require additional information, such as monitoring how students do in subsequent courses, on other assessments of similar constructs, in other programs of study, or professionally.

Higher education professionals who use assessments want to make decisions based on the results—decisions to reteach a unit, to accelerate or repeat instruction, to group students, to assign grades, or to evaluate a program of study and inform accreditation. The *Standards* provides the industry's best practices. In addition to the three chapters on the foundational concepts of validity, reliability, and fairness, the *Standards* includes 10 additional chapters, ranging from test design and development to the rights and responsibilities of the test takers. Chapter 13 of the *Standards*, which focuses on program evaluation and accountability, might be especially relevant in situations where higher education professionals are involved in the accreditation process. Practical issues, such as specifics on how to develop a test that leads to valid use of the resulting scores for the desired purpose, issues around test administration such as setting accommodations conditions, and test security issues, are also discussed. The purpose of the *Standards* is to facilitate providing the best data possible, not to make the decisions or influence policy outcomes.

Conclusion

Colleges use assessments in the following ways: to admit students; to assess learning and assign credit; and for program evaluation, accreditation, and accountability. Some of these uses entail assessments individual professors have little to do with (e.g., standardized national admission examinations) and some that they have virtually complete control over (e.g., individual course quizzes). Many assessments fall somewhere in between, such as those designed to measure program effectiveness, which typically involve a group of professors, and perhaps additional experts.

Professors developing classroom tests, and even groups of professors developing accountability assessments, seldom have the resources at their disposal that, say, a testing company would have. However, that does not lessen the need for the assessments they develop and base decisions on to be reliable and valid. All those who give assessments want to make some decision based on the results. It is important to keep in mind that the evidence of reliability and validity required should be aligned with the nature of the use of the resulting assessment scores; an assessment to determine what to teach tomorrow has arguably much lower stakes, because of much lower consequences if one gets it wrong, than the assessment used to assign a grade to a student, or decide whether a program of study is effective in terms of student benefits and outcomes. The *Standards for Educational and Psychological Testing* (AERA, APA, & NCME, 2014) provides a framework for considering validity and reliability as well as guidelines around the development of instruments that facilitate valid score use and appropriate interpretation of the resulting assessment data.

References

American Educational Research Association, American Psychological Association, & National Council on Measurement in Education. (2014). *Standards for educational and psychological testing.* Washington, DC: American Educational Research Association.

Feldt, L. S., & Brennan, R. L. (1989). Reliability. In R. L. Linn (Ed.), *Educational measurement* (3rd ed., pp. 105–146). New York. NY: American Council on Education and Macmillan.

Haertel, E. H. (2006). Reliability. In R. L. Brennan (Ed.), *Educational measurement* (4th ed., pp. 65–110). Westport, CT: American Council on Education/Praeger.

Kane, M. (2006a). Content-related validity evidence in test development. In S. Lane, M. Raymond, T. M. Haladyna, & S. M. Downing (Eds.), *Handbook of test development* (pp. 131–151). Mahwah, NJ: Lawrence Erlbaum Associates.

Kane, M. (2006b). Validation. In R. L. Brennan (Ed.), *Educational measurement* (4th ed., pp. 17–64). Washington, DC: American Council on Education/Praeger.

Lissitz, R. W., & Samuelsen, K. (2007). A suggested change in terminology and emphasis regarding validity and education. *Educational Researcher, 36*, 437–448.

Markus, K. A., & Borsboom, D. (2013). *Frontiers of test theory: Measurement, causation, and meaning.* New York, NY: Routledge.

Messick, S. (1989). Validity. In R. Linn (Ed.), *Educational measurement* (3rd ed., pp. 13–103). Washington, DC: American Council on Education.

Thompson, B. (Ed.). (2003). *Score reliability: Contemporary thinking on reliability issues.* Thousand Oaks, CA: Sage.

Wise, L. L., & Plake, B. S. (2015). Test design and development following the standards for educational and psychology testing. In S. Lane, M. Raymond, T. M. Haladyna, & S. M. Downing (Eds.), *Handbook of test development* (2nd ed., pp. 19–39). New York, NY: Routledge.

PART TWO

DIRECT AND INDIRECT
ASSESSMENT

3

DIRECT ASSESSMENT
METHODS

Terrel Rhodes, Association of American Colleges & Universities

Jennifer Bergeron, Harvard University

Since the twentieth century, assessment has played an increasingly important role in American higher education. Compared to other academic disciplines, the study of assessment and the study of its underlying theories are relatively nascent, reflected by the variety of definitions referenced in the literature. This is partially attributed to the diversity of people studying assessment who come from different academic backgrounds (Suskie, 2009), and partly due to the negative attributions and narrow definitions and uses often associated with systems of government-mandated accountability in education. Many faculty still equate assessment with testing and grading.

Although the language used to define *assessment* has not been standardized, researchers and practitioners in higher education describe assessment as a continuous process aimed at improving student learning (Allen, 2004; Suskie, 2009; Walvoord, 2004). According to Miller, Linn, and Gronlund (2013), assessment is the systematic process of gathering, analyzing, and using information from multiple sources to draw inferences about the characteristics of students, the curriculum, and programs for the purposes of making informed decisions to improve learning. Key to its purpose and meaning is that assessment (a) relies on multiple measures to provide broad descriptions about student characteristics, unlike tests, which represent only a sample of behavior, and (b) is specifically linked to outcomes or standards, making it easy to identify student- or program-level strengths or weaknesses. The process of developing or selecting measurement methods that are reliable and valid for the specified purposes or interpretations is thus key to the meaning and criteria for good assessment.

In higher education, assessment can occur at different levels within an institution (i.e., classroom, program, and institutional levels) and can be locally or externally developed (i.e., published tests). Locally developed assessments are created internally by members of an academic program to measure student learning tied to specific programmatic learning outcomes. These assessments can be administered at the classroom level and then rolled up to the program level. Although published assessments have established reliability and validity and offer the ability to yield norm-referenced scaled scores that can compare student performance over time, between groups, and across institutions, they are not widely used by institutions for the purposes of evaluating program-level learning outcomes because they don't easily align with programmatic outcomes. The advantages of embedded assessments are that they are a part of the typical routine in a course they do not require additional student time, can be tied to grades so that student motivation does not become a source of irrelevant variance, and can be easily aligned with the curriculum.

Assessment can also serve different purposes (i.e., placement, formative, diagnostic, summative assessment), measure different levels of achievement (i.e., simple versus complex), and take different forms (direct versus indirect). Most researchers and practitioners distinguish between two forms of assessments that are either indirect or direct. Chapters 5 and 6 illustrate how indirect measures solicit student self-reports of their perceived changes in attitudes or behaviors. Common examples of indirect measures in higher education include surveys; end-of-semester course evaluations; focus groups; and interviews, which largely focus on satisfaction, self-reported learning gains, changes in attitudes, and agreement with value statements. Indirect assessments may also include general indicators of learning such as graduation rates, retention rates, grades, and enrollment. Sometimes indirect assessments are the only way to capture latent constructs such as attitudes because they are difficult to observe directly. Direct measures, however, always require demonstration of knowledge, skill acquisition, and ability. Direct measures produce data with greater impartiality than indirect measures of latent constructs as there are not assumptions to make about how well student perceptions match their actual performance.

Although none of the regional accrediting bodies dictate specific assessment approaches, they are now placing greater emphasis on assessment practices that incorporate both direct and indirect types of assessments to evaluate learning in a more holistic way (Provezis, 2010). Indirect assessment results may shed light on the interpretation of direct assessment results whereas direct assessment results may lend validity to the interpretation of student opinions or self-reports. Although multimethod approaches are viewed as the gold standard, this is not always the case in practice. For example, universities still rely heavily on surveys to evaluate students' learning because surveys are easier to construct and administer, can be analyzed relatively quickly, and make it easier to track changes across time to explore trends (Kuh, Jankowski, Ikenberry, & Kinzie, 2014). In a report issued by the National Institute for Learning Outcomes Assessment in 2014, researchers reported that although surveys still remain the most popular tool for assessment, the range of assessment approaches has expanded significantly as institutions are starting to rely more on direct assessments (Kuh et al., 2014).

In this chapter we focus on direct assessments. We begin by identifying and explaining the different types of direct assessments most commonly used in higher education. We then explore development, administration, and scoring with a special emphasis on introducing approaches that will minimize sources of error. We introduce a special project under way to evaluate the Valid Assessment of Learning in Undergraduate Education (VALUE) rubrics under the leadership of the Association of American Colleges & Universities (AAC&U) and then end with a discussion on issues surrounding validity and reliability.

Types of Direct Assessment

Assessment practitioners usually distinguish between two formats of direct assessment: fixed choice and performance based. Formats differ based on the types of inferences that can be drawn about students' skills, level of achievement, and cognitive processes. Most commonly, cognitive taxonomies have been used to classify intended depth of students' processing and levels of achievement. Employing taxonomies in test construction and validation helps ensure coverage and representativeness of different levels of achievement. Although there are other cognitive taxonomies in the literature, Bloom's Taxonomy continues to be featured prominently in the assessment literature. Bloom's work is premised on the importance of content mastery, a higher level of thinking, in lieu of memorization. Each domain consists of progressively advanced levels (i.e., knowledge and comprehension represent lower cognitive skills versus synthesis and evaluation, which represent higher level cognitive skills) of learning that, according to Bloom, must be mastered in sequence (Johnson, Penny, & Gordon, 2009).

Fixed-Choice Assessments

Fixed-choice formats are most commonly used to measure learning outcomes based on knowledge or comprehension, but they can also be used to assess beyond these simple learning outcomes with items that require students to interpret, apply knowledge, and identify patterns and relationships that underpin novel problems. There is a wide range of these formats in terms of how items are structured and the levels of knowledge they can elicit. Multiple-choice (MC), alternative response (i.e., true-false; yes-no), and short-answer and completion items are all examples of this format. Alternative response items allow students to choose between diametrically opposed alternatives (e.g., yes-no; correct-incorrect; true-false) in response to a declarative statement. This is equivalent to a two-option MC item. The most popular of the two-option formats are true-false items. These items test students' ability to identify the correctness of statements, facts, terms, propositions, and/or cause-and-effect relationships. Short-answer and completion items vary on a continuum in terms of the types and level of learning outcomes they assess. The more controlled the response, the lower the item falls on the cognitive hierarchy. Completion items measure knowledge of simple terminology, facts, principles, and/or procedures. Short-answer items fall somewhere in the middle of the continuum and allow for solving problems and manipulating mathematical formulas. These formats make guessing less likely and can sample a broad range of knowledge outcomes.

MC items are probably the most widely used item format (Miller et al., 2013). In higher education this format is widespread in large introductory courses. The main advantages are in the flexibility and ease of administration and scoring and that the items can sample a wide range of content. When properly constructed, these items can also be more reliable. The biggest disadvantage is that they do not allow for easy detection of where learning difficulties may be occurring because they elicit a single correct response and thus provide less diagnostic value compared to other formats. Although MC items are widely used, the construction of good items is an art. Haladyna, Downing, and Rodriguez (2002) introduced a revised set of 31 MC item-writing guidelines, presented in Appendix 3A, which they validated through a process of reviewing textbooks on educational testing and research articles.

In this review, the coauthors also discuss the validity of different types of fixed-choice formats including conventional MC; complex MC; alternate choice; true-false and its variation, the multiple true-false; matching; and context dependent. Examples of the different item types are presented in Table 3.1 and the benefits and challenges are presented in Table 3.2.

Performance-Based Assessment

Although performance assessments are not limited to one side of the cognitive spectrum, they are most often used to assess students' higher order

TABLE 3.1
Fixed-Item Formats

Item Format	Example
Conventional MC	What is a group of organisms at any particular level in a classification system called? A. Species B. Genus C. Taxon D. Phylum

Context-Dependent Item Set—presents a stimulus (i.e., a graph, data, or a reading passage) and a set of multiple-choice test items	Mr. Smith wants his students to truly understand American Civil War battles. He engages the help of a local historical reenactment society and assigns each of his students to the Union or Confederate side. His students join the reenactors from 7 a.m. to 7 p.m. for a full day of activities, including marching a long distance (complete with rudimentary battle gear), setting up camp, cooking over campfires, scouting territory, and engaging in a historically representative battle.
	
	1. The teacher's strategy is most representative of which of the following learning theories:
	  a. Behaviorism
	  b. Cognitivism
	  c. Social cognitivism
	2. Mr. West is using which of the following strategies:
	  a. Maintenance
	  b. Shaping
	  c. Multisensory teaching
	  d. Negative reinforcement

True-False	Biologists currently recognize three kingdoms: Plants, animals, and protists. T/F
Multiple True-False (MTF)	The set of scores 4, 5, 5, 7, 8, 9, 9, 15 has (T) _ a. A median of 7.5 (F) _ b. A symmetric shape (T) _ c. More than one mode (T) _ d. A larger mean than median
Matching	Match the cell part to its function. 1. Serves as the cell's protective barrier 2. Builds proteins by putting together long chains of amino acids 3. Power house of the cell; converts glucose to ATP A. Cell wall; B. Mitochondria; C. Ribosomes; D. Golgi body

(*Continues*)

TABLE 3.1 *(Continued)*

Item Format	Example
Complex MC	Which of the following are classical era composers? 1. Joseph Haydn 2. Franz Schubert 3. Johann Pachelbel A. 1 & 2; B. 2 & 3; C. 1 & 3; D. 1, 2, & 3

TABLE 3.2
Benefits and Challenges of Fixed-Item Formats

Format	Benefits and Challenges
Conventional MC	• Can measure a broad range of learning outcomes across the cognitive spectrum (more difficult to measure recall, ability to present ideas and ability to organize) • Can be presented as a question or direct statement • Challenges include developing the correct number of plausible distractors and avoiding cueing in the answer stem (Miller et al., 2013)
Context-Dependent Item Set	• Useful for measuring complex achievement (i.e., interpretive skills, problem-solving, reasoning, and understanding) • Takes students longer to complete • Difficult to construct • Can't measure integrated problem-solving process as compared to performance-based tasks; can measure different aspects of the problem-solving process but do not allow for integration of these skills (Haladyna et al., 2002; Miller et al., 2013)
True-False	• Useful in measuring knowledge, cause and effect, relationships, and distinguishing between fact and opinion • Require that course material is phrased in a true-false; yes-no; correct-incorrect; fact-opinion format; in some subject areas this is not possible • Susceptible to guessing (a scoring formula for chance guessing may correct for this) (Frisbie & Becker, 1991; Haladyna et al., 2002; Miller et al., 2013) • Lower reliability compared to MC formats; more items may help address this (Frisbie & Becker, 1991) • Susceptible to response sets (Frisbie & Becker, 1991; Haladyna et al., 2002; Miller et al., 2013)

TABLE 3.2 (*Continued*)

Format	Benefits and Challenges
Multiple True-False	• Have been restricted to measuring knowledge and recall of facts (Downing, Baranowski, Grosso, & Norcini, 1995; Frisbie, 1992; Haladyna, 1994; Haladyna et al., 2002) • Produces more reliable scores as compared to traditional multiple choice (Downing et al., 1995; Frisbie, 1992)
Matching	• Restricted to outcomes that measure factual information • Material in a matching exercise requires homogeneous series of ideas from list and alternatives • Research is scant on the quality of this type of item format; however, in their review of MC formats, Haladyna et al., (2002) do not recommend against using this format
Complex MC	• Not recommended as they take students longer to answer than other formats and have been shown to be susceptible to clueing, which may artificially increase scores and decrease reliability (Albanese, Kent, & Whitney, 1979; Haladyna, 1994; Haladyna et al., 2002)

thinking skills such as their ability to perform tasks, evaluate relationships, synthesize information, and apply knowledge to solve realistic and novel problems. Performance tasks require students to develop their own solutions and are designed to mimic the actual context and conditions under which the knowledge and skill sets are to be executed. Examples include science experiments and lab work that students design, implement, analyze, and report on; computer programming that students develop and test; research projects that require a written and/or oral presentation or demonstration; language interviews where students are asked to demonstrate their ability to communicate in a foreign language; essays that prompt students to apply historical knowledge or literary critique; and studio assignments and performances that document student achievement in the fine arts. Regardless of the subject matter under consideration, performance assessment usually consists of the following three parts: a task, a scoring guide or rubric, and a set of administration guidelines. Tasks may vary in terms of cognitive complexity and the depth of content knowledge required to complete the task. Tasks that are more open and allow learners to develop their own strategies and processes to solve the problem and require substantial content knowledge require more complex thinking skills compared to tasks that are more structured and lean on only content knowledge (Baxter & Glaser, 1998).

It should be noted that performance assessments, similar to fixed-response formats, can be used for different purposes. Because of their thorough nature and ability to look at both product and process, they can be used to diagnose what students know and where they need help; monitor their progress; and, when combined with other kinds of assessment, make summative judgments. In fact, reliance on performance assessments has been shown to have a positive effect on instructional practice and learning. Koretz, Mitchell, Barron, and Keith (1996) found that when teachers moved to performance-based assessment, they changed their instructional strategies to incorporate more student-centered practices that emphasized cooperative work, communication, problem-solving, and hands-on learning as opposed to rote learning. Moreover, a preponderance of evidence has shown that how students are assessed plays an important role in how they learn (Herman, 1992; Resnick & Klopfer, 1989). An overreliance on measures that focus primarily on acquisition of basic skills and knowledge results in students who are not easily able to solve complex problems and employ higher order skills. Performance assessment can also be used for both small- (i.e., formative assessment in a classroom) and large-scale purposes (i.e., educational reform by policymakers using state tests).

A primary emerging approach in performance assessment is the use of student or course portfolios, or electronic portfolios, also called ePortfolios. Portfolios of student work have existed in higher education for decades in such fields as architecture, art, and education; however, ePortfolios are web-based frameworks for collecting and representing student work presented in response to assignments and activities associated with the curriculum and cocurriculum and can capture a broad range of student performance activities, including audio, video, and graphical representations. A key component of successful ePortfolios is students' ownership or voice through reflection and articulation of their own learning exhibited through the work in the portfolios and the ability to have the work examined and assessed by faculty and other external evaluators. Portfolios enable institutions and faculty to see beyond the transcript list of courses, titles, and grades and to delve into the students' demonstrated learning. When students' work in the ePortfolio is evaluated using rubrics, it is possible to chart improvement of students' knowledge, capacities, and skills over time and to note skills that still need improvement. However, ePortfolios are not without weaknesses. They cost time and money, and if not set up properly can easily become electronic filing cabinets that achieve little other than archiving student work.

In summary, although the benefits of these direct formats are many, as highlighted in this section, creating good performance assessments takes considerable thought and work in their development and scoring. Like fixed-item formats, performance tasks must have verifiable content representation and alignment with the learning outcomes being measured, and scoring must be reliable and objective. Human scoring and content underrepresentation are the largest threats to validity. Careful attention must be dedicated to creating scoring rubrics and training raters in order to minimize these threats. The creation of test specifications can also help to minimize the threat of content underrepresentation.

Designing the Assessment: Table of Specifications

Earlier in this chapter we outlined the different types of direct assessments commonly used to evaluate student learning outcomes. In this section we describe how a table of specifications, or test blueprint, can be used in assembling both fixed-choice and performance-based assessments to ensure that items are (a) aligned with learning outcomes and (b) representative of the content domain and cognitive skills to be measured (Crocker & Algina, 1986; Fives & DiDonato-Barnes, 2013; Miller et al., 2013). A table of specifications is also useful if designing a test to measure change over time to ensure that content remains comparable. A table of specifications is a two-way table. Across the top of the table is usually a list of outcomes with associated cognitive levels of Bloom's Taxonomy, and across the side, a list of the substantive content areas. Learning outcomes can help identify the relevant types and levels of behaviors that students should be able to demonstrate as a result of instruction. At the same time it is also important to identify the relevant instructional topics that define the subject domain emphasized in the curriculum that will be comprehensive enough to allow for appropriate sampling of test content. It is noteworthy that large-scale testing organizations identify the content and cognitive processes and publish content standards.

Once the learning outcomes and content have been determined, instructors can formulate a plan for assigning the relative coverage that each of these components should receive. Topics covered in more detail should be given more weight. Determining the number of items to include on the assessment depends on how much time is given to students to complete the assessment. Even though longer tests allow for greater content coverage, thus increasing the reliability of the assessment, there is a trade-off with test fatigue. Faculty should use their best judgment when determining how many test items to include. Because it's impossible for an examinee to complete every conceivable item that represents all subject matter at all levels of achievement on a single assessment, sampling must be done. Sampling of items should be done to cover a broad range of content and behaviors that have been emphasized in the curriculum and are most important. This is more difficult to do with performance assessments as compared to MC exams because there are fewer tasks from which to sample, and each one is unique (Haertel & Linn, 1996).

Once the table of specifications is complete, the faculty member must decide what type of item formats to use. In general, item formats should be appropriate for the type of learning outcome and content being measured, free from irrelevant cues, and at the appropriate levels of difficulty for the students for whom the assessment is being constructed so that the assessment will yield trustworthy results (see Table 3.3). It should be noted that a table of specifications can also be used when selecting published tests. Many publishers will include a detailed description of their test specifications in their testing manual so that it is easier to link program-level outcomes to what is being measured by the assessment (Miller et al., 2013).

Scoring

Related to the issue of scoring is reliability. *Reliability* refers to the consistency of scoring that allows for valid interpretations of results. Unless there is consistency over items, over time, over forms of a test, and across raters, we can have little faith in our result. There are different methods for estimating reliability depending on the types of consistency information needed to be collected. For example, to assess stability across administrations of the same test, test-retest reliability is computed. To examine equivalency across different samples of equivalent tasks, equivalent forms of reliability are computed. Reliability can also be calculated for a single administration of an assessment to examine internal consistency or the degree to which items on a single assessment measure similar characteristics. For objective tests that have only a single administration, reliability is typically computed using Cronbach's alpha. As noted in chapter 2, reliability can be increased by including enough items to provide an adequate sample of the content domain and behaviors, assuming the items are well written and the length of the test does not cause extraneous effects such as examinee fatigue. The magnitude of a reliability coefficient should be determined largely by the types of decisions to be made. Higher reliability is needed to justify test uses with high-stakes decisions.

Interrater reliability provides a measure of consistency across raters and can be enhanced by utilizing good scoring rubrics, rater training, and calibrations. As with internal consistency, interrater reliability needs to be

TABLE 3.3
Table of Specifications for an Exam in Epidemiology

Reporting Category	Knowledge	Application	Analyze	Evaluation	Total
	MC	Student-Produced Response	Brief Constructed Response	Extended Constructed Response	Points per Category
	1 pt	1 pt	3 pts	4 pts	
Understand public health and medical literature	8	1	0	1	13
Develop judgment about which statistical technique to use in a situation	10	3	0	1	17
Critically evaluate public health and medical literature, including identifying sources of bias and confounding	4	2	2	0	12
Design and carry out a study	4	0	1	1	11
Total	26	6	3	3	53

higher for higher stakes uses. For example, a program-level assessment in a postsecondary institution that does not include high-stakes uses for students would not require the same level of reliability as the high-stakes use of the assessment for student placement. In Table 3.4 we present different methods for estimating reliability that are adapted from Miller and colleagues (2013).

Scoring fixed-choice formats is relatively straightforward. There is an answer key and items are usually marked correct or incorrect. Scoring performance assessments, on the other hand, is a more complicated process, as it is highly susceptible to human error. To minimize this threat to validity,

TABLE 3.4
Determining Reliability

Method	Type of Reliability	Way of Estimating
Test-retest	Stability over time	Give same assessment twice to the same group of students. Resulting scores are correlated.
Equivalent forms	Equivalence across forms	Give different forms of an assessment with the same set of test specifications to the same group of students. Resulting scores are correlated.
Internal consistency	Degree to which items on a single assessment measure similar characteristics	Give the assessment once and compute Kuder-Richardson-20 (for dichotomously scored items) or coefficient alpha
Interrater	Consistency across raters	Have two or more raters independently score assessment. Calculate percent agreement and correlation values.

Note. Adapted from Miller and colleagues (2013).

scholars and practitioners have identified a number of methods to increase scoring accuracy including developing rubrics, benchmarking responses to provide proficiency levels, introducing scorer training, establishing reliability, and monitoring rater drift during scoring.

Developing scoring rubrics is the most important step in ensuring score consistency and accuracy. Rubrics typically contain a specified set of dimensions that describe characteristics expected in student work, short descriptors of what each dimension entails, and a set of levels at which a student might perform in demonstrating the dimensions of learning.

There are two varieties of scoring rubrics: holistic and analytic. Holistic scoring rubrics are constructed to provide a score for overall performance. Although they do provide specific criteria for performance like the analytic scoring rubric, scores for each criterion do not have to be specified (see Figure 3.1). Raters weigh the relative strengths and weaknesses among the various criteria and arrive at an overall assessment of performance, which makes scoring efficient and economical. However, a

Figure 3.1. Holistic rubric examples.

INQUIRY:
The ability to explore issues or topics through the ethical and responsible collection, analysis, and use of information as evidence that results in informed conclusions/judgments.

Expert = 3
• Identifies a focused, feasible, and significant topic that thoroughly addresses all relevant aspects of the topic, which may identify innovative aspects of this area of inquiry. • Accesses information using effective, well-designed strategies and comprehensive sources. Demonstrates ability to refine search. Analyzes own and others' assumptions and carefully evaluates the relevance of contextual factors when presenting a position. • Synthesizes in-depth information from relevant sources representing various points of views/approaches. • Consistently employs the expected information use strategies, including use of citations and references; choice of paraphrasing, summary, or quoting; use of information in ways that are true to the original context; distinguish between common knowledge and ideas that require attribution. Consistently employs the expected information use strategies with virtually no errors in use of citations and references. Appropriately chooses paraphrasing, summary, and quoting. Uses information in ways that are true to original context. Clearly distinguishes between common knowledge and ideas that require attribution.

Practitioner = 2
• Identifies a focused and feasible topic that broadly addresses the relevant aspects of this area of inquiry. • Accesses information using a variety of search strategies and some relevant sources. Demonstrates ability to conduct an effective search. Identifies own and others' assumptions and several relevant contextual factors while presenting a position. • Presents in-depth information from relevant sources representing various points of view/approaches. • Consistently employs the expected information use strategies with only a minimal number of errors in use of citations and references. May show imbalance in choice of paraphrasing, summary, and quoting. Uses information in ways that are true to original context. Clearly distinguishes between common knowledge and ideas that require attribution.

Novice = 1
• Identifies a topic that is far too general and wide ranging to be feasible or is too narrowly focused and leaves out relevant aspects of the topic. • Accesses information using simple search strategies and retrieves information from limited sources. Questions some assumptions. Identifies several relevant contextual factors when presenting a position. May be more aware of others' assumptions than one's own (or vice versa). • Presents information from relevant sources representing limited points of view/approaches. • Inconsistently employs of the expected information use strategies with a high number of errors in use of citations and references. May show overreliance on quoting versus paraphrasing and summarizing. Extrapolates information beyond original context. Distinguishes between common knowledge and ideas that require attribution in an unclear manner.

Note. Adapted from the inquiry and analysis VALUE rubric at Virginia Polytechnic Institute and State University.

major disadvantage of this scoring technique is that it offers limited diagnostic feedback.

Analytic scoring rubrics require raters to score each of the noted performance indicators (or criteria), which provides more feedback than holistic judgments. Performance can be scored on a rating scale or by a checklist in which a simple yes-no response is provided for each component task (see Appendix 3B). Analytic rubrics allow raters to focus on different components of a task rather than having to create an overall assessment of performance. Because of this, it is often more time consuming to create them and to train raters. However, their major advantage is in the detailed feedback they can provide along the different competencies that can be used by faculty to improve their teaching, and by students to enhance their learning. Analytic scoring rubrics can also be used as a valuable teaching tool when provided in advance to students to ensure that students understand expectations to meet standards of quality. Students can use rubrics to assess their own work and the work of others as part of the learning process.

There is conflicting evidence regarding the reliability of these two approaches (Johnson et al., 2009). Johnson and colleagues (2009) suggest selecting rubrics and rubric types based on the intended use of information generated from the scores. It is recommended that holistic scoring rubrics be used for assessing performance that relies on a single trait or when reporting requires a single score. Analytic scoring rubrics, in contrast, should be used for more high-stakes assessments in which detailed feedback is needed about the components of performance. Sometimes raters will provide an overall holistic rating along with analytic ratings of each proficiency level.

When developing scoring rubrics there are different considerations. The first consideration is to ensure alignment between content standards and learning outcomes specified in the rubric, which increases content validity. The second consideration is determining the number of scale points, which can affect the reliability of scoring. Although there should be enough scale points to differentiate between levels of performance, there should not be so many that categories become indistinguishable. Reliability has been shown to increase up to a 12-point scale assuming they are clearly defined (Johnson et al., 2009). Interrater reliability coefficients ranging from .79 to .96 have been shown on advanced placement exams using 12-point scales (Johnson et al., 2009). However, most scoring rubrics rely on 4-point to 6-point scales, which yield underestimated reliability coefficients. The use of measurement procedures (i.e., score augmentation) can correct for this bias, but this is beyond the scope of this chapter (Johnson et al., 2009). The third consideration is creating descriptors that are written in enough detail to distinguish between ability levels. In creating the descriptors it is helpful to start by defining the low, middle, and high ends of the scale points. The scales can then be further divided. Once the score points have been decided, pilot testing can be used to identify scoring ambiguity. Scoring rubrics in large-scale testing often go through a rigorous validation process.

Currently, the most widely used set of programmatic (e.g., content-specific disciplines) or institutional-level (e.g., general education) rubrics in higher education are the VALUE rubrics (Finley & Rhodes, 2013). The VALUE rubrics are utilized at thousands of institutions in the United States and abroad. The VALUE rubrics provide faculty and institutions the ability to assess a variety of student work. The VALUE rubrics were created by a group of interdisciplinary, interinstitutional teams of faculty and other educational professionals. They were developed as metarubrics (rubrics that can be broadly applied within and across disciplines to examine learning such as written communication or critical thinking) to evaluate 16 learning outcomes expected of college graduates as expressed by both faculty and employers with the purposes of being used at institutional or programmatic levels of assessment and to follow student progress over time. Users have been encouraged to modify the original VALUE rubrics to reflect their own institutional mission and program emphasis or to translate the rubric dimensions into course and assignment rubrics that can be used for grading. Through these translation and alignment processes, student learning assessments can be designed at multiple levels and to measure multiple dimensions of learning outcomes. The AAC&U VALUE rubrics have allowed for multiple audiences to see and use evidence of student attainment, including the students themselves.

Scoring of performance assessments may be conducted by raters or by automated scoring systems that have been calibrated by human scoring. We choose to focus on human scoring. Raters may differ in terms of how they understand, interpret, and apply the scoring rubrics, which can affect content representation of the assessment. Through rater training, inconsistency and bias can be minimized, and calibration can lead to rich faculty discussions about what matters most in curriculum and pedagogy. This usually begins by having raters review the task, scoring rubrics, and examples of student work that serve as benchmarks for typical performance (usually the midrange) at each scale point on the rubric. The raters are then given practice sets that are scored and calibrated. These exercises allow raters to recognize the highs and lows of each score point and to correct their scoring. The number of practice sets that each rater will complete can vary (i.e., they can include 10–20 exercises for large-scale assessments). Qualifying sets are then used to determine if raters meet a specified criterion (i.e., percent agreement). During actual scoring sessions, raters complete monitoring sets to ensure that rating remains consistent and that additional training is not needed.

The VALUE rubrics, for example, were developed by groups of faculty experts and novices for each of 16 learning outcomes. For each outcome, the faculty developers examined and analyzed research on the elements or dimensions of learning for each rubric and the analysis of rubrics that had already been developed by faculty and others. From the beginning, this gave the VALUE rubrics high content and face validity. In addition, through testing the rubrics with student work on multiple campuses (a total of more than 100 colleges and universities), the validity of the VALUE rubrics had been established prior to their release in fall 2009.

Surveys of scorers who participated in a multistate collaborative (MSC) for learning outcomes assessment project using the VALUE rubrics to score student work across 12 states, 60 institutions, and multiple disciplines responded in broad agreement on the validity of the rubric dimensions:

- Ninety percent of participating faculty believed that the VALUE rubrics were a useful tool for evaluating student work quality.
- Greater than 80% indicated that the rubrics contained a sufficient range of criteria, the descriptors were understandable, and the descriptors were relevant for making judgments about levels of learning.
- Seventy-five percent of scorers indicated the dimensions encompassed the core meaning of the learning outcome.

In reality, scores might not always fit neatly into categories, or the surveys are not easy to read, are incomplete, or are left blank; in these cases, decision rules must be created to address these issues in a systematic way to maintain scoring consistency and fairness. In addition to scorer inconsistency, there are the issues that comprise rater bias such as the halo effect, central tendency (i.e., assigning scores around the middle of the scale), leniency or severity, scoring fatigue, skimming (i.e., failing to read the whole response), language (i.e., assigning scores based on language usage or grammar as opposed to the construct of interest), or clashing values (assigning lower scores to work that conflicts with the personal views of the rater). Training sessions should help address these issues by making raters aware of these possible threats.

The techniques described in this section should help increase the reliability of scoring and minimize the threats of scoring bias, which is a perfect segue into the discussion that follows in the next section on utilizing psychometrics to enhance assessment interpretation and use.

Score Interpretation and Use: Psychometrics in Assessment

Key to the purpose of assessment is the ability to draw inferences about the characteristics or performance of students, the curriculum, and/or the program in order to make informed decisions that can be either low stakes or high stakes. Therefore, collecting evidence to ascertain whether interpretations drawn from assessment results are suitable for their intended use is critical. As discussed in chapter 2, validity is not a property of the assessment itself but rather a property of the interpretations and inferences drawn from results, and it is linked to the specific uses and purposes of the assessment. Not all assessments are valid for all purposes. For example, a mathematics performance assessment designed to evaluate mathematical problem-solving ability but that requires a high level of reading ability will affect the validity and fairness of score interpretation for English language learners being placed into the appropriate math class. Selecting and designing assessments requires determining their purposes and intended uses, designing tasks that fit these purposes, and then collecting validity evidence to support their intended uses.

Crucial to the evaluation of the validity of test use and interpretation are the concepts *construct underrepresentation* and *construct-irrelevant variance* (AERA, APA, & NCME, 2014; Messick, 1993). Validity can be reduced when scores are affected by irrelevant factors, such as in the case of item design when cues within item stems lead to selecting the correct response as a result of those cues; reading or language ability, which are ancillary factors that may contribute to performance on assessments designed to test other skills such as math and science; and when raters score performance on ancillary factors (i.e., grammar, handwriting, score length, clashing values) that do not adhere to the rubric and affect scoring. This can be minimized through rater training as previously addressed. Validity can also be reduced when the assessment does not fully capture the construct of interest, rendering score inference nongeneralizable to the larger content domain from which the construct represents.

There are a variety of ways to gather validity evidence. Validity criteria that are most essential for evaluating the quality of direct assessments include evidence based on test content and the outcomes from which the assessment was developed, evidence based on the cognitive processes that were used by students to perform the tasks, and evidence based on the degree to which assessment results are related to other valid measures of performance and consequential validity (AERA, APA, & NCME, 2014; Messick, 1993).

Evidence based on content—or content representativeness—involves determining the adequacy of the test content in sampling from the knowledge and skill domains that are relevant and representative of the construct of interest. For performance assessment, test content also includes the task and item formats, as well as scoring procedures. As previously mentioned, establishing content representativeness is more difficult for performance-based formats due to the small number of items as compared to MC exams. As a result, many large-scale assessments rely on a combination of performance-based tasks with MC items. In addition, performance assessments that are administered at multiple points throughout the year will allow for greater content representation across assessments (Lane, 2010).

It is also important to ensure that cognitive skills of the target domain are represented. It should not be assumed that performance assessments always capture higher order skills; evidence is needed to determine the extent to which the assessment and scoring rubrics are getting at the cognitive skills and processes represented by the construct. Qualitative approaches such as protocol analysis and analysis of reasons can be used to verify whether the construct of interest is being represented in the assessment task (Lane, 2010). With these approaches, students are asked to do think-aloud processing as they solve problems and provide rationales for their responses. Finally, as previously discussed, using a table of specifications when designing assessments and scoring rubrics will help ensure that items are aligned with learning outcomes, ensuring that the items provide a representative sample of the content domain and cognitive skills. This alignment is crucial to establishing the validity of the assessment.

Assessment and Psychometrics Example

A major initiative currently under way is the aforementioned MSC project developed to examine whether the performance appraisals using the VALUE rubrics for assessing student learning over multiple learning outcomes are possible. Twelve states and more than 100 two- and four-year public institutions are collaborating in the MSC under the leadership of the AAC&U and the State Higher Education Executive Officers Association. This project, supported by a grant from the Bill & Melinda Gates Foundation, is also addressing the content validity of the rubrics within the context for which they are being used. Evaluating alignment among the learning objectives, learning activities, and assessment techniques provides the foundation for the validity argument.

Through the MSC project, extensive research is being conducted to substantiate the different types of interpretations that can be drawn from the VALUE rubrics in light of their intended purposes. The study provides an evaluation of the processes by which the rubrics were developed and their varied and broad application across a spectrum of courses, programs, and disciplines on campuses, both during and since their development. This project, along with two parallel projects involving private liberal arts colleges in Minnesota and the Great Lakes Colleges Association, addresses the reliability and validity (construct and content) of the VALUE rubric approach to assessing student learning.

The MSC project also aims to address scoring issues, which were examined by surveying faculty during and after the training and rating process and through the analysis of interrater reliability. A generalizability study is also planned to estimate the multiple sources of error that can be differentiated to determine which sources of error variance are most influential on the dependability of scores. For example, the use of multidimensional rubrics to evaluate student work samples at the institutional level can generate several potential sources of error beyond differences in raters, including differences among students within institutions, differences among raters' scores, differences between institutional means, differences in assignment prompts, and the interactions of these differences. Testing these sources of error using a family of analysis of variance (ANOVA) models will allow for the estimation of each component of variance to determine the percentage of overall variance applicable to any one source. For example, varying the number of raters, prompts/assignments, and students will affect the dependability of an institutional mean. Accordingly, we need to determine the appropriate sampling of students, artifacts/assignments (including whether the work comes from the beginning, midpoint, or near end-point of the student's time in college), and raters to generate dependable scores for assessing student-; institutional-; and, for the MSC, state-level performance.

In the MSC pilot year, activities were devoted to testing the protocols and processes for collecting student work and scoring. The pilot year initiative involved 11,000 distinct pieces of student work submitted for course assignments, generated by 1,600 unique assignments from 45 different majors at 100 two- and four-year colleges and universities located in 12 states. The student artifacts were scored by 190 raters who had gone through a calibration procedure to use the VALUE rubrics.

The process of establishing the validity and reliability of the VALUE rubrics is complex and difficult to compare to the process of establishing the validity and reliability of standardized testing. Nonetheless, establishing the validity—credibility and transferability—and reliability of the VALUE rubrics is a key priority for MSC during the full-implementation year.

During the pilot year, interrater reliability was explored by examining the percent agreement among raters using the Intraclass Correlation Coefficient (ICC-1) to test agreement beyond chance. The ICC-1 is often used to examine ordered categorical data, such as the scale date developed for the VALUE rubrics, and it is appropriate when you do not have fully crossed raters for all artifacts. For example, on the quantitative literacy rubric dimension of application/analysis, the ICC-1 was .552 and the Cronbach's alpha was .550, indicating moderate reliability. Perfect score agreement was 40%, indicating that 40% of the essays received the same rating. The score agreement within one column was 79%, indicating that 79% of the essays received the same rating within one point of one another.

Chapter 4 provides a more comprehensive discussion of reliability and validity, but it is worth emphasizing that these important psychometric principles and analyses are important considerations in constructing assessments and developing scoring procedures that will maximize the utility of the results. There are many factors that can affect the validity of score interpretations. Although many of these concepts and approaches have been applied to large-scale assessments, in everyday situations, such as in the classroom or assessment at the program level, it is important to consider the types of validity evidence that are available, reasonable to collect, and most appropriate within one's context, and the inferences to be made. This involves—at minimum—determining what is to be assessed and what factors could influence results and then controlling for them so that inferences drawn from the data can be meaningful. Educators attempt to minimize construct underrepresentation and construct-irrelevant variance as potential threats to the validation process by careful consideration of the evidence and arguments (Messick, 1993).

Conclusion

Direct assessments can play a major role in the instructional process and in decisions being made about student learning in higher education. From an instructional standpoint direct assessments can be used to determine students' prerequisite skills, their learning progress and difficulties, and their overall mastery of objectives. From a policy standpoint, they can be used to identify gaps in student achievement and produce information to inform university systems, school districts, states, and the federal government. When used in combination with indirect measures of student learning, they are a powerful tool.

As illustrated in this chapter, there are many different considerations in developing and implementing direct assessments including determining what needs to be assessed, deciding on the substantive content areas and skill levels to sample from, designing a sampling strategy to ensure that test content is representative of the larger domain of interest, determining what item formats should be used in light of the characteristics to be measured, developing a scoring strategy, and then deciding whether inferences drawn from the assessment are meaningful and valid.

Attempting to justify score interpretation involves designing assessments and scoring procedures that minimize the presence of plausible rival interpretations of score meaning and then collecting evidence to justify conclusions. The use of a table of specifications, development of scoring rubrics, and rater trainings can help minimize sources of error that are irrelevant to the construct of interest. The MSC project examination of the VALUE rubrics is one such example. Measurement models and procedures can also be used to model and control error in the estimation of student scores.

Finally, there are several rival interpretations to consider when drawing inferences about test scores. Whereas it is not always practical or feasible to conduct validation studies for a classroom or programmatic use, awareness of rival factors can be preventative. This includes thinking about the relevance and representativeness of test content in relation to the larger content and cognitive domains, the cognitive processes that underlie responses, the relationships of test score with other measures, the dependability and consistency of scores across raters and across tasks, and the unintended and intended social consequences of test use that might affect the meaning of test scores.

References

Albanese, M. A., Kent, T. H., & Whitney, D. R. (1979). Cluing in multiple-choice test items with combinations of correct responses. *Journal of Medical Education, 54,* 948–950.

Allen, M. (2004). *Assessing academic programs.* Boston, MA: Anker.

American Educational Research Association, American Psychological Association, & National Council on Measurement in Education. (2014). *Standards for educational and psychological testing.* Washington, DC: Author.

Anderson, L. W., Krathwohl, D. R., Airasian, P. W., Cruikshank, K. A., Mayer, R. E., Pintrich, P. R., Raths, J., & Wittrock, M. C. (2001). *A taxonomy for learning, teaching and assessing: A review of Bloom's taxonomy of educational objectives* (abbreviated ed.). Upper Saddle River, NJ: Pearson Education.

Baxter, G. P., & Glaser, R. (1998). Investigating the cognitive complexity of science assessments. *Educational Measurement: Issues and Practice, 17*(3), 37–45.

Cole, N. S., & Moss, P. A. (1989). Bias in test use. In R. L. Linn (Ed.), *Educational measurement* (3rd ed., pp. 201–220). New York, NY: American Council on Education and Macmillan.

Crocker, L., & Algina, J. (1986). *Introduction to classical modern test theory.* Orlando, FL: Harcourt Brace Jovanovich.

Downing, S. M., Baranowski, R. A., Grosso, L. J., & Norcini, J. N. (1995). Item type and cognitive ability measured: The validity evidence for multiple true-false items in medical specialty certification. *Applied Measurement in Education, 8*(2), 187–197.

Finley, A., & Rhodes, T. (2013). *Using the VALUE rubrics for improvement of learning and authentic assessment.* Washington, DC: Association of American Colleges & Universities.

Fives, H., & DiDonato-Barnes, N. (2013). Classroom test construction: The power of a table of specifications. *Practical Assessment Research & Program Evaluation, 18*(3), 1–7.

Frisbie, D. A. (1992). The multiple true-false item format: A status review. *Educational Measurement: Issues and Practice, 11*(4), 21–26.

Frisbie, D. A., & Becker, D. F. (1991). An analysis of textbook advice about true-false tests. *Applied Measurement in Education, 4*(1), 67–83.

Haertel, E. H., & Linn, R. L. (1996). Comparability. In G. W. Phillips (Ed.), *Technical issues in large-scale performance assessment* (NCES 96-802). Washington, DC: U.S. Department of Education.

Haladyna, T. M. (1994). *Developing and validating multiple-choice test items.* Hillsdale, NJ: Lawrence Erlbaum Associates.

Haladyna, T. M., Downing, S. M., & Rodriguez, M. C. (2002). A review of multiple-choice item-writing guidelines for classroom assessment. *Applied Measurement in Education, 15*(3), 309–334.

Herman, J. L. (1992). *A practical guide to alternative assessment.* Alexandria, VA: Association for Supervision and Curriculum Development.

Johnson, R., Penny, J., & Gordon, B. (2009). *Assessing performance: Designing, scoring, and validating performance tasks.* New York, NY: Guilford.

Koretz, D. M., Mitchell, K., Barron, S. I., & Keith, S. (1996). *The perceived effects of the Maryland School Performance Assessment Program: Final report* (CSE Technical Report No. 409). Los Angeles: University of California, Center for the Study of Evaluation.

Kuh, G. D., Jankowski, N., Ikenberry, S. O., & Kinzie, J. (2014). *Knowing what students can do: The current state of student learning outcomes assessment in U.S. colleges and universities* (NILOA Occasional Paper No. 6). Urbana: University of Illinois and Indiana University, National Institute for Learning Outcomes Assessment.

Lane, S. (2010). *Performance assessment: The state of the art* (SCOPE Student Performance Assessment Series). Stanford, CA: Stanford University, Stanford Center for Opportunity Policy in Education.

Messick, S. (1993). *Foundations of validity: Meaning and consequences in psychological assessment* [Research Report]. Princeton, NJ: Educational Testing Service.

Miller, M. D., Linn, R. L., & Gronlund, N. E. (2013). *Measurement and assessment in teaching* (11th ed.). Boston, MA: Pearson.

Provezis, S. (2010, October). *Regional accreditation and student learning outcomes: Mapping the territory* (NILOA Occasional Paper No. 6). Urbana: University of Illinois and Indiana University, National Institute for Learning Outcomes Assessment.

Resnick, L., & Klopfer, L. (Eds.). (1989). *Toward the thinking curriculum: Current cognitive research.* Alexandria, VA: Association for Supervision and Curriculum Development.

Suskie, L. (2009). *Assessing student learning: A common sense guide* (2nd ed.). San Francisco, CA: Jossey-Bass.

Walvoord, B. E. (2004). *Assessment clear and simple: A practical guide for institutions, departments, and general education.* San Francisco, CA: Jossey-Bass.

Revised Taxonomy of Multiple-Choice Item-Writing Guidelines

Content Concerns

1. Every item should reflect specific content and a single, specific mental behavior, as called for in test specifications (two-way grid, test blueprint).
2. Base each item on important content to learn; avoid trivial content.
3. Use novel material to test higher level learning. Paraphrase textbook language or language used during instruction when used in a test item to avoid testing simply for recall.
4. Keep the content of each item independent from content of other items on the test.
5. Avoid overspecific and overgeneral content when writing multiple-choice (MC) items.
6. Avoid opinion-based items.
7. Avoid trick items.
8. Keep vocabulary simple for the group of students being tested.

Formatting Concerns

9. Use the question, completion, and best-answer versions of the conventional MC, the alternate choice, true–false (TF), multiple true–false (MTF), matching, and the context-dependent item and item-set formats, but *avoid* the complex MC (Type K) format.
10. Format the item vertically instead of horizontally.

Style Concerns

11. Edit and proof items.
12. Use correct grammar, punctuation, capitalization, and spelling.
13. Minimize the amount of reading in each item.

Writing the Stem

14. Ensure that the directions in the stem are very clear.
15. Include the central idea in the stem instead of the choices.
16. Avoid window dressing (excessive verbiage).
17. Word the stem positively; avoid negatives such as *not* or *except*. If a negative word is used, use the word cautiously and always ensure that the word appears capitalized, and boldface [or italicized].

Writing the Choices

18. Develop as many effective choices as you can, but research suggests three is adequate.
19. Make sure that only one of the choices is the right answer.
20. Vary the location of the right answer according to the number of choices.
21. Place choices in logical or numerical order.
22. Keep choices independent; choices should not be overlapping.
23. Keep choices homogeneous in content and grammatical structure.
24. Keep the length of choices about equal.
25. "None-of-the-above" should be used carefully.
26. Avoid "all-of-the-above."
27. Phrase choices positively; avoid negatives such as "not."
28. Avoid giving clues to the right answer, such as the following:
    a. Specific determiners including always, never, completely, and absolutely.
    b. Clang associations, choices identical to or resembling words in the stem.
    c. Grammatical inconsistencies that cue the test taker to the correct choice.
    d. Conspicuous correct choice.
    e. Pairs or triplets of options that clue the test taker to the correct choice.
    f. Blatantly absurd, ridiculous options.
29. Make all distractors plausible.
30. Use typical errors of students to write your distractors.
31. Use humor if it is compatible with the teacher and the learning environment.

Quantitative Literacy VALUE Rubric

Association
of American
Colleges and
Universities

The VALUE rubrics were developed by teams of faculty experts representing colleges and universities across the United States through a process that examined many existing campus rubrics and related documents for each learning outcome and incorporated additional feedback from faculty. The rubrics articulate fundamental criteria for each learning outcome, with performance descriptors demonstrating progressively more sophisticated levels of attainment. The rubrics are intended for institutional-level use in evaluating and discussing student learning, not for grading. The core expectations articulated in all 15 of the VALUE rubrics can and should be translated into the language of individual campuses, disciplines, and even courses. The utility of the VALUE rubrics is to position learning at all undergraduate levels within a basic framework of expectations such that evidence of learning can be shared nationally through a common dialog and understanding of student success.

Definition

Quantitative literacy (QL)—also known as numeracy or quantitative reasoning (QR)—is a "habit of mind," competency, and comfort in working with numerical data. Individuals with strong QL skills possess the ability to reason and solve quantitative problems from a wide array of authentic contexts and everyday life situations. They understand and can create sophisticated arguments supported by quantitative evidence and they can clearly communicate those arguments in a variety of formats (using words, tables, graphs, mathematical equations, etc., as appropriate).

Quantitative Literacy Across the Disciplines

Current trends in general education reform demonstrate that faculty are recognizing the steadily growing importance of quantitative literacy (QL) in an increasingly quantitative and data-dense world. AAC&U's recent survey showed that concerns about QL skills are shared by employers, who recognize that many of today's students will need a wide range of high level quantitative skills to complete their work responsibilities. Virtually all of today's students, regardless of career choice, will need basic QL skills such as the ability to draw information from charts, graphs, and geometric figures, and the ability to accurately complete straightforward estimations and calculations.

Preliminary efforts to find student work products which demonstrate QL skills proved a challenge in this rubric creation process. It's possible to find pages of mathematical problems, but what those problem sets don't demonstrate is whether the student was able to think about and understand the meaning of her work. It's possible to find research papers that include quantitative information, but those papers often don't provide evidence that allows the evaluator to see how much of the thinking was done by the original source (often carefully cited in the paper) and how much was done by the student herself, or whether conclusions drawn from analysis of the source material are even accurate.

Given widespread agreement about the importance of QL, it becomes incumbent on faculty to develop new kinds of assignments which give students substantive, contextualized experience in using such skills as analyzing quantitative information, representing quantitative information in appropriate forms, completing calculations to answer meaningful questions, making judgments based on quantitative data, and communicating the results of that work for various purposes and audiences. As students gain experience with those skills, faculty must develop assignments that require students to create work products which reveal their thought processes and demonstrate the range of their QL skills.

This rubric provides for faculty a definition for *QL* and a rubric describing four levels of QL achievement which might be observed in work products within work samples or collections of work. Members of AAC&U's rubric development team for QL hope that these materials will aid in the assessment of QL—but, equally important, we hope that they will help institutions and individuals in the effort to more thoroughly embed QL across the curriculum of colleges and universities.

Framing Language

This rubric has been designed for the evaluation of work that addresses quantitative literacy (QL) in a substantive way. QL is not just computation, not just the citing of someone else's data. QL is a habit of mind, a way of thinking about the world that relies on data and on the mathematical analysis of data to make connections and draw conclusions. Teaching QL requires us to design assignments that address authentic, data-based problems. Such assignments may call for the traditional written paper, but we can imagine other alternatives: a video of a PowerPoint presentation, perhaps, or a well-designed series of web pages. In any case, a successful demonstration of QL will place the mathematical work in the context of a full and robust discussion of the underlying issues addressed by the assignment.

Finally, QL skills can be applied to a wide array of problems of varying difficulty, confounding the use of this rubric. For example, the same student might demonstrate high levels of QL achievement when working on a simplistic problem and low levels of QL achievement when working on a very complex problem. Thus, to accurately assess a student's QL achievement it may be necessary to measure QL achievement within the context of problem complexity, much as is done in diving competitions where two scores are given, one for the difficulty of the dive, and the other for the skill in accomplishing the dive. In this context, that would mean giving one score for the complexity of the problem and another score for the QL achievement in solving the problem.

QUANTITATIVE LITERACY VALUE RUBRIC

Reprinted with permission from "VALUE: Valid Assessment of Learning in Undergraduate Education." Copyright 2017 by the Association of American Colleges & Universities (http://www.aacu.org/value/index.cfm)

Evaluators are encouraged to assign a zero to any work sample or collection of work that does not meet benchmark (cell 1) level performance.

	Capstone	Milestones		Benchmark
	4	3	2	1
Interpretation *Ability to explain information presented in mathematical forms (e.g., equations, graphs, diagrams, tables, words)*	Provides accurate explanations of information presented in mathematical forms. Makes appropriate inferences based on that information. *For example, accurately explains the trend data shown in a graph and makes reasonable predictions regarding what the data suggest about future events.*	Provides accurate explanations of information presented in mathematical forms. *For instance, accurately explains the trend data shown in a graph.*	Provides somewhat accurate explanations of information presented in mathematical forms, but occasionally makes minor errors related to computations or units. *For instance, accurately explains trend data shown in a graph, but may miscalculate the slope of the trend line.*	Attempts to explain information presented in mathematical forms, but draws incorrect conclusions about what the information means. *For example, attempts to explain the trend data shown in a graph, but will frequently misinterpret the nature of that trend, perhaps by confusing positive and negative trends.*
Representation *Ability to convert relevant information into various mathematical forms (e.g., equations, graphs, diagrams, tables, words)*	Skillfully converts relevant information into an insightful mathematical portrayal in a way that contributes to a further or deeper understanding.	Competently converts relevant information into an appropriate and desired mathematical portrayal.	Completes conversion of information but resulting mathematical portrayal is only partially appropriate or accurate.	Completes conversion of information but resulting mathematical portrayal is inappropriate or inaccurate.

Calculation	Calculations attempted are essentially all successful and sufficiently comprehensive to solve the problem. Calculations are also presented elegantly (clearly, concisely, etc.).	Calculations attempted are essentially all successful and sufficiently comprehensive to solve the problem.	Calculations attempted are either unsuccessful or represent only a portion of the calculations required to comprehensively solve the problem.	Calculations are attempted but are both unsuccessful and are not comprehensive.
Application/Analysis *Ability to make judgments and draw appropriate conclusions based on the quantitative analysis of data, while recognizing the limits of this analysis*	Uses the quantitative analysis of data as the basis for deep and thoughtful judgments, drawing insightful, carefully qualified conclusions from this work.	Uses the quantitative analysis of data as the basis for competent judgments, drawing reasonable and appropriately qualified conclusions from this work.	Uses the quantitative analysis of data as the basis for workmanlike (without inspiration or nuance, ordinary) judgments, drawing plausible conclusions from this work.	Uses the quantitative analysis of data as the basis for tentative, basic judgments, although is hesitant or uncertain about drawing conclusions from this work.
Assumptions *Ability to make and evaluate important assumptions in estimation, modeling, and data analysis*	Explicitly describes assumptions and provides compelling rationale for why each assumption is appropriate. Shows awareness that confidence in final conclusions is limited by the accuracy of the assumptions.	Explicitly describes assumptions and provides compelling rationale for why assumptions are appropriate.	Explicitly describes assumptions.	Attempts to describe assumptions.
Communication *Expressing quantitative evidence in support of the argument or purpose of the work (in terms of what evidence is used and how it is formatted, presented, and contextualized)*	Uses quantitative information in connection with the argument or purpose of the work, presents it in an effective format, and explicates it with consistently high quality.	Uses quantitative information in connection with the argument or purpose of the work, though data may be presented in a less than completely effective format or some parts of the explication may be uneven.	Uses quantitative information, but does not effectively connect it to the argument or purpose of the work.	Presents an argument for which quantitative evidence is pertinent, but does not provide adequate explicit numerical support. (May use quasi-quantitative words such as "many," "few," "increasing," "small," and the like in place of actual quantities.)

4

VALIDITY AND RELIABILITY
OF DIRECT ASSESSMENTS

Jon S. Twing, Pearson

Kimberly J. O'Malley, Pearson

Most practitioners, stakeholders, and users of assessment understand (to some degree) that the concepts of validity and reliability are fundamental to the field of measurement and fundamental to measures themselves. Samuel Messick (1994) argues the importance of these concepts even beyond measurement:

> Such basic assessment issues as validity, reliability, comparability, and fairness need to be uniformly addressed for all assessments because they are not just measurement principles, they are social values that have meaning and force outside of measurement wherever evaluative judgments and decisions are made. (p. 13)

Despite this understanding, evidence suggests that technical aspects of these foundational concepts are not well understood. In his presidential address to the National Council on Measurement in Education, David Frisbie (2005) stated,

> For a concept that is the foundation of virtually all aspects of our measurement work, it seems that the term validity continues to be one of the most misunderstood or widely misused of all. (p. 21)

Frisbie (2005) goes on to cite examples of how and why he feels this is the case and claims a parallel can be found regarding the concept of reliability:

Some of what I said earlier about validity has a parallel with reliability. Not only do introductory students of measurement confuse validity and reliability with each other, but they also develop a very limited view of how to use the two ideas. (p. 25)

Frisbie implies that this misunderstanding is not limited to measurement students but practitioners and users of assessment as well.

To add to the confusion, the measurement of student knowledge and progress is changing. Three key trends driving the change are (a) the move to using direct assessments, where measurement "relies on the student's ability to demonstrate clearly defined and measurable competencies in a designated program" (Southern Association of Colleges and Schools Commission on Colleges [SACSCOC], 2013); (b) digital transformation, which offers opportunities to gather and combine new forms of data (e.g., time and clickstream data) in real time; and (c) the emphasis on combining multiple measures of student learning (McClarty & Gaertner, 2015; U.S. Department of Education, 2015). If the concepts of validity and reliability challenged us before, they will certainly test understanding in the next generation of assessments.

In this chapter, we will share ways in which psychometric concepts of validity and reliability will need to evolve in the context of direct assessment as measured using multiple measures and applied in a digital-first world. As with the *Standards for Educational and Psychological Testing* (AERA, APA, & NCME, 1985, 1999, 2014; subsequently referred to as the *Standards*), we tackle validity for next-generation assessments first and follow with a discussion of reliability.

Validity

Brennan (2006) shows dispensation for the lack of complete agreement regarding many evolving but fundamental topics in educational measurement and cautions that readers should not assume consensus among experts within the field.

The authors of this chapter, serving as reviewers and public commentators on the most recent edition of the *Standards*, cannot help but speculate that one of the areas Brennan is referencing is what is commonly known as *consequential validity*. There seems to be at least two areas of consensus, but there is still much disagreement in this regard. First is the area expressed in the *Standards* that echoes the chapter on validity by Samuel Messick (1989), which states, "It is the interpretation of test scores required by proposed uses that are evaluated (as part of validation), not the test themselves" (p. 9). This first standing suggests that both intended and unintended consequences of test score use must be considered. The second standing is the notion that validity is the continuous collection of evidence in defense of inferences drawn from assessment results, about which there is little disagreement or controversy.

The "controversy of consequences" has been debated in the measurement literature for quite some time (Cizek, 2012, 2015; Crocker, 1997; Lissitz & Samuelsen, 2007; Mehrens, 1997; Shepard, 1997; Sireci, 2016). For example, in her editorial to the 1997 edition of *Educational Measurement: Issues and Practice*, Linda Crocker stated, "The debate presented here has been brewing in psychometric circles for nearly a decade" and "the essential nature of validity as a psychometric construct, and what properly constitutes validation activities, has been opened for question" (p. 4). She further stated, "The question is whether the investigation of possible consequences of administering and using an assessment should be defined as an integral part of the validation plan" (p. 4).

In fact, this debate arguably expanded as articulated in a special issue of the *Journal of Educational Measurement* as anchored by Kane's (2013a) citations in the article "Validating the Interpretations *and Uses* of Test Scores" (emphasis added). Presumably, Kane chose this provocative title to generate the very debate we have been presenting—and as seen in the subsequent articles in that special issue it succeeded (Borsboom & Markus, 2013; Brennan, 2013; Haertel, 2013; Kane, 2013b; Moss, 2013; Newton, 2013; Sireci, 2013).

As seen later in this chapter, some prominent psychometricians continue arguing this question, insisting that justifications of a specific test use and validation of intended score inference are indeed separate and not combinable (Cizek, 2015). Other equally prominent psychometricians claim that the debate Crocker referenced in 1997 is over and should not be revisited. Sireci (2016), for example, suggested that "we move past the academic debate over what validity refers to and accept the AERA et. al., (2014) definition" (p. 15). Sireci (2016) stated, "It is not helpful to our profession, or to the science and practice of psychometrics to restrict validity to the theoretical realm of score interpretations. Actions and uses need to be validated, not interpretations that exist somewhere in the netherworld, never to be acted upon" (p. 15).

Both Cizek (2015) and Sireci (2016) have their followers, supporters, and detractors, but two things can be gleaned from their debate at least by these authors. First, clearly the "open question" Crocker (1997, p. 4) referred to is certainly not closed and the debate about the use of test scores and/ or consequences continues. This debate might be even more critical now as assessments move to digital formats and evolve into much more complicated scenarios regarding purpose, construct, and evidence. Second, and less clearly, there exists a gap between Cizek's needs in separating validity of inferences and evidence of appropriate use and Sireci's claim that they are one and the same. This is explored further in later sections of this chapter.

Reliability

The term *reliability* was coined by the English poet Samuel Taylor Coleridge in 1816 in a poem he wrote to his friend Robert Southey (Saleh & Marais, 2006). He noted: "He bestows all the pleasures, and inspires all that ease of mind on those around him or connected with him, with perfect consistency, and (if such a word might be framed) absolute reliability" (Coleridge, 1983). In measurement, *reliability* is defined as the consistency of a measure under different measurement conditions, where the construct remains unchanged. Features about the measurement of the construct that cause inconsistency, error sources, come from all matters of occasions. Some of those error sources are considered random whereas others are systematic errors.

Debates around reliability are less prevalent than those for validity. However, they exist. Disagreement tends to focus more on the ways to measure reliability than the concept or definition. Regarding the concept, one area of debate is whether the target of reliability is a single measure or measurement of a student learning outcome (SLO) via multiple measures. The concept of reliability in the 1930s was clearly focused on a single test and not on the combination of measures. Kuder and Richardson (1937) noted that "the theoretically best estimate of the reliability coefficient is stated in terms of a precise definition of the equivalence of two forms of a test" (p. 151). Although reliability was discussed in terms of measurement in the standards, for all practical purposes, it was applied at the test level. Over time, the concept of reliability has expanded to one more of measurement than of test forms. The 2014 *Standards* states: "Lengthening the assessment, and thereby increasing the size of the sample of tasks/items (or raters or occasions) being employed, is an effective and commonly used method for improving reliability/precision" (AERA, APA, & NCME, 2014, p. 38). Even though the concept of reliability goes beyond a single test to measurement including different tasks, items, raters, or occasions, debate about reliability of measurement with multiple measures from multiple sources is in its infancy.

The more pointed debate about reliability has been around how to measure or estimate it. Even in the first official published standards of achievement tests by a professional body (American Psychological Association, 1954), the lack of clarity about how to measure reliability was obvious. The 1954 *Standards* notes that *reliability* "is a generic term referring to many types of evidence. The several types of reliability coefficient do not answer the same questions and should be carefully distinguished" (p. 27). From classical test theory (CTT) reliability to item response theory (IRT) to generalizability theory (G theory), the ways to estimate reliability and, more precisely, sources of error variance have evolved.

With direct assessment measurement, the concept and estimation of reliability will need to evolve even more. No longer will the focus of measurement be on an individual assessment such as information literacy, but the measurement will be of more discrete SLOs, such as applying research principles and methods to gather and scrutinize information. The only way we will be able to reach acceptable levels of reliability and estimate different error sources will be to combine data across multiple sources on multiple types of educational activities that assess the competency of interest.

As we will see in later sections of this chapter, the science of reliability is how to draw such measures minimizing the sources of error impacting the resulting inferences.

Direct Assessment

This chapter is the authors' attempt to explain the evolution in the state of the art regarding the psychometric concepts of validity and reliability in the context of direct assessment. *Direct assessment* can be defined as assessments that directly measure SLOs that are competency based (SACSCOC, 2013). The measurement of specific SLOs is at a more granular level than traditional constructs for which our current psychometric methods were developed; therefore, changes to the ways in which we conceptualize and measure reliability and validity must be made.

Direct assessments focus on student competencies and do not incorporate student behaviors or compliance information. "Direct assessment competency-based educational programs use the direct assessment of student learning in lieu of measuring student learning in credit or clock hours" (SACSCOC, 2013, p. 1). Although these measures might appear objective, they may also involve human judgment typically seen in large-scale assessment when rubrics are often used to score a multitude of student performance measures. Direct assessment does not include grades, self-report measures, or many generalized survey instruments. Direct assessment does not include other surface measures of learning such as "seat time" (i.e., time on task), grades, attendance, or other noncompetency-based measures of cognitive outcomes (e.g., tacit knowledge).

The SACSCOC (2013) provides the following additional clarification:

> Federal regulations define a direct assessment competency-based educational program as an instructional program that, in lieu of credit hours or clock hours as a measure of student learning, uses direct assessment of student learning relying solely on the attainment of defined competencies, or recognizes the direct assessment of student learning by others.

Validity Defined

There is no single universal definition of *validity, validity evidence, validity theory,* or the *validation process,* but as Cizek (2015) points out, there are many aspects of the concept of validity that the measurement community seems to be in agreement about, including the following:

1. Validity pertains to the inferences intended to be made from test scores or their intended interpretations.
2. Validity is a unitary concept—despite the literature being replete with different types and kinds of validity.
3. Validity is not a state but reflects a continuum of evidence to support intended inferences made from test scores.
4. Validation is a continuous process.
5. Validation is an inherently value-laden process.

This simple five-step definition should not be too controversial for measurement specialists and others who have some familiarity with validity research in the field. For example, it is in agreement (for the most part) with what Cizek (2015) calls "perhaps the most . . . oft-cited description of validity" (p. 3):

> Validity is an integrated evaluative judgment of the degree to which empirical evidence and theoretical rationales support the adequacy and appropriateness of inferences and actions based on test scores of other modes of assessment. Broadly speaking, then, validity is an inductive summary of both the existing evidence for and the potential consequences of score interpretations and use. Hence, what is to be validated is not the test or observation device as such but the inferences derived from test scores or other indicators—inferences about score meaning or interpretation and about the implications for action that the interpretation entails. It is important to note that validity is a matter of degree, not all or none. Inevitably, then, validity is a continuing process. (Messick, 1989, p. 13)

Notice, however, that Messick's (1989) definition contains one additional phrase, "and the potential consequences of," related to the interpretation of test scores. This simple phrase has been at the heart of more recent debates of how best validity theory should evolve.

Evolution of Validity Theory

Brennan (2006) arguably provided the best summary of how the concept of validity has changed and evolved over the years. Cureton (1951) stated that validity was "how well a test does the job it is employed to do" (p. 621). This concept is similar to what many of us learned in measurement training, namely, that validity is the evidence that a test measures what it purports to measure. It is also not far from what Ebel (1983) described as *intrinsic rational validity*:

> The basis for the validity of any mental measurement lies in the rationale for the means used in making the measurement. Given the ability that the test is intended to measure, one can make rational inferences about the kind of tasks to be included in it, tasks that will require the ability to be measured. The more of this ability an examinee possesses, the more of the test tasks the examinee should be able to complete successfully. This is intrinsic validity because it is built into the test. It is rational validity because it is derived from rational inferences about the kind of tasks that will measure the intended ability. (p. 7)

Ebel (1983) goes on to link this concept to the *validity* definitions of the day by summarizing the notions of Thorndike (1918), Bridgman (1927), and Flanagan (1951) to emphasize the importance of establishing the limitations of score interpretation. Ebel (1983) and Cureton (1951) both offer aspects of validity theory that are well articulated elsewhere and are fundamental aspects of validity evidence, namely, content/construct-related evidence as well as criterion (correlational)-related for measures of direct assessment. This latter type of evidence shows the test samples from the domain of tasks or competencies desired and whether there is evidence that similar measures correlate to a positive degree and that dissimilar measures correlate inversely.

Brennan (2006) goes on to outline how the 1996 edition of the *Standards* (AERA, APA, & NCME) explicitly defines *validity categories*—content, criterion, and construct, which were called *aspects* or *concepts* of validity (p. 2). This trinitarian point of view was first defined by Guion (1980) and became one of the fundamental and dominating definitions of *validation* during this time. Brennan (2006) further outlines the evolution of validity theory. For example, Cronbach (1971) brings forward the notion that validity applies to the inferences made from the test scores and not the tests or the scores themselves. He states the following:

> Validation is the process of examining the accuracy of a specific prediction or inference made from a test score. To explain a test score, one must bring to bear some sort of theory about the causes of the test performance and about its implications. (p. 443)

As Brennan (2006) points out, Cronbach (1971) goes on to add another seminal aspect of validation, namely, that it is one unifying theory as opposed to the discrete types previously thought about (i.e., content, construct, and criterion aspects). He notes: "For purposes of exposition, it is necessary to subdivide what in the end must be a comprehensive, integrated evaluation of a test" (p. 445).

Hence, according to Brennan (2006) the evolution of validity theory has moved thus far in the timeline from three or four discrete types or aspects to one unified theory about the inferences made from test scores as supported by different types of evidence—content related, criterion related, and construct related.

This evolution has set the stage well for what some measurement experts contend is the penultimate discussion of validity and validity theory, namely, Messick's chapter in the third edition of *Educational Measurement* (Messick, 1989):

> Validity is an integrated evaluative judgment of the degree to which empirical evidence and theoretical rationales support the adequacy and appropriateness of inferences and actions based on test scores or other modes of assessment. Broadly speaking, then, validity is an inductive summary of both the existing evidence for and the potential consequences of score interpretation and use. Thus the key issues of test validity are the interpretability, relevance and utility of scores, the import or value implications of scores as a basis for action, and the functional worth of scores in terms of social consequences of their use. (p. 13)

As Brennan (2006) underscores: "Messick's treatment of the subject is notable on many levels. Perhaps most importantly, he repeatedly emphasizes that validity is an integrated evaluative judgment concerning inferences and *social consequences* (emphasis added) of test use" (p. 2). Brennan (2006) also points out that the most recent edition of the *Standards* (AERA, APA, & NCME, 2014) agrees with Messick in this regard:

> Validity refers to the degree to which evidence and theory support the interpretations of test scores entailed by proposed uses of tests. The process of validation involves accumulating evidence to provide a sound scientific basis for the proposed score interpretations. It is the interpretations of test scores required by proposed uses that are evaluated, not the test itself. (p. 9)

Sireci (2016) supports this argument by claiming that both the 1999 edition (AERA, APA, & NCME) and most recent edition (AERA, APA, & NCME, 2014) of the *Standards* remove any lack of clarity regarding the definition of *validity* and clearly define the term as both "clear test interpretation" and "test use" and calls these concepts "inseparable" (p. 8).

This debate about consequential validity does not appear to be a "clarifying" one or a debate about vocabulary or definition. Rather it seems that Cizek (2015) is purporting that the very definition of current *validity theory* is wrong and needs a correction. In contrast, Sireci (2016) is essentially saying that all we need to do is implement the existing definition and move on. This debate is very important for builders, owners, policymakers, and stakeholders of direct assessments, and this will be explored further in the next section. However, note that the five aspects about current validity theory discussed at the beginning of this section should still provide those involved in direct assessment with a sensible framework to identify, collect, and report the evidence required to defend inferences made from direct assessments in many contexts.

Consequential Validity

As alluded to in previous sections of this chapter, the debate about the role consequential validity plays in the continuing evolution of validity theory is still ongoing. The most recent online publication of *Assessment in Education* (Cizek, 2015; Kane, 2016; Markus, 2016; Moss, 2016; Newton, & Shaw, 2016; Sireci, 2016) contains the most recent set of articles engaging in this debate.

As test builders, scientists, and defenders of assessment globally, the authors of this chapter find the logic of the Cizek (2015) article to be the most helpful in articulating the problems direct assessment developers have had with the notion of consequential validity since Messick's original text (1989). These problems have not been around the concept of consequences—those of us who often appear in court, at legislative hearings, and in media events to defend the use of measures and assessments know all too well both the anticipated and unanticipated consequences of assessment—it is the *mixing of the different types of evidence needed* (evidence to defend the measure and evidence of how that measure is used) that has been muddled in the evolution of validity theory to date. As Cizek (2015) points out in his eloquent argument:

> For clarity, the two essential aims of defensible test development and use can be simplified as straightforward research questions:
>
> Q1: What do these scores mean?
> Q2: Should these scores be used for X (where X is a specific test use)? (p. 3)

Practical examples of these questions are illustrated in Table 4.1.

It is these interrogatories that represent both the dilemma for test builders and the challenges the authors of this chapter have struggled with for years. For example, when we were building the assessments in Texas (Smisko, Twing, & Denny, 2000), we followed standard protocols and procedures for collecting validity evidence for achievement tests. Namely, we collected countless sources of evidence in the "old" areas of content-, construct-, and criterion-related validity evidence. We showed correlations with other measures; correlations with grade point averages; and longitudinal analyses showing student performance improvement, particularly as related to remediation and recovery efforts. But to justify the policymakers' decisions to use the assessment results in the accountability system for Texas or to link it to graduation would require entirely different evidence, evidence beyond the purview of the assessment.

Cizek (2015) points out that what we had accomplished "was a necessary first-step—but not a sufficient condition—for the justification of test use," (p. 4) at least not as the current definition of *validity* stands. Cizek goes on to describe the second half of a two-step process and proposes a revised framework for defensible testing by outlining a way to collect justification of intended test use. The authors of this chapter agree with Cizek (2015) when he states:

> Policy implications or other social consequences of testing are invoked as bearing on the validity of a test when they have no relationship whatsoever to the meaning of the test scores. (p. 5)

We find connecting policy implications and testing consequences to the concept of validity unwise and illogical. Yet, the current status of validity

TABLE 4.1
Practical Examples of Defensible Test Development and Use

Score Meaning	Score Use
Q1: Do these end-of-course capstone project scores reflect mastery of a degree program's content standards?	Q2: Should these end-of-course capstone scores be used for awarding a program degree?
Q1: Do these ACT/SAT scores measure high school preparation for success in college?	Q2: Should these ACT/SAT scores be used for college admission decisions?

theory indicates this as best practice. That is why we also agree with Cizek (2015) that a new revised framework for the two types of evidence needed (evidence for intended score inference *and* justification of intended score use) is needed "for defensible testing" (p. 5).

A new framework with two evidence types benefits users of direct assessments. It is not the case that inferences about scores resulting from assessments in the context of competency-based educational programs will be the end of how the assessment information will be used. Rather, given the very nature of a competency-based decision, it is likely that all sorts of uses of these results will be desired. Hence, Cizek's (2015) "revised framework for defensible testing" (p. 5) provides a theory of action users of direct assessments can follow for collecting evidence for both score inference and test use.

Unfortunately, Cizek's (2015) framework has not been met with universal acceptance. Perhaps its largest critic is Sireci (2015), who argues, "To ignore test use in defining validity is tantamount to defining validity for 'useless' tests" (p. 1). Sireci's argument misses the point and illustrates a misunderstanding with the two-step process described by Cizek (2015):

> To understand my point, it is helpful to ask the question "Can we have test interpretation without test use?" That is, can someone interpret a test score but never act upon that interpretation? I must admit it is possible, but why would we develop a test that we expect will never be used for a practical purpose? (p. 12)

No one is arguing that test use is not part of the process or the theory of validity. Rather, we are arguing that two different types of evidence are required, one traditionally associated with validation in the collection of evidence to support the inferences made from test scores and the other to justify its use. As Cizek (2015) points out, the first is a required but insufficient condition to justify use. The authors of this chapter find it particularly ironic that Sireci (2016) refers to this as validity of useless tests but never solves the interrogatories that are so simple and yet so powerful that Cizek (2015) offers as questions.

The Evolution of Reliability

The history of the measurement concept called *reliability* is described in three stages. In the first stage, focus is on the reliability of a single measure and error (unreliability) is investigated one potential source at a time. The second stage also focuse on reliability of a single measure but differs from the first

TABLE 4.2
Three Stages in the Evolution of Reliability

Stage	Reliability Focus	Error Analysis
1	Single measure	Single error source
2	Single measure, distribution wide	Multiple error sources
3	Multiple measures	Multiple interrelated error sources

stage by expanding the error analysis to more than one source simultaneously and conditioning reliability across the score distribution. The third stage, the one on which most current literature is focused, expands reliability beyond single measures to the combination of data from multiple measures involving multiple sources of non-independent error sources. This third stage is very application oriented, looking at the reliability of the combination of data from multiple methods and sources. Table 4.2 presents a summary of the three stages.

Stage 1: Single Measure, Single Error Source

The first stage of reliability was characterized by the use of CTT to define *reliability*. From a CTT perspective, reliability was based on a true score model, where an observed score variance is composed of two independent variance sources, the true score plus error. In CTT, the expected value of the error is assumed to be zero, which means that the errors are independent or random. In simple terms, this means there is no reason to believe that we can predict with accuracy the probability of a correct response to, say, question number two on an assessment if we know the examinee's response to question number one, other than position of the latent trait being measured.

In CTT, *reliability* is defined as a coefficient of the true score variance divided by the observed score variance. To make reliability (and its counterpart, unreliability of error) more relevant, it can be expressed in terms of a measurement scale or standard error of measurement (*SEM*):

$$\sigma_e = \sigma_x \sqrt{(1 - \rho_{xt}^2)}$$

Here the *SEM* is the average size of the measurement errors for the observed score of the random variable being studied.

CTT focuses on different types of errors separately, leading to many estimates of reliability for the same measure, such as test-retest reliability, focused on error introduced by time; alternate forms reliability, focused on error introduced by forms; different internal consistency reliability, focused on errors due to items; and interrater reliability, focused on rating judgment errors.

Stage 2: Single Measure, Distribution Wide, Multiple Error Sources

Stage 2 characterized reliability using two newer theories of measurement, generalizability theory (G theory) and item response theory (IRT). Fortunately, technology expanded to help measurement experts investigate multiple error sources during this second stage of the evolution of the concept of reliability. This enhanced researchers' ability to conduct more sophisticated analyses and led to a deeper understanding about how to control error and, hence, increase reliability of a particular measure.

Generalizability Theory

Introduced in 1972 by Lee Cronbach (Cronbach, Gleser, Nanda, & Rajaratnam, 1972), generalizability extended the idea of measurement variance (under CTT, conceptualized as only two components—true score variance and error variance) to multiple sources of variance. In G theory, variance due to raters, items, time, and other factors (or facets) can be disaggregated and estimated into different sources of variance. Analysis of variance (ANOVA) procedures estimate these variance components (Brennan, 1992). Through the process of identifying the particular error sources, G theory offers the opportunity to diagnose causes for error and ways to reduce them, thereby increasing reliability.

Unlike CTT, G theory does not make distributional assumptions about the measure. It assumes only randomly parallel tests, where conditions are considered a sample from the universe of admissible conditions such that variance components in the sample can be connected or *generalized* to the universe of variance components. The connection enables an estimate of the dependability of the measurement in the broader universe (Brennan, 2001; Shavelson & Webb, 1991).

Also unlike CTT, G theory decomposes the variance by different error sources *simultaneously*, resulting in a reliability estimate for the entire set of measures and associated sources of error.

Besides these differences with CTT, G theory helped the evolution of reliability in several ways. In G theory, the types of decisions to be made using the measures are taken into account, and separate estimates of reliability are provided differently for relative (e.g., comparing student writing samples) versus absolute decisions (e.g., determining whether a student has met writing proficiency). Because G theory is a variance decomposition model, it also allows for analysis of fixed, random, nested, and crossed facets or variance components.

Item Response Theory

In IRT, reliability is conceptualized as information, or precision for distinguishing learners on a construct (e.g., lower and higher ability). This conceptualization differentiates how IRT treats reliability from CTT because now the error is conditional on ability or skill level, not generalized across the entire score distribution. The information comes from the items on the measure, and the information is expected to vary dependent on the location in the score distribution. Reliability is calculated as a function, called the information function. The information function is directly related to the *SEM* in a matter analogous to the *SEM* in CTT. In IRT, however, the information is conditional on the location in the score distribution; reliability is not uniform for all scores. Specifically, error is calculated as the inverse of the information function, where the standard error of the estimate (*SEE*) is expressed as follows:

$$SEE(\theta) = 1/\sqrt{I(\theta)}$$

Thissen (2000) illustrated that a more traditional reliability coefficient (in the form of a correlation coefficient) can be calculated as follows:

$$r = 1 - (1/I(\theta))$$

Limitations

Although at the onset it appears IRT and G theory offer marked improvements to how sources of error are analyzed when compared to CTT, they are not without the following limitations:

- *Complexity:* To dissect different error variances, the data collection design requires sufficient replications over the error sources. For example, to calculate errors due to raters or occasions, a study design would need to include a sufficient number of raters and occasions (often more than is practical in real-world circumstances) to estimate these error variances.
- *Limited focus:* IRT advanced the concept of nonuniform reliability across the score distribution but it limited the focus on errors due to test questions and is difficult without multidimensional extensions

to capture other facets of the measure (e.g., raters, occasions, or question types).

- *Single measures*: Despite the advances of G theory and IRT, reliability focus continued to be on a single measure. Reliability was conceptualized as a reliability of a measure. Additional measures of the construct were typically used to evaluate the reliability of the single measure instead of creating a combination to strengthen measurement.

Stage 3: Multiple Measures, Multiple Interrelated Error Sources

One of the largest needs in measurement, typically driven by the integration of technology with almost all aspects of learning, is the need to directly measure student competencies using new measures, such as technology-enhanced performance assessments, portfolios, and performance in simulations and games. Another complicating factor is the overwhelming amount of digital data and the proliferation of methods for combining different measures, especially those measures collected electronically. For these reasons, the way reliability is conceptualized and measured continues to evolve. This evolution is characterized as reliability of measurement, not the separate reliability of measures, and assumes all measurement will go beyond a single measure.

With direct assessments, faculty members capture a sample of what students can do using direct methods, such as pre- and postassessments, portfolio evaluations, capstone projects, and internship evaluations. To determine whether students have mastered the defined competencies, faculty must combine evidence from these multiple measures. A faculty member's decision, or inference, about whether the student demonstrations meet the minimum level of competency will be based on multiple sources of evidence. Making judgments based on multiple measures will push the measurement community to evolve both the definition and measurement of *reliability*.

The focus on direct assessments, or the need to measure defined student competencies (Accrediting Commission for Community and Junior Colleges, 2016; SACSCOC, 2013), encourages assessment using less traditional formats, relying often on technology-enhanced or -enabled performance assessment. In the past, researchers raised reliability concerns related to performance assessments. Phillips (1996) noted:

> The number of [performance] tasks is inversely related to the error variance in most generalizability studies—the fewer the tasks the larger the error variance. One approach to reducing error variance might be to nar-

row the domain of tasks so that each is a slight modification of the others (*thereby increasing replicants of sampled behaviors such that a clear and more reliable picture of student latent ability can be inferred*). The other approach is to increase the number of tasks (say to 10 or more) to reduce the error (*thereby increasing replicants of sampled behaviors directly*). Although this may be a costly alternative, it often makes more sense than restricting the domain. (p. iv)

Phillips's perspective is based on the idea that limited information comes from performance assessments in the form of rubric scores or teacher ratings, where the output information is a summary evaluation of the performance. Moss (1994) also noted the challenge of reliability in what she called "less standardized forms of assessment" such as portfolios when she wrote that these types of assessment "present serious problems for reliability, in terms of generalizability across readers and tasks as across other facets of measurement" (p. 6).

When investigating the liability of performance assessment, most current research makes two primary assumptions. First, it is assumed that scores from performance measures "stand alone" and are not combined with other measures. Second, there is the tendency to assume that information from these assessments is in the form of summary scores or overall ratings of the performance. If only one or a few scores result from performance assessments, then lower evidence of reliability is a real issue, making reliability of the inferences a concern (as described by Phillips, 1996).

However, in digital learning environments, there is a new opportunity. Literally all data regarding student performance can be collected (e.g., clickstream, time, and performance data), and sophisticated and sometimes real-time data analytics can be generated. This allows for the use of very rich student performance information while learning is taking place. Furthermore, this information does not have to be limited to only student performance or summative-type scores. A variety of many different measures and aspects or facets of a construct can be brought together. For example, this might entail measures of not if but how students solve problems during classroom learning activities, streaming data from games and simulations, teacher ratings, evaluations and grades on the competencies, and performance on homework or tutorials.

If we intend to measure the more granular competencies that are called for in direct assessment, we will have to pull data from multiple sources and draw on rich digital learning data, or what DiCerbo and Behrens (2014) call the *digital ocean*, to reliably measure these competencies.

Suppose the goal is to measure students' physical science knowledge of solids, liquids, and gases. Operating in this third stage of the evolution of measurement reliability does not focus on individual measures separately— instead, student performance from all of these measures is combined, resulting in increased measurement precision. Importantly, the increased measurement precision will be necessary if more granular aspects of learning are to be inferred. The following are examples of multiple measures to be used:

- Student performance data extracted from simulation activities where students drag pictures of solids, liquids, and gases into the correct categories
- Teacher grades on the completed student in-class activities
- Student homework data from an activity where students take pictures from their environment of solids, liquids, and gases
- Group performance ratings by students on activities requiring students to describe particle motion in solids, liquids, and gases
- Student physical science summative testing scores

Researchers are implementing a variety of methods to estimate the reliability of measurement from these combined sets of data. If the goal is to calculate a measure of student ability at one time, structural equation modeling techniques can be used (Zanella & Cantaluppi, 2013). More recently, researchers are using Bayesian inference networks, or Bayes nets, to use evidence to measure more granular concepts in a learning progression via a competency model. These Bayes nets allow continuous updates to the probability models so that researchers can model in real-time student understanding of each competency. This level of complexity to determine the reliability of the combined data sets would need to be evaluated within the context of a particular setting or degree program to determine the relevance of the reliability estimate to the particular test use or interpretation.

Real-time data collection as evidence of student mastery of competencies should challenge the users of direct assessment models as the evolution of not only reliability theory under this third stage but also the measures themselves. Direct assessment users will need to determine learning data that indeed directly measure each of the defined competencies and combine those to form a reliable measure of the mastery. Table 4.3 summarizes the reliability concepts across different theories for the different stages.

From a variance decomposition perspective, combining evidence from multiple sources measuring a construct will increase the true score variance, or latent trait variance, and reduce error variance. By decomposing total

TABLE 4.3
Summary of Reliability Concepts Across Different Theories

Theory	Statistical Model	Reliability Concept	General Formula	Applied to a Score (e.g., student score)
Classical (Stage 1)	True score	Ratio of true score variance to observed score variance	$\rho_{xt}^2 = \dfrac{\sigma_t^2}{\sigma_x^2}$	Standard error of measurement
Generalizability Theory (Stage 2)	Factorial analysis of variance	Reliability considered in the context of the measurement situation	Many formulas	Generalizability (G) coefficient
IRT (Stage 2)	Probabilistic		$r = 1 - (1/I(\theta))$	Standard error of the estimate (conditional on ability estimate)
Multiple Measures (Stage 3)	Structural equation model, probabilistic	Reliability strengthened by bringing rich data from many sources together to enhance true score, or latent score, variance	Can use a variety of formulas	Dependent on the methods deployed

variance into more aspects related to the construct (that would otherwise fall into error variance), less and less of the total variance will be attributed to error (random or systematic). This is analogous to adding more test questions on a simple multiple-choice test—increasing the observations of student performance tells us more accurately about that performance and this is translated into improved reliability.

Guide to Validity and Reliability of Direct Assessments

This section provides some suggestions or guidelines intended to focus the reader on the evidence collection needed to defend the reliability and

Figure 4.1. Conceptual map showing the structure of measurement.

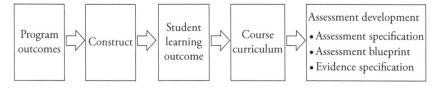

validity of direct assessments. To frame this section of the chapter, it is important to offer a *conceptual map* (see Figure 4.1) showing the relationship between the *construct* (the broadest definition of what is to be measured) and the *evidence* (the test item or evidence of direct measure in the narrowest definition).

For example, using Figure 4.1, consider the development of a mathematics program. First, the faculty articulate program outcomes. This step provides the broad framework from which all curriculum and assessment decisions will be made. The second step entails the identification of the construct, which is a "grand representation" of what is being taught and measured—say, for example, business mathematics. In the third step, from this construct? the SLOs are defined in order to specify the student outcomes expected at the completion of the course requirements of the degree program. The fourth step is based on the SLOs, with which faculty specify the learning targets and, as a result, the course curriculum is developed. After the curriculum has been used to operationalize the SLOs, the content for the assessment of the SLOs is identified through content standards. The final step in this process is the development of the assessment.

Once the measurement content or direct assessment evidence is determined, rules for how the evidence will be measured are defined as part of the assessment specifications. For example, it might be decided that multiple measures may be utilized such that 60% of the assessment composite will use objective measures, 20% will use portfolio evaluation data, and only 20% will require performance tasks. Once the assessment specifications are defined, the assessment blueprint will again clarify, or narrow, what is being measured by implementing operational aspects of the assessment. For example, the assessment blueprint outlines how many direct assessment measures, of what type, measuring which subskills of the content standards. Finally, evidence specifications define what is and is not allowed regarding specific test questions or direct assessment evidence of the competency. For example, item or evidence specifications might state that only the evaluation from independent student performance is included. As is evident from this conceptual map, the generation of the assessment involves a set of finer and finer judgments that actually operationally define what is being measured and evidence supporting mastery. As such, these cascading judgments are very important as we consider the evidence we will need to show both reliability and validity of the direct assessment.

As presented previously in this chapter, validity is established with the collection of evidence to defend the inferences drawn from the results of an assessment, or drawn from the compilation of direct measures. As such, to improve the strength of the validity argument in support of an assessment, the string of this evidence should be continuously reviewed, updated, and improved. Table 4.4 provides some examples and steps that will likely lead to improvements in the defensibility of this evidence.

Unlike validity, reliability is concerned with the identification and removal of error from the collection of student responses to the assessment. Literally, everything that can be done to reduce error—from internal aspects of a direct assessment such as increasing the amount of evidence for a competency and standardized procedures for assigning a portfolio score—will likely lead to error reduction and hence improved reliability. Table 4.4 provides some ways in which such error can be minimized.

Conclusion

As the concept of assessment evolves from holistic grades that incorporate learning of a particular construct with compliance factors (e.g., seat time) to assessment of the specific SLOs using direct assessments, so should the concepts of validity and reliability. Specifically, we need to evolve the framework of validity of direct assessments to one that requires collecting evidence for both score inference and assessment. We need to evolve the concept of reliability to one of measurement (not of the measures themselves), where we combine information from multiple sources and multiple measures to strengthen true score variance. We need to leverage the power of digital data throughout the learning process to bring sufficient evidence from multiple direct measures of student competencies so that the reliability of defining whether students have met the minimal level of a competency is not arbitrary. The tools and data for evolving traditional psychometric principles to the modern problem of direct assessment in competency-based education exist. We must embrace them and apply them, so that we can support the direct assessments needed for next-generation learning.

TABLE 4.4

Ideas to Improve Validity and Reliability of Direct Assessments

Validity Evidence	Considerations	Comments
Content	What is the relationship between the SLO as operationally defined by the evidence source and the curriculum and content standards?	Ensure alignment with the instruction, SLO, and assessment(s).
Concurrent/ external	How well do measures of the SLO relate to similar independent measures?	Relationship between professional certification results or other independent measures and the assessment of the SLOs.
Content	Is the direct assessment difficulty appropriately aligned to the content standards being assessed?	Evidence gathered from performance tasks and other measures of direct assessment that are appropriate in difficulty as determined by the instructional objective they are trying to measure.
Administration specifications	Have direct assessment methods been designed with clear directions and specifics about what learning evidence is appropriate?	Examinees might not automatically understand the types of evidence needed to illustrate their learning competencies so clarity in the types of evidence they need to produce will improve both the reliability and validity of direct assessment; sharing a scoring rubric in advance is considered a best practice.
Speededness	Has sufficient time been allotted for students to produce evidence that they have mastered the competencies? (If time is part of construct being measured, this consideration may be less applicable.)	Unless speed of response is part of the construct being measured by definition (i.e., "perceptual speed and accuracy"), then allow enough time for the students to produce direct evidence of mastering competencies without time pressure.

References

Accrediting Commission for Community and Junior Colleges, Western Association of Schools and Colleges. (2016). *Accreditation reference handbook*. Retrieved from http://www.accjc.org/wp-content/uploads/2016/08/Accreditation_Reference_Handbook_July_2016.pdf

American Educational Research Association, American Psychological Association, & National Council on Measurement in Education. (1999). *Standards for educational and psychological testing*. Washington, DC: American Educational Research Association.

American Educational Research Association, American Psychological Association, & National Council on Measurement in Education. (2014). *Standards for educational and psychological testing*. Washington, DC: American Educational Research Association.

American Psychological Association. (1954). Technical recommendations for psychological tests and diagnostic techniques [Supplement]. *Psychological Bulletin, 51*(2), 1–38.

American Psychological Association, American Educational Research Association, & National Council on Measurement in Education. (1966). *Standards for educational and psychological tests and manuals*. Washington, DC: American Psychological Association.

Borsboom, D., & Markus, K. A. (2013). Truth and evidence in validity theory. *Journal of Educational Measurement, 50*(1), 110–114.

Brennan, R. L. (1992). *Elements of generalizability theory*. Iowa City, IA: American College Testing.

Brennan, R. L. (2001). *Generalizability theory*. New York, NY: Springer Verlag.

Brennan, R. L. (2006). Editor's preface. In R. L. Brennan (Ed.), *Educational measurement* (4th ed., pp. xv–xvii). Westport, CT: Praeger.

Brennan, R. L. (2013). Commentary on validating the interpretations and uses of test scores. *Journal of Educational Measurement, 50*(1), 74–83.

Bridgman, P. W. (1927). *The logic of modern physics*. New York, NY: Macmillan.

Cizek, G. J. (2012). Defining and distinguishing validity: Interpretations of score meaning and justifications of test use. *Psychological Methods, 17*, 31–43.

Cizek, G. J. (2015). Validating test score meaning and defending test score use: Different aims, different methods. *Assessment in Education: Principles, Policy & Practice, 23*(2), 212–225.

Coleridge, S. T. (1983). Biographia literaria. In J. Engell & W. J. Bate (Eds.), *The collected works of Samuel Taylor Coleridge*. Princeton, NJ: Princeton University Press.

Crocker, L. (1997). The great validity debate. *Educational Measurement: Issues and Practice, 16*, 4.

Cronbach, L. J. (1971). Test validation. In R. L. Thorndike (Ed.), *Educational measurement* (2nd ed., pp. 443–507). Washington, DC: American Council on Education.

Cronbach, L. J., Gleser, G. C., Nanda, H., & Rajaratnam, N. (1972). The dependability of behavioral measurements. New York, NY: Wiley & Sons.

Cureton, E. E. (1951). Validity. In E. F. Lindquist (Ed.), *Educational measurement* (1st ed., pp. 621–694). Washington, DC: American Council on Education.

DiCerbo, K. E., & Behrens, J. T. (2014). *The impact of the digital ocean on education* [White paper]. London: Pearson. Retrieved from https://research.pearson.com/digitalocean

Ebel, R. L. (1983). The practical validation of tests of ability. *Educational Measurement: Issues and Practice, 2*(2), 7–10.

Flanagan, J. C. (1951). The use of comprehensive rationales in test development. *Educational and Psychological Measurement, 11*, 151–155.

Frisbie, D. A. (2005). Measurement 101: Some fundamentals revisited. *Educational Measurement: Issues and Practice, 24*(3), 21–28.

Guion, R. M. (1980). On Trinitarian conceptions of validity. *Professional Psychology, 11*, 385–398.

Haertel, E. (2013). Getting the help we need. *Journal of Educational Measurement, 50*(1), 84–90.

Kane, M. T. (2013a). Validating the interpretations and uses of test scores. *Journal of Educational Measurement, 50*(1), 1–73.

Kane, M. T. (2013b). Validation as a pragmatic, scientific activity. *Journal of Educational Measurement, 50*(1), 115–122.

Kane, M. T. (2016). Explicating validity. *Assessment in Education: Principles, Policy & Practice, 23*(2), 198–211.

Kuder, G. F., & Richardson, M. W. (1937). The theory of the estimation of test reliability. *Psychometrika, 2,* 151–160.

Lissitz, R. W., & Samuelsen, K. (2007). A suggested change in terminology and emphasis regarding validity and education. *Educational Researcher, 36*, 437–448.

Markus, K. A. (2016). Alternative vocabularies in the test validity literature. *Assessment in Education: Principles, Policy & Practice, 23*(2), 252–267.

McClarty, K. L., & Gaertner, M. N. (2015). *Measuring mastery: Best practices for assessment in competency-based education.* AEI Series on Competency-Based Higher Education. Retrieved from https://www.aei.org/publication/measuring-mastery-best-practices-for-assessment-incompetency-based-education/

Mehrens, W. L. (1997). The consequences of consequential validity. *Educational Measurement: Issues and Practice, 16*, 16–18.

Messick, S. (1989). Validity. In R. L. Linn (Ed.), *Educational measurement* (3rd ed., pp. 13–103). New York, NY: Macmillan.

Messick, S. (1994). The interplay of evidence and consequences in the validation of performance assessments. *Educational Researcher, 23*(2), 13–23.

Moss, P. A. (1994). Can there be validity without reliability? *Educational Researcher, 23*(4), 5–12.

Moss, P. A. (2013). Validity in action: Lessons from studies of data use. *Journal of Educational Measurement, 50*(1), 91–98.

Moss, P. A. (2016). Shifting the focus of validity for test use. *Assessment in Education: Principles, Policy & Practice, 23*(2), 236–251.

Newton, P. E. (2013). Two kinds of argument? *Journal of Educational Measurement, 50*(1), 105–109.

Newton, P. E., & Shaw, S. D. (2016). Disagreement over the best way to use the word 'validity' and options for reaching consensus. *Assessment in Education: Principles, Policy & Practice, 23*(2), 316–318.

Phillips, S. E. (1996). Legal defensibility of standards: Issues and policy perspectives. *Educational Measurement: Issues and Practice, 15*(3), 5–13.

Saleh, J. H., & Marais, K. (2006, February). Highlights from the early (and pre-) history of reliability engineering. *Reliability Engineering and System Safety, 91*(2), 249–256.

Shavelson, R. J., & Webb, N. M. (1991). *Generalizability theory: A primer.* Thousand Oaks, CA: Sage.

Shepard, L. A. (1997). The centrality of test use and consequences for test validity. *Educational Measurement: Issues and Practice, 16*, 5–13.

Sireci, S. G. (2013). Agreeing on validity arguments. *Journal of Educational Measurement, 50*(1), 99–104.

Sireci, S. G. (2016). On the validity of useless tests. *Assessment in Education: Principles, Policy & Practice, 23*(2), 319–321.

Smisko, A., Twing, J. S., & Denny, P. (2000). The Texas model for content and curricular validity. *Applied Measurement in Education, 13*(4), 333–342.

Southern Association of Colleges and Schools Commission on Colleges. (2013). *Direct assessment, competency-based educational programs* [Policy statement]. Retrieved from http://www.sacscoc.org/pdf/081705/DirectAssessmentCompe tencyBased.pdf

Thissen, D. (2000). Reliability and measurement precision. In H. Wainer (Ed.), *Computerized adaptive testing: A primer* (2nd ed., pp. 159–184). Mahwah, NJ: Lawrence Erlbaum Associates.

Thorndike, E. L. (1918). The nature, purposes and general methods of measurement of educational products. In *The measurement of educational products* (17th Yearbook, Part II, pp. 16–24). Chicago, IL: National Society for the Study of Education.

U.S. Department of Education. (2015). *Fact sheet: Testing action plan.* Retrieved from http://www.ed.gov/news/press-releases/fact-sheet-testing-action-plan

Zanella, A., & Cantaluppi, G. (2013). *Global evaluation of reliability for a structural equation model with latent variables and ordinal observations.* Dipartimento di Scienze Statistiche, Università Cattolica del Sacro Cuore. Retrieved from http://meetings.sis-statistica.org/index.php/sis2013/ALV/paper/viewFile/2728/429

5

INDIRECT ASSESSMENTS IN HIGHER EDUCATION

Thomas F. Nelson Laird, Indiana University

Allison BrckaLorenz, Indiana University

I n the previous chapters, the authors focused on the direct assessment of student learning. In this chapter, we focus on indirect assessments as they are used in higher education. The purpose of this chapter is to define *indirect assessment*, explain common ways in which it is conducted, and offer a summary of the strengths and limitations of different versions of this type of assessment.

Before providing definitions, consider an example. Pandora, a student at a liberal arts college in Iowa, took a critical thinking test as she entered college in the fall of her first year and each spring until she graduated. In addition, just prior to graduation, Pandora was asked to indicate on a questionnaire how much her collegiate experience had helped her to learn to think critically. For our purposes, the testing of her critical thinking skills over time during college is a direct assessment of an aspect of learning whereas the questionnaire item should be considered an indirect assessment. It is worth noting that assessments of learning likely fall on a continuum from completely direct to completely indirect with very few situated at the far ends of the spectrum (Ewell & Jones, 1993). For example, the test of critical thinking in our example is likely estimating only true or actual learning, but that test, which should be asking the student to *use* the skill being tested, is more direct than a questionnaire item about perceived learning.

Indirect assessments in higher education gather evidence about learning rather than attempting to measure learning directly (Allen, 2004; Palomba & Banta, 1999). Although it is tempting to view indirect assessments as proxy measures, or substitutes for direct measures, users of indirect assessments should accept that indirect assessments most likely capture aspects of the learning process or perceptions of learning, not actual student learning. Indirect assessments are unlikely to provide the evidence needed to make judgments about, for example, the amount a student learned to think critically. This is because they are not intended to do so (the exception, of course, is when a strong relationship between indirect and direct assessments has been established). For example, Pandora may think that she is far more (or less) advanced in learning to think critically than the test of her critical thinking skills shows. A lack of relationship between direct and indirect measures is not, however, necessarily cause for concern. In our particular example, Pandora may overestimate (or underestimate) her critical thinking skills relative to what her test scores show because Pandora and the test may define *critical thinking* quite differently.

Indirect assessments can be made by asking for information from students about their experiences and attitudes or from the perceptions of those who work with students, such as faculty, staff, parents, and administrators. People in higher education commonly ask students about their experiences, study habits, satisfaction, and perceptions of learning, and also gather information about the courses they take, their grades, and whether they have declared a major. All of these indirect assessments give us insight into students' learning processes.

Indirect methods of assessment provide information about students' perceptions of their performance and their academic environment, as well as how they feel their institution contributes to their learning. An indirect assessment can show how much students feel their experience at the institution has contributed to their growth in areas like critical thinking skills. Indirect assessments may also help to explain students' performance levels. For example, through other questions asked of Pandora, we may learn the course characteristics; in-class and out-of-class activities; and personal dispositions that relate to Pandora's growth in critical thinking skills, including things like how much Pandora's coursework emphasized the use of higher order thinking. Although indirect assessments do not directly measure facets of learning, they should be used when there is a desire to understand the processes and attitudes that are correlated with the development of that aspect of learning. Even when the connection between direct and indirect assessments of a particular aspect of learning is well established through extensive review of previous literature and rigorous research studies across a wide variety of contexts, results from indirect assessments should still be interpreted with caution and should never be viewed as a complete substitute for direct knowledge of student learning, particularly for individual students.

In this chapter, we write about closed-ended questioning, open-ended questioning, and archival records, as it is through questioning and accessing records that indirect assessment occurs. First, we define each of these three categories. Second, we explain how these types of questions or records get developed and what methods are used to gather information using these types of questions or records. Third, we summarize the strengths and limitations of each.

Definitions

In this section, we define *closed-ended* and *open-ended questioning* as well as *archival records*. The definitions are fairly straightforward, and readers are likely aware of each. We also draw from our experience as the designers of indirect assessments to help illustrate each definition.

Closed-Ended Questioning

Closed-ended questions generally contain questions, items, and a predetermined set of responses from which a respondent chooses. Responses are often brief, and questions can usually be answered simply and quickly (Allen, 2004; Dillman, 2000; Groves et al., 2004). Responses can be considered correct or incorrect or can be perceptions or opinions, but ultimately the direction of the responses is in the control of the researcher or assessment professional (i.e., the question asker). The intention for closed-ended questions is often to quickly gather consistent information from respondents rather than allow respondents to provide unique or unanticipated answers. Common formats of closed-ended questions include selecting one response from a list, selecting all responses that apply from a list, or selecting a rating on a scale continuum of responses. Because closed-ended questions can be asked of many people, their responses can be used to categorize people into groups or they can be analyzed statistically. Closed-ended questions can be relatively simple, asking students to report their age or whether they live on or off campus. Demographic questions are often asked as closed-ended questions. Closed-ended questions, however, can also require more thought, such as asking students how many hours per week they typically spend preparing for class or how many pages of writing they completed for assignments in their most recent semester. Response options can also be vague, such as asking students how often they have given a course presentation during the current school year (very often, often, sometimes, or never) or to rate on a scale from 1 (not at all) to 7 (very much) the extent to which courses have challenged them to do their best work. Response options can also be very specific, like asking for a count of the number of times students met with an adviser (Allen, 2004; Dillman, 2000).

Open-Ended Questioning

In contrast to closed-ended questions, open-ended questions often ask respondents to create longer and more thoughtful replies. Within the boundary of the question, respondents construct their own response, often allowing for answers that were not anticipated by the researcher or assessment professional (Allen, 2004; Groves et al., 2004). The intention for open-ended questions is often exploratory in nature, either to start a conversation with respondents or to gather more information about a respondent's experiences. Often open-ended responses are reflective, contain opinions or feelings, and are descriptive of respondents' personal experiences; the direction of the responses to open-ended questions is more in the control of respondents. Common open-ended question prompts begin with "how," "why," or "describe." Questions can be very specific, asking for more detail about a particular experience, or relatively generic, such as asking for any additional comments from the respondent or asking for any additional information that the respondent may want the researcher or assessment professional to know. Although open-ended questions generally ask for in-depth and detailed responses, they can be shorter, such as if researchers or assessment professionals are trying to supplement the response list of a closed-ended question by examining responses that do not align with the predetermined list of response options (i.e., "other, please specify"; Dillman, 2000).

Archival Records

Archival records are academic records and official documentation that accumulate over time; they are related to teaching and learning and are kept to show the goals and accomplishments of individuals or organizations at an institution. These records can be very specific to individual students, such as course plans, transcripts, average GPA, awards, certifications, participation in academic experiences or cocurricular activities, and capstone portfolios or theses. These records can be course level, such as course descriptions, course syllabi, learning outcomes, course evaluation ratings, grading rubrics, and prerequisite requirements. Academic programs or departments may have their own archival records, such as general education or major requirements, departmental learning goals, the availability of electives, or program admission requirements. Institutions will also have archival records, such as admissions requirements, graduation requirements, student services records, mission statements, and accreditation documentation (Ewell & Jones, 1993; Maki, 2002; Suskie, 2009).

Developing Questions and Records

In this section, we describe how open-ended and closed-ended questions as well as archival records get developed for indirect assessments and what characteristics they should have. We highlight, using examples, good practice and things to try to avoid.

Closed-Ended Questioning

Good closed-ended questions should be unambiguous, simple, and written with language that is clear to respondents (Allen, 2004; Erwin, 1991). Any ambiguous terms, such as *learning community*, should be defined, particularly if terms are not clearly understood by respondents. Questions should not be leading, biased, or threatening to students. Asking students about whether they ever cheated on an exam may make them uncomfortable or encourage students to intentionally provide inaccurate information. Questions should be written so they can be understood on their own and are asking about only a single thing at a time. For example, the question "To what extent do you feel your instructors and institution are supportive of your learning?" is asking respondents for information about both their instructors and institutions. It is possible that students find their instructors but not their institution supportive, making this question difficult for respondents to answer (Allen, 2004; Groves et al., 2004).

Questions will also be easier for respondents and may elicit more accurate information if they are placed in a reasonable time frame (Banta & Paloma, 2015; Erwin, 1991). Senior students, for example, are more likely to be able to accurately recall how many papers they wrote in the previous semester than how many papers they wrote during their entire college career. It will be easier for respondents to answer related questions together, but the ordering of questions can be important. Asking students about the quantity of their writing assignments directly before a question about how challenging their coursework is may elicit different responses if questions about students' use of quantitative reasoning skills precede the question about challenging coursework. Students may think differently about challenging coursework depending on their thoughts about writing versus quantitative reasoning (Dillman, 2000).

Researchers and assessment professionals must carefully consider the response options of closed-ended questions. It is extremely important for closed-ended questions to include all possible response categories, and response categories should not overlap (Groves et al., 2004). If researchers or assessment professionals are unsure if they have included all possible response options, an "other" or "none of the above" response option should be included so that all respondents can provide an answer to the question. Because these kinds of response options do not necessarily elicit helpful information, an "other, please specify" response option with a text box for a brief explanation from respondents can provide more helpful information. Closed-ended questions should also allow for respondents to answer with a nonanswer, such as "not applicable," if the question content will not apply to all respondents. If students respond "never" to a question asking them how often they visit the financial aid office, it is not possible to tell if the student never visits because he or she calls the office versus if the student never visits because financial aid is not needed. A not-applicable type of response can help clarify this distinction. Because closed-ended questions are often designed with predetermined response options, it is relatively easy to quantify the information. Response options are often easy to code and tabulate (Allen, 2004).

Although responses to individual items from closed-ended questions can be used, often a group of items is used to ask about different aspects of a concept. For example, the following from the National Survey of Student Engagement (NSSE) measures different ways that students learn together (NSSE, 2015):

- During the current school year, about how often have you done the following?
  o Asked another student to help you understand course material
  o Explained course material to one or more students
  o Prepared for exams by discussing or working through course material with other students
  o Worked with other students on course projects or assignments

Each of these items can be used individually to learn more about the individual practices, but together they give a better-rounded picture of the idea of working with peers. Students' responses are given a numerical value (very often = 4, often = 3, sometimes = 2, never = 1) so that the scores of groups of students can be averaged, compared statistically, and used in statistical modeling. Often, when groups of questions are asking about facets of a construct, items can be grouped together to make a single score representing a measure of that construct. These aggregate scores can be created in a variety of ways, but most popularly, items are averaged together into a scale score or added together into an index. The previously mentioned items, for example, are averaged together to create what NSSE calls the *Collaborative Learning Engagement Indicator*.

Open-Ended Questioning

When asking multiple open-ended questions, it can help to begin the questions with items that are straightforward and comfortable for respondents. Although questions are intended to allow students to respond spontaneously, responses will be more useful if questions have a focus or defined boundaries. Asking students what they think about their classes may not provide as useful information as asking students what teaching styles are most and least helpful to their understanding of course concepts. It is important, however, that open-ended questions are actually open ended. Asking students if they find the recreation center convenient can be easily answered with a yes or no. Asking students what aspects of the recreation center are more or less convenient should provide more useful information. It will also be easier for respondents to talk about their own perspectives or experiences rather than abstract concepts or complicated issues. It is more difficult for students to respond to a question about how advising is helpful than it would be to answer a question about what experiences with their adviser have been more or less helpful to students in navigating course selection. Although boundaries and direction are important in eliciting useful information from open-ended questions, it can be illuminating to allow students some freedom to respond in later questions. General questions asking students for any additional comments, thoughts, or important things they have not had a chance to say can inform researchers and assessment professionals of issues they had not previously thought about (Allen, 2004).

The analysis of qualitative information elicited from open-ended questions often begins with a thorough review of responses. Verbal responses are often transcribed so that responses can be read and sorted. It may be helpful to initially remove or code any irrelevant comments at the beginning of analysis. Next, comments should be reviewed for common themes, which may later be assigned numeric values. Individual comments may end up with more than one code if they touch on more than one theme. Often the reviewing and coding is an iterative process where initial codes may be refined, combined, or broken out as responses are continuously reviewed. It can be helpful to start with many categories and themes, which can later be narrowed down. Having an "other" category can be helpful for responses that are relevant but do not easily fit into the rest of the more defined categories. With such a coding process, qualitative responses become more like quantitative responses, which can lead to overall descriptions of responses and the examination of patterns in responses. Important points can be highlighted with quotes from responses to help support the findings of the researcher or assessment professional.

Archival Records

Archival records are developed for many reasons, but generally not for assessment purposes. These records are often developed to assist with key institutional functions and/or track important information. For example, admissions offices record application information to help with the admissions process and to begin an institution's tracking of student characteristics. In addition, the registrar tracks courses taken, grades, and other information critical to determining student eligibility, progress, honors, and graduation requirements met, which help with advising and determining who graduates at a particular time.

Such records are so common on college and university campuses that many institutions are compiling vast amounts of data across many areas and functions. In our current era, much of this information is being captured in commercially supplied and serviced or homegrown databases. However, some records (e.g., departmental syllabi) may be collected and stored in electronic or physical files, although the digital storage of information is more common and ranges from faculty collecting student assignments to institutions compiling ePortfolios for every student. Institutions should consider creating such databases in easy to access and store formats. Suskie (2009) recommends reviewing records such as departmental syllabi every five years or so to make sure courses are aligned with current learning goals.

As suggested in the preceding examples, development of archival records occurs at nearly every level of an institution (e.g., individual, program/department/office, school/college, and campus wide). This dispersion of records creates challenges for accessing information along two fronts. First, when centralized, records are often difficult to access due to privacy or ownership concerns. Second, when records are dispersed (e.g., syllabi), getting adequate representation from across a campus can be a daunting task because, although one knows the records exist, it may not be clear whom to ask for such records or where they are stored, which can hinder assessment efforts. Allen (2004) notes that with some important assessment questions, the pursuit of such preexisting databases can be worth the effort.

It is worth noting that when used for assessment purposes archival records often need to be transformed into a format suitable for the assessment task. This might be as simple as transforming grades into grade points and as complicated as rating the difficulty of a course based on the information in a syllabus. As with transforming any data, transforming archival records should be done with great care, making sure to preserve the original record, track the transformation process, and double-check that the transformation occurred correctly.

Another difficulty of using archival records for assessment purposes is the complexity of the task. Ratcliff and Jones (1993) describe their detailed procedures for examining learning through the analysis of patterns detected in student transcripts. Their model accounts for difficult situations to examine, such as how to handle transfer credits, general education requirements, major prerequisites, multicampus institutions, and periodically changing course offerings.

Methods of Collection

In the following sections, we discuss ways in which responses to closed-ended and open-ended questions and archival records are collected. We focus on the main methods of collection used in higher education and offer examples to illustrate the methods. Where appropriate, we touch on benefits and challenges of these methods; however, the penultimate section of the chapter provides more detail.

Closed-Ended Questioning

Closed-ended questions can be collected in several forms. The advantage of closed-ended questions is that simple algorithms can be used for scoring.

Questionnaires

Questionnaires are one method of gathering information from a large group of individuals and are particularly useful for gathering information about people's values, beliefs, attitudes, experiences, perceptions, and satisfaction. They are a relatively fast, inexpensive, and efficient method for collecting informal assessment information from a wide variety of audiences (Allen, 2004). Students, alumni, faculty, staff, and administrators are just some of the groups of people who could be reached through a questionnaire administration. Additionally, using the results from more than one audience can help provide a variety of perspectives on the teaching and learning environment. Although many questionnaires are now completed electronically, they can be completed through the mail, over the phone, or in person. With the widespread use of the Internet and e-mail, questionnaires can be administered and completed relatively easily by most participants, which is particularly advantageous for distant respondents such as alumni or students and instructional staff at remote campuses. If questionnaires are repeated periodically or before and after specific initiatives, results can be viewed over time to look for evidence of change or trends.

Generally, questionnaires provide information that is quantitative in nature, but often in a variety of forms. People can respond to questions about the frequency of their participation in activities, the importance they place on particular services, the likelihood they would attend certain events, or their level of agreement on various issues. Similarly, they can rank the importance of various options, choose their most valued option, or indicate the approximate value they hold for each option. A wide variety of topics can be covered in a questionnaire, and the format of questions is highly flexible. Questionnaire results from these types of questions and items are fairly straightforward to tabulate and generally easy to interpret. Questionnaires in which students cannot be identified by a student ID number or personalized e-mail link are likely to include a variety of demographic questions so that responses can be analyzed by groups of students with different characteristics. One potential difficulty for questionnaires is the desire for large respondent counts and representative samples. In many circumstances, getting enough respondents who represent the desired population can be difficult and take considerable effort.

Although one benefit of a questionnaire administration is that it can be large scale, smaller, more localized questionnaires can be beneficial as well. Angelo and Cross (1993) give two examples of such questionnaires: course-related self-confidence surveys (p. 275) and teacher-designed feedback forms (p. 330). Student self-confidence questionnaires can help to give instructors an idea of how confident students are about their ability to learn course material and skills. With an understanding of students' perceived confidence, instructors can structure assignments to build that self-confidence and potentially avoid activities that might lower students' self-confidence (Angelo & Cross, 1993). Teacher-designed feedback forms are basically a midterm course evaluation that instructors use to collect detailed feedback from students early enough that midcourse changes can be made and such adjustments can be discussed and implemented by both instructors and students. Midcourse feedback can improve learning, show students that faculty find their feedback and learning to be important, and help students take more responsibility and actively participate in their learning (Angelo & Cross, 1993).

There are several benefits to using published questionnaires in higher education assessment and research. Using standardized instruments can allow researchers and assessment professionals to compare the experiences and perceptions of students on one campus to those at other colleges and universities. Such comparisons can give researchers and assessment professionals a sense of students' responses relative to groups of students at other institutions, sometimes being able to define one's own comparison group of institutions. External audiences may also feel that results are more legitimate coming from an externally created collection source, which can have well-written and well-tested items created by questionnaire experts. Additionally, because published instruments are created by someone else, local researchers and assessment professionals will not have to expend the energy and resources required to create their own instruments. Because they are created by external sources, however, published instruments may not exactly measure what local constituents would like to examine, might be inappropriate for special subpopulations of students, and may be costly to administer. It is important to consider different options when deciding whether to use published instruments or locally created instruments. Several examples of published instruments that indirectly assess learning in higher education can be found in Figure 5.1.

Interviews

Interviews are another method of collecting responses to closed-ended questions. Interviews can take the form of an unstructured conversation, a formal list of questions and answers, or anything in between (Banta & Palomba, 2015; Erwin, 1991). More structured interviews can be held where the

Figure 5.1. Examples of published instruments for indirect assessment in higher education.

Center for Community College Student Engagement (www.ccsse.org/center)
- Community College Survey of Student Engagement
- Community College Faculty Survey of Student Engagement
- Survey of Entering Student Engagement

Center for Postsecondary Research (cpr.indiana.edu)
- National Survey of Student Engagement
- Faculty Survey of Student Engagement
- Beginning College Survey of Student Engagement
- Law School Survey of Student Engagement

Center for Studies in Higher Education (www.cshe.berkeley.edu)
- Student Experience in the Research University

Higher Education Research Institute (www.heri.ucla.edu)
- CIRP Freshman Survey
- Your First College Year
- Diverse Learning Environments
- College Senior Survey
- HERI Faculty Survey

---

interviewer asks very specific questions and anticipates responses, possibly using predetermined checklists or response categories. Most often, structured interviews are conducted over the phone. Less structured interviews can provide interviewers with more spontaneous responses, but more structured interviews are more likely to be consistent in terms of each student receiving the same questions (Allen, 2004; Erwin, 1991).

Open-Ended Questioning

Open-ended questions can be collected in several forms. Open-ended questions imply that the data collected need interpretations for scoring, or ratings by scorers.

Writing Prompts

Asking for people to reflect on and write about their experiences can be a valuable form of indirect assessment. Although reading through reflection writing can be time consuming, and results can be difficult to summarize, Rogers (2001) writes that "perhaps no other concept offers higher education as much potential for engendering lasting and effective change in the lives of students as that of reflection" (p. 55). Students could be asked to reflect on broader teaching and learning experiences, such as describing how their academic program could be improved to increase their learning, how their courses could be changed to better prepare them for their anticipated career, or what types of teaching styles have been more or less helpful to their learning. As an indirect assessment, such questions could be embedded in a questionnaire experience, an interview, or a focus group, but reflection writing could be easily assigned as part of coursework or other educational experiences. Creating a writing assignment that gives the students time to reflect and focus on the specific issue in question, as opposed to making the reflection part of another exercise, might result in deeper, more thoughtful responses. Longer reflection assignments could help to give insight on specific student experiences, to provide feedback about program initiatives, or even to raise important issues for a campus overall (Allen, 2004).

Reflection can be integrated relatively easily into coursework and course experiences. Ash and Clayton (2004) use reflection writing with service-learning experiences with the ultimate goal of helping "students explore and express what they are learning through their service experiences so that both the learning and the service are enhanced" (p. 139). They use these student reflections to answer a variety of questions about student learning, such as how learning varies with differing service experiences (a single service-learning experience versus multiple experiences, students' class level, discipline, etc.) and how students can better meet learning objectives. Another example of reflection as a course assessment is the use of reflection writing as part of student portfolios. Students can reflect on their own work, such as the process of creating a portfolio of their work, the products contained in their portfolio, or their achievement in relation to course goals. They can also reflect on their successes and challenges in the course, which parts of the course were beneficial to their learning, and what they can do in the future to increase their success in other courses or their future careers. Using reflective exercises to create hypotheses about how learning could be improved can help students take more responsibility for their learning and can help instructors make decisions about what to change about future courses.

Angelo and Cross (1993) outline how to take advantage of brief reflection-writing exercises, which they call "minute papers" (p. 149). In these brief papers, students are asked such things as what they believe are the most significant things about what they are learning, and to describe their major questions or confusions. This feedback can be a way for instructors to quickly gather some useful feedback for what students are learning and what they may need more time to learn. This feedback can also give instructors ideas for the kinds of instructional changes to make to increase student learning. Measurement experts usually suggest a variety of questions for reflection, such as asking students what they learned from their experiences that is not reflected in their coursework, or what their goals are for the next semester and how they plan to reach them, or if they were to start over (with an assignment, a course, a program, etc.) what they would do differently next time. All of these questions can help instructors learn about ways to assist students in learning. Students can also reflect on their process in completing an assignment, referred to as "process analysis" (p. 307) by Angelo and Cross (1993). With such an assignment, students record the process they follow when completing course assignments and comment on their approach, particularly where they may be struggling. Reviewing students' processes can help instructors be informed of how students are completing their coursework as well as give them insight into how to help with additional direction in areas of difficulty.

Questionnaires

Questionnaires can also have open-ended or partially open-ended writing prompts. Results from such questions can be more difficult to summarize but can be made manageable if the questions are specific and ask for brief responses (or limit the number of words or characters that can be included in a response). Open-ended questionnaire results can be used to add detail and context to other questions and can bring up new information that may not have been covered in closed-ended questions. Because open-ended questionnaire items are more mentally challenging and time consuming for respondents to answer, they should be used only when necessary and when questions can be answered briefly (Allen, 2004; Dillman, 2000; Suskie, 2009).

Interviews

Interviews are another method that can be used to gather open-ended information about people's experiences, attitudes, and beliefs. Interviews can be conducted in person, over the phone, or by using an Internet-based service such as Skype. Interviews can be more expensive and time consuming than questionnaires, but they have the added benefit of allowing the interviewer to ask and answer clarifying questions, or ask additional follow-up questions based on students' responses. Interviews can take place once; be conducted periodically; or be held with students before, during, and after the implementation of initiatives to help chart historical changes in students' experiences. Interviews can also provide a sense of importance and personal attention that might be hard to achieve with a questionnaire format. Because interviewers may inadvertently influence interviewee responses (introducing bias, asking leading questions, etc.), it is very important that interviewers be trained and have adequate experience with the interview experience (Allen, 2004; Banta & Palomba, 2015).

Hilgers and Bayer (1994) studied student experiences with writing-intensive (WI) courses using interviews. Students were asked what they saw as the benefits of the WI courses, how the WI courses related to their major, what made a successful WI instructor, what students thought of the small WI class sizes, and how the students would improve writing instruction. Researchers found that students were generally positive about their WI experiences and made several suggestions for improvement. They used student interview responses to create a guide for faculty teaching WI courses and to make changes to how the course was structured to improve students' understanding of the value of taking WI courses. Even though their work was used for research purposes, the process used by Hilgers and Bayer (1994) could easily be repeated for assessment purposes in many contexts.

Focus Groups

Focus groups have become increasingly popular for educational improvement, suggesting "they are of clear value to educators, place reasonable demands on resources, and provide information in a timely manner" (Tipping, 1998, p. 153). Similar to interviews, focus groups are another indirect assessment method where facilitators interact with participants. However, in a focus group setting, facilitators ask questions of small groups of participants at the same time to gather information about their collective experiences, attitudes, and beliefs. Like interviews, focus groups allow the facilitator to ask clarifying or follow-up questions based on participants' responses, and focus groups can also range from unstructured conversations to more formalized lists of questions and discussion points. Focus groups can also be time consuming and expensive to set up, facilitate, and analyze, but they can provide important feedback, particularly in regard to group consensus. Unlike interviews, focus groups allow participants to hear and respond to each other's responses, comments, and questions. Facilitators can use the agreements and disagreements among participants to help guide the conclusions that can be made from the focus group discussion (Allen, 2004). Focus groups can also be easily integrated within course time; outside of course participation, however, it can be difficult to recruit and schedule groups of people. Additionally, groups of participants can be created so that they are demographically representative of the institution overall to provide a more generic assessment, or student groups can be created with targeted students to provide specific feedback such as from historically marginalized groups, at-risk students, or students in specific departments or programs.

Focus groups can be used more locally for course planning or understanding student satisfaction or concerns, or more broadly by gathering information about particular academic programs, educational improvement efforts, or general policies and procedures. Krueger and Casey (2009) outline three ways in which focus groups could be used in the educational improvement process. One way, focus groups can be used by researchers and assessment professionals to gain understanding about particular issues through the lens of the participants. This can be particularly useful in learning about the understanding and values that students have about particular topics. The focus group can also provide researchers and assessment professionals with the language that students use when talking about these topics. This information can be especially useful when intending to create other forms of assessment such as questionnaire items. Knowing language that is familiar to students in regard to the issues being studied will help researchers and assessment professionals to create clear and unambiguous questionnaire items. Once researchers and assessment professionals better understand students' views and values on a topic, new programs or educational interventions can be planned. Another way in which focus groups can be useful is to use them to pilot-test the ideas behind newly developed programs and interventions. Focus group participants can help discuss the pros and cons of new plans as well as give further advice about program development. A final way in which focus groups can be useful to researchers and assessment professionals is to check in with participants after having experienced the new programs or interventions. Focus group participants can provide an evaluation of changes to see if processes and outcomes have improved. Walvoord (2010) suggests the following three key questions that could be beneficial for department-level assessment using focus group participants:

1. How well did you achieve each of the following departmental learning goals?
2. What aspects of your education in this department helped you with your learning, and why were they helpful?
3. What might the department do differently that would help you learn more effectively, and why would these actions help? (p. 60)

Archival Records

Another method of indirect assessment could take the form of analyzing archival records of student participation in various experiences or being exposed to certain practices. Although students or instructional staff could report this information through another form of indirect assessment, it may be helpful to examine primary sources of information that are intended to guide students' learning. An examination of the curricula at an institution can be a good start in determining whether the intentions an institution has for learning are aligned with students' experiences. Because curricula exist at many different levels (course, department, discipline, institution, etc.) it is especially important to pay close attention to providing a coherent plan for student learning. Palomba and Banta (1999) write that "curriculum aware-ness is a process of looking at programs rather than at students and making sure appropriate conditions for learning exist" (p. 272). Course catalogues are another source of information about program structure, prerequisites, and available course options. Institution mission statements or statements of learning objectives should be examined alongside curricula to check for alignment but can also be independently examined as an indirect measure of the students' general environment. Examining students' understanding and knowledge of institution mission statements or statements of learning objec-tives can be another way to assess the clarity and understanding that students have of an institution's goals and intentions for learning.

Additionally, students' transcripts, plans of study, or course syllabi could be examined to gain a sense of course taking and learning objectives. Ratcliff and Jones (1993) describe a process of examining student transcripts to clus-ter students into patterns based on achievement and coursework. Through this analysis, they were able to find relationships between specific kinds of learning and particular course sequences as well as how these relationships changed for differing kinds of students. Course syllabi could also be a source of information for the quality of such things as quantitative literacy, intensive writing experiences, or collaborative learning opportunities. For example, Bers, Davis, and Taylor (1996) conducted a syllabus analysis for all of the courses in two departments focusing on aspects of writing, critical thinking, appreciation for diversity, and appreciation for lifelong learning. They found instances of inconsistency and lack of clarity in expectations or coursework resulting in a set of guidelines and ideas for faculty to use in future syllabi.

Looking at students' assigned coursework could also highlight expectations of faculty and the experiences of students. Records of participation in various high-impact practices, advising experiences, or use of learning support services could also provide insight into students' learning environments. Although transcripts may include some of this information, such as participation in an internship or service-learning experience, other offices on campus may have information about participation in other academic experiences, such as residence hall activities or campus or department events that are beneficial to student learning. The use of institutional resources and implementation of institutional mission as part of student learning could be examined by records such as class sizes; general education, major, and graduation requirements; and availability and use of learning support services. Although these primary sources of information about what students are learning may only be written indicators of intentions for learning, they can provide additional context to student experiences especially when examined with other sources of information about student learning.

Strengths and Limitations

A summary of the strengths and limitations of closed-ended and open-ended questions as well as archival records is presented in Table 5.1. The table is followed by a discussion of some of the advantages and disadvantages of indirect assessment in general and some of the methods commonly used for indirect assessment.

Indirect assessment is not a substitute for the direct assessment of student learning. It is, however, a valuable means to complement direct assessments by helping to provide context about student learning, why student learning may or may not be occurring, and what can be done to maintain or improve student learning. Direct assessments provide information about what students have or have not learned, but they generally do not provide guidance on what should be done to maintain or improve learning. Indirect assessments can quickly provide evidence about student learning and inform the development of direct assessments, which can be more time consuming to create. One of the biggest benefits of using indirect assessments to evaluate student learning is that, relative to the creation of direct assessments,

TABLE 5.1

Strengths and Limitations of Closed-Ended Questions, Open-Ended Questions, and Archival Records

	Strengths	Limitations
Closed-Ended Questions	• Questions are brief so many questions can be asked. • Questions can easily be asked of many people. • Questions can easily be asked in different contexts or over time. • Responses are easy to turn into quantifiable data. • Responses are easy to tabulate and report. • Responses can provide general information to direct more in-depth, open-ended questioning.	• Researchers and assessment professionals must be able to anticipate all potential responses. • Respondents are unlikely to reveal unanticipated responses. • Responses do not likely give insight into why respondents give their particular responses. • Respondents are limited in what information they can share. • "Other" or "None of the above" responses can be uninformative.
Open-Ended Questions	• Questions can ask for in-depth and reflective information. • Questions can easily be asked in different contexts or over time. • Responses are spontaneous and can reveal unanticipated results. • Responses can provide insight into respondent experiences, beliefs, and attitudes. • Responses can provide information to improve quantitative questions. • Responses can reveal a wide variety of beliefs, opinions, and experiences. • Respondents are allowed to respond using their own words.	• Analyzing responses can be difficult, time consuming, and costly. • Questions can be difficult and time consuming to answer so fewer questions are asked. • Responses are often not clearly grouped as there can be overlap in responses. • Responses can be difficult to report. • Analysis of responses relies on the interpretation of the researcher or assessment professional.

TABLE 5.1 (*Continued*)

Archival Records	• Data often already exist. • Data are factual and may be easily quantifiable. • Data may be more accurate than respondent memories or self-reports.	• Data may be difficult to find, access, and/or transform. • Analyzing data can potentially be difficult if they is difficult to quantify. • More data may be available than needed and choosing which data to use may be difficult.

indirect assessments are less difficult to create, implement, and analyze. Indirect assessment methods can more efficiently gather data and can be more quickly evaluated. A questionnaire of students' experiences with writing in their courses can be far more quickly tabulated than reading and grading hundreds of students' essays. This is especially beneficial when periodic assessments are to be made over time. Indirect assessments are also very flexible in nature. Questionnaire items, reflection prompts, interview questions, and focus group discussions can all be specifically tailored to meet assessment objectives. Indirect assessments, particularly questionnaires, can be an inexpensive way to reach wide and distant audiences in a variety of format options.

One disadvantage of indirect assessments is that they often rely on students' memories of what happened in the past. These memories may be distorted from what actually happened, particularly if the memory to be recalled is distant (Banta & Palomba, 2015; Dillman, 2000; Erwin, 1991; Groves et al., 2004). Participants in the indirect assessment might also interpret the questions or discussion in ways that the researchers or assessment professionals did not intend. Researchers and assessment professionals must be particularly careful to have clear, unambiguous questions, as they regularly do not have the opportunity to clarify what is actually meant when there are misunderstandings. It is also possible that students may report things that might not represent what they actually do or believe. Therefore, it is important to ensure that students feel comfortable with interviewers, facilitators, or questionnaire items so that they feel they can give accurate responses. The validity of indirect assessments relies directly on the quality of questions, prompts, and discussion facilitated by those doing the assessment. It is important that researchers and assessment professionals have the proper training to conduct indirect assessments to avoid inaccuracies due to bias or misinterpretation. In any indirect assessment, there is also the possibility that certain kinds of experiences, attitudes, and beliefs will be overlooked based on who participates in the assessment. Specific subpopulations, hard-to-reach students, or unique perspectives may not be assessed if large sample sizes are not realized. Motivating students to participate in indirect assessments, which is often optional, can also be difficult. Creating a culture where assessments are valued and used to make improvements can be one way to encourage participation (Dillman, 2000; Palomba & Banta, 1999; Suskie, 2009). Whereas questionnaires are an efficient way to collect a lot of data, reflection writing, interviews, focus groups, and archival records can be more time consuming to administer or gather and analyze. These processes can be especially time consuming if rigorous coding or transcripts are used in the analysis of responses, and especially expensive if facilitators and/or participants are to be paid. One larger-picture drawback to using indirect assessments is the potential perceived lack of credibility in usefulness (Allen, 2004; Ewell & Jones, 1993). People may not see the value of looking at results that are *about* student learning but not direct evidence of student learning. A basic understanding of the purpose of the indirect assessment and the intention to use the indirect information as a supplement to direct knowledge may help with people's use and understanding of findings.

Conclusion

Although indirect methods of assessment may be somewhat removed from students' coursework and course activities, they can complement the findings of direct assessments by providing more context to students' learning. Looking at the results from indirect and direct assessments, or multiple indirect assessments, can help to tell a more complete story of not only what students are learning but also how and why they are learning. Instructional staff who know that students are not accomplishing important learning objectives may not know why students are struggling. Indirect assessments are one way to gain such important insights. Students' coursework and test scores coupled with focus group or interview information can give faculty ideas on how and where exactly student learning needs to be supported. Walvoord (2010) writes that "ideally, standardized tests and surveys will be one of several sources of data about student learning, each augmenting, correcting, and amplifying the others, to lead to appropriate action" (p. 47).

The experiences of students who are less successful in college can be examined to look for patterns of participation so that interventions can be made. Other indicators of students' experiences such as students' completed coursework, participation in cocurricular activities, archival records, and engagement in high-impact practices can be viewed alongside the results of other indirect assessments to further add context to students' learning. Using multiple data points alongside indirect assessments is also an excellent way to establish the validity of measurements. If the findings from an indirect assessment align with findings from direct assessments, users can feel more assured that the indirect assessments are reflective of aspects of learning.

Indirect assessments can help provide information on how to make sense of direct assessments in order to make changes. The combination of findings from direct and indirect assessments can also help institutions to evaluate teaching practices, curricula, learning support services, and other programs and events intended to enhance student learning. When connections are made between students' experiences (through indirect assessment) and student learning (through direct assessment), successful pedagogies and practices can be identified and expanded. For example, one could find that directly assessed critical thinking scores are low in a course where indirectly assessed collaborative learning levels (indirectly assessed through questionnaires) are also low, and focus groups reveal students think faculty give poor instructions for collaborative assignments and students have low motivation for working together. If a positive relationship exists between collaborative learning and critical thinking, then improving assignment instructions and increasing motivation for working collaboratively will likely lead to improved collaborative learning, which will, in turn, lead to improvements in critical thinking. This is an illustration of how classrooms or almost any higher education context "can be used as laboratories to observe and study students in the process of learning, and then to modify teaching to make it more effective" (Angelo & Cross, 1993, p. 381). Students' perceptions of their learning environment can help provide instructional staff with ideas and insight on what might be changed or improved. Similarly the perceptions and experiences of instructional staff can contribute to broadening the conversation on the improvement of the teaching and learning process. Indirect assessments are also a good way to solicit feedback and advice from colleagues and stakeholders on improving the teaching and learning process. Given the vast variability in education on multiple levels (course, department, institution, etc.) it especially makes sense to collect information about the context of student learning in order to make adjustments. Such information collected from indirect assessments can be used to guide improvement processes and advise on where to best deploy time and other resources.

References

Allen, M. J. (2004). *Assessing academic programs in higher education*. Bolton, MA: Anker.

Angelo, T. A., & Cross, K. P. (1993). *Classroom assessment techniques: A handbook for college teachers* (2nd ed.). San Francisco, CA: Jossey-Bass.

Ash, S. L., & Clayton, P. H. (2004, Winter). The articulated learning: An approach to guided reflection and assessment. *Innovative Higher Education, 29*(2), 137–154.

Banta, T. W., & Palomba, C. A. (2015). *Assessment essentials: Planning, implementing, and improving assessment in higher education.* San Francisco, CA: Jossey-Bass.

Bers, T., Davis, D., & Taylor, W. (1996). Syllabus analysis: What are we teaching and telling our students? *Assessment Update, 8*(6), 1–2.

Dillman, D. A. (2000). *Mail and internet surveys: The tailored design method.* New York, NY: John Wiley & Sons.

Erwin, T. D. (1991). *Assessing student learning and development: A guide to the principles, goals, and methods of determining college outcomes.* San Francisco, CA: Jossey-Bass.

Ewell, P. T., & Jones, D. P. (1993). Actions matter: The case for indirect measures in assessing higher education's progress on the national education goals. *Journal of General Education, 42*(2), 123–148.

Groves, R. M., Fowler, F. J., Couper, M. P., Lepkowski, J. M., Singer, E., & Tourangeau, R. (2004). *Survey methodology.* Hoboken, NJ: John Wiley & Sons.

Hilgers, T., & Bayer, A. S. (1994). Student voices and the assessment of a new core writing requirement at the University of Hawaii. *Assessment Update, 5*(4), 4–5.

Krueger, R. A., & Casey, M. A. (2009). *Focus groups: A practical guide for applied research* (4th ed.). Thousand Oaks, CA: Sage.

Maki, P. (2002, January). Using multiple assessment methods to explore student learning and development inside and outside the classroom. *NASPA Online.* Retrieved from http://www.apu.edu/live_data/files/333/multiple_assessment_methods_to_explore_student_learning_and_deve.pdf

National Survey of Student Engagement. (2015). *Engagement insights: Survey findings on the quality of undergraduate education—Annual results 2015.* Bloomington: Indiana University Center for Postsecondary Research.

Palomba, C. A., & Banta, T. W. (1999). *Assessment essentials: Planning, implementing, and improving assessment in higher education.* San Francisco, CA: Jossey-Bass.

Ratcliff, J. L., & Jones, E. A. (1993). Coursework cluster analysis. In T. Banta (Ed.), *Making a difference: Outcomes of a decade of assessment in higher education.* (pp. 256–268). San Francisco, CA: Jossey-Bass.

Rogers, R. R. (2001). Reflection in higher education: A concept analysis. *Innovative Higher Education, 26*(1), 37–57.

Suskie, L. (2009). *Assessing student learning: A common sense guide.* San Francisco, CA: Jossey-Bass.

Tipping, J. (1998). Focus groups: A method of needs assessment. *Journal of Continuing Education in the Health Professions, 18,* 150–154.

Walvoord, B. E. (2010). *Assessment clear and simple: A practical guide for institutions, departments, and general education* (2nd ed.). San Francisco, CA: Jossey-Bass.

6

VALIDITY AND RELIABILITY OF INDIRECT ASSESSMENTS

M. David Miller, University of Florida

John P. Poggio, University of Kansas

When using direct or indirect assessments, any test or assessment should provide psychometric evidence that shows the test is an effective measure of the student learning outcomes (SLOs) or relevant constructs (see chapter 4 of this book, on validity and reliability of direct assessments). That is, evidence should be provided that shows the intended uses and interpretations of the test are appropriate or suitable; the test is sufficiently stable, dependable, or reliable; and the uses or interpretations of the tests are equitable across subpopulations (see chapter 2 of this book for a summary of the *Standards* [AERA, APA, & NCME, 2014]). Evidence for test use and interpretation should be based on the three foundational areas in the *Standards*: validity, reliability, and fairness. Adherence to the *Standards* becomes more vital and proper as the importance and stakes of the decisions and uses of the tests grow more substantial to individuals or groups. In the case of accountability, tests should be considered of high importance and high stakes when they are used to make decisions about program and institutional accreditation. Thus, in the situations described throughout this book, providing evidence of the psychometric properties of the tests becomes particularly imperative because "adhering to the *Standards* becomes more critical as the stakes for the test taker and the need to protect the public increase" (AERA, APA, & NCME, 2014, p. 3).

Program accountability can take many forms in higher education. However, accrediting agencies typically require (a) the specification of SLOs that define what students will know or be able to do at program completion, (b) direct assessments that specifically measure the SLOs and the student learning that would be expected at program completion, and (c) indirect assessments that measure outcomes that are not specific to explicit SLOs but are reasonable expectations inferred at program completion (e.g., achievements, aptitudes, attitudes, beliefs, dispositions). Defining characteristics and examples of indirect and direct assessments are discussed in chapters 3 and 5 of this book.

The three foundational areas of the *Standards* (AERA, APA, & NCME, 2014) provide guidance and direction on the types of evidence that need to be considered when adopting or developing a test for accreditation purposes. Consequently, tests should closely examine evidence that addresses the consistency of the scores (reliability) and the uses or interpretations of the scores (validity). In addition, "fairness is a fundamental validity issue" (p. 49) that deals with the appropriateness and use of test scores for all individuals within any subpopulation (e.g., gender, ethnicity, disabilities, cultural, linguistic).

Although the *Standards* is broadly applicable to a wide range of types of tests and test uses and interpretations, it is also clear that all standards are not always applicable and that specific standards will be used in different contexts. As the *Standards* makes clear, the application of the standards is a matter of professional judgment, and decisions about validity, reliability, and fairness need to be linked to specific contexts, uses, and interpretations. Thus, it is reasonable and expected that different evidence is needed for direct assessments than for indirect assessments. Furthermore, different indirect assessments may necessitate different types of evidence of reliability, validity, or fairness. Discussed in this chapter are key psychometric methods that would have wide applicability with indirect assessments.

Indirect Assessments

Indirect assessments are assessments that measure any of the expected outcomes of a program other than those that are direct measures of the SLOs. These assessments can include perceptions, attitudes, opinions, or behaviors that are a result of program participation and that are related to student knowledge, skills, and learning. As pointed out in chapter 5, indirect assessments can also assume multiple assessment formats including selected or closed-response and constructed or open-response options. However, it is clear and deserves recognition that the outcomes being measured by indirect assessments only allow us *to infer* indirectly that learning is occurring or that the conditions for learning are occurring. This contrasts with direct assessments that directly and explicitly measure the SLOs and allow us *to confirm* that learning is occurring. Historically, as related to the areas of cognitive appraisal, achievement tests have been commonly thought of as direct assessments, whereas aptitude and ability measures are indirect assessments regardless of the format.

In their tips on assessment, ABET, formerly known as the Accreditation Board for Engineering and Technology, further defines *indirect assessments* in the following way:

> Indirect assessments of student learning ascertain the perceived extent or value of learning experiences. They assess opinions or thoughts about student knowledge or skills. Indirect measures can provide information about student perception of their learning and how this learning is valued by different constituencies. (Rogers, 2006, p. 1)

Consequently, when planning indirect assessments, there are a wide range of alternatives. With each option, it is important to consider the psychometric quality of the assessment. The first decision that needs to be made in planning an assessment is whether, pragmatically, tests are already available to be adopted or adapted. Adopting an existing assessment has many advantages. Besides the obvious advantage of having a test that is already available, existing tests may have known psychometric properties for your audience, less time is needed for test development and examining/estimating psychometric properties, comparative data will be available from other users of the test, and interpretations of the results can be expected to be established already. However, the adoption of existing tests may be more problematic in other ways, especially in their alignment with the targeted goals of the program. Development procedures can be expected to be specifically aligned with the goals of the program, whereas the alignment of local program goals and the assessment may not be as exact or focused, or at least more difficult to ensure, when adopting an existing assessment. Regardless, whether to adopt a preexisting test requires careful and deliberate consideration of the psychometric properties.

Adopting Existing Tests

When adopting an existing measure, the key issues are those outlined in chapter 2: validity, reliability, and fairness. The strongest feature for adopting an existing test is that information and data on these three criteria already exist and have been reported for the instrument. However, the responsibility of the adopters/users would be to review the available information to see if it meets their use criteria for validity, reliability, and fairness, and whether additional information is needed.

In 2014, the University of Florida (UF) developed a quality enhancement plan (QEP) (Miller, Villalon, & Brophy, 2014) for its Southern Association of Colleges and Schools Commission on Colleges (SACSCOC) review. The QEP at UF focused on internationalizing the undergraduate experience. When planning the indirect assessments, the international task force and the appointed assessment committee found seven existing indirect measures of the three SLOs. The seven instruments measured the perceptions, attitudes, skills, and behaviors of internationalization that were used at other colleges/universities. For each instrument, technical reports summarizing the reliability, validity, and fairness of the instruments were examined. The review by UF of the indirect assessments focused on the following four criteria:

1. How well did the content and objectives of the instrument align with the SLOs developed for the UF Learning Without Borders: Internationalizing the Gator Nation program?
2. What other evidence was available for the validity of the instrument?
3. What was the level of reliability of the scales or subscales? What type of reliability was reported?
4. Was the instrument suitable for large-scale use at UF?

The documentation for the seven instruments based on the four criteria was developed by faculty and graduate students to include (a) descriptions of the content of the instruments; (b) a summary of validity information reported in any technical reports for each instrument including content reviews, correlations with other instruments, and behaviors; (c) any reported reliability in technical reports for each instrument; and (d) the contexts in which each instrument had been used. The international task force and its assessment committee used the following criteria to determine if an instrument was useful: (a) whether the content of the instruments related to the SLOs developed for the program in a way that changes in the measured perceptions, attitudes, skills, and behaviors were likely to occur for the planned program (sensitivity to content); (b) whether the validity and reliability evidence supported the planned use of the instruments; and (c) whether the contexts in which the instruments had been used were similar to the large-scale use being planned or whether the planned use would be feasible with the instruments. The reviews were conducted in group meetings that were required to reach consensus on the usefulness of the instruments. The review regarded alignment and reliability to be the most important evidence. Thus, content needed to match the goals and objectives of the program. In addition, fairness was not addressed in the previous questions. It was assumed that content reviews of fairness and other evidence would need to be established because evidence of fairness was not included in the seven technical reports. Finally, it was assumed that the use of assessments in a large-scale context involved complexities that would affect the validity and reliability evidence. The reviews by the international task force and the assessment committee resulted in a recommendation not to adopt most of the existing instruments primarily due to a lack of alignment (i.e., validity shortcomings) with the program goals, objectives, and SLOs and not being used previously in a large-scale environment. As a result, the program decided to develop its own instruments. The process for this development is described in the following section.

As an institution considers adopting existing instruments, similar reviews need to be conducted. The key parts of the review are as follows: (a) an expert review panel needs to be established that has the expertise to understand the content and skills taught in the program being assessed, and what evidence of validity, reliability, and fairness would be expected for the planned use or interpretation of the assessment; and (b) criteria need to be specified and agreed upon for instrument selection. This procedure would lead to the following likely conditions: (a) adopting instruments where the reliability, validity, and fairness evidence is convincing; (b) not adopting an instrument where the evidence is not convincing; or (c) adopting an instrument provisionally where additional studies or modifications are needed to provide sufficient evidence for adoption. For example, if the content-related alignment evidence for the instruments being considered by UF QEP had been convincing, the instruments could have been provisionally adopted while local data examining fairness were collected, reviewed, and evaluated for a UF adoption.

Developing Indirect Assessments

In the absence of usable existing tests, programs may find it necessary to build assessments to measure their SLOs with direct or indirect assessments. Building assessments are based on principles of test and item construction that are commonly covered in many standard measurement textbooks (e.g., Miller, Linn, & Gronlund, 2013). Previous chapters have discussed varying item formats that have been used for indirect or direct assessments, focusing on differences such as open-ended or closed-ended response items. It is during the test development phase that many of the issues of reliability, validity, and fairness are first addressed (Crocker & Algina, 1986; Schmeiser & Welch, 2006). *Reliability* is defined in terms of the consistency of examinee scores on the assessment. Thus, it is important to write items that are consistent measures of the construct. This consistency is accomplished through careful consideration of the purpose of the test item and the types that will be used, and careful development of a test blueprint and item specifications.

In addition, it is important to have a large enough pool of items to have a reliable assessment even after eliminating items during pilot testing, content and fairness review, and field testing.

Schmeiser and Welch (2006) argue that the foundation for validity evidence begins with test design and development by asking at the outset, "What should constitute content-related evidence of validity for the knowledge and skills to be measured?" (p. 313). We would hasten to add that a complete and comprehensive definition of the intended, often indirect construct in the case of desired noncognitive behavior measures and their change deserves considerable attention and operational definition. Test development will begin addressing the validity issue through test specifications that define the purpose of the testing and the test content and skills that need development. The item types will also define the response process, which can be an important component of establishing the validity of the test. The test development process further includes formal reviews by testing and content experts and clients/examinees that provide information along with formal and informal data to address validity and fairness. Such reviews should systematically and deliberately include a review for content coverage and skills accuracy, fairness, and editorial style as perceived by the examinees.

Validity Evidence

As has been noted, the *Standards for Educational and Psychological Testing* (AERA, APA, & NCME, 2014) identifies three foundational areas of assessing tests: validity, reliability, and fairness. *Validity* is "the degree to which evidence and theory support the interpretations of test scores for proposed uses of tests. Validity is, therefore, the most fundamental consideration" (p. 11). Although validity is a unitary concept and does not have distinct types, the *Standards* emphasizes the ongoing nature of validation and use of multiple sources of evidence based on the theoretical work of Messick (1989). Selection of the sources of evidence that are needed will depend on the particular uses and interpretations of the results. Kane (2006) suggested an argument-based approach to validation that is based on the rationale or the claims made for the test. Thus, any argument for validity begins with a clear statement of the purposes and uses of the test.

The five sources of validity evidence in the *Standards* are meant to address different aspects of the validity argument. The five sources of evidence are as follows:

1. Evidence based on content
2. Evidence based on response processes

3. Evidence based on internal structure
4. Evidence based on relations to other variables
5. Evidence based on consequences of testing

Each of these sources of evidence may be needed to understand the proposed interpretations and uses of tests. However, not all sources of evidence are necessary for any proper and thus particular interpretation or use. The selection of the most relevant and meaningful sources of evidence will be based on the purposes and uses of the tests and will be a matter of professional judgment. It also bears recognition and realization that validation can be expected to occur over time, not just during the creation of the measure. Thus, capturing information and data within the context of short-, mid-, and long-term plans can have very desirable features and properties. Demonstrating how content-related evidence is maintained or may have to change over time, or that consequential evidence may become available and supportive only following a period of test use, speaks to the ongoing nature and a desirable feature of test validation.

Evidence based on content is usually one of the core sources of evidence in accreditation, as it should be. The main purpose of testing for accreditation is to show that the content of the program is covered whether using direct or indirect assessments. Thus, evidence based on content will almost always be collected to support the validity argument in educational assessment. Content evidence can be gathered as part of the test development process and by expert judgments during and after test development. As a result, this core evidence can be collected and used for existing or newly developed tests. Content evidence is typically a matter of expert judgment, and as such, evidence is collected by clearly specifying the purposes and uses of the test, specifying in detail the exact content measured and taxonomic levels of skills expected, identifying expert reviewers, and articulating the judgments needed. The purposes and uses of the test are identified by specifying the accreditation process and how particular tests will fit into the overall reporting system. The content is ordinarily identified through the specification of test blueprints and item specifications. Expert reviewers in the context of accreditation are the faculty and others involved in program implementation who have knowledge about the content of the program or the assessment process. Finally, systematic questions will be used to guide the judgment process and will focus on the alignment of items with the test specifications and the purposes and uses of the test, as well as the declaration by content experts of what is not covered on the test but should be. Multiple questions can be used to provide alignment ratings and can also involve judgments about item fit with the specified content, the match between items and item specifications, and technical accuracy of the items. Fairness can also be addressed during this process by asking questions about differences in interpretations or offensiveness, insensitivity, or bias with reference to impacted subpopulations (fairness is explored further later). Expert judgments can be recorded and summarized or discussed through group interactions and eventual decisions.

Evidence based on response processes would be used for indirect assessments when an important part of the testing includes the processes engaged in by test takers. Thus, closed-ended responses may not provide evidence based on response processes but open-ended responses may need the evidence. For example, this source of evidence may become unnecessary when the test taker is completing a multiple-choice direct assessment or a Likert-type scaled indirect assessment. In contrast, evidence based on response processes may be important to test score use or interpretation for open-ended responses where the response process is a central part of the definition of the purpose of the testing. Test takers' response process might be important to measuring open-ended responses such as participating actively in group tasks, conducting or participating in experiments, detailing experiences as work was planned or carried out, or participating in performances. Each might be measured using an indirect assessment where the process engaged in is as important as the knowledge, skills, abilities, and attributes (KSAs) measured. Under these conditions, multiple assessment strategies or approaches might be used to provide evidence of the response process, including the recording of observations by raters, open-ended survey questions of examinees, or test taker guided reflections.

Evidence based on internal structure shows the extent to which relationships between items and test components conform to what is being measured. Thus, this source of evidence is potentially important whenever the test consists of more than one item or component. Analyses of internal structure include a variety of empirical methods to examine the relationships of items or components with other items, components, or test scores (Crocker & Algina, 1986; Kane, 2006; Messick, 1989). Two of the more commonly used approaches for examining internal structure are item analysis and factor analysis. Item analysis shows the relationship between individual items or test components and the test score using classical test theory (CTT) or the latent score using modern-day item response theory (IRT). Each provides a clear understanding of the relative importance of specific items/components in score interpretation. Similarly, an exploratory or confirmatory factor analysis estimates the relationship between the items/components and the underlying factors. Internal structure would be important for indirect assessments such as attitude scales but would not be appropriate when using a single question or item as the indicator.

Evidence based on relations to other variables suggests that the interpretations or uses of a test may imply that the construct may be empirically related to other variables. For example, completion of certain components of a program (an indirect assessment) may lead to learning that should result in increased scores on a professional certification exam. Cronbach (1988) argued for the importance of hypothesis testing as a source of validity evidence. Thus, empirical relationships are hypothesized based on test interpretations or uses and tested to provide evidence that supports the validity argument. Hypotheses for indirect measures of program effectiveness and the specific variables will differ across programs. Relationships of an indirect assessment could be hypothesized for other indirect assessments, direct measures of the SLOs, student grades, and other outcomes of the program. For example, an attitude, disposition, or belief assessment might be hypothesized to have a positive relationship with other attitude measures, the learning outcomes (i.e., direct assessment), student course grades, or graduation. Confirming the hypothesized relationships would provide additional support for the validity argument for the attitude, disposition, or belief assessment. A well-known, complex, and elegant empirical design for this orientation to validation is referred to as the convergent-divergent validation approach discussed by Campbell and Fiske (1959). In this model for validation, the researcher would first propose those characteristics or traits that should correlate or fail to correlate and, further, the levels of relationship expected. In addition, expected relationships are specified for the methods/procedures of direct and indirect assessment that would or would not support, interfere, or compromise the measurement of the traits. Results are then used to support or fail to support the validity of the measure being evaluated.

Evidence based on the consequences of test use is especially relevant in high-stakes testing environments where the high stakes lead to changes in test-taking behaviors, which, in turn, lead to changes in score interpretations and uses. Accreditation, program review, and decision-making (e.g., admissions, placement) are higher education environments where consequences potentially change the interpretations and uses of tests with ongoing assessments. Thus, the initial validity evidence will provide a validity argument for test use and interpretation, but that validity argument may need to be updated or meaningfully altered when high-stakes testing has an effect on test use or test preparation behaviors that result in changes in the interpretations of test scores. In a high-stakes environment, this is an ongoing concern that suggests the need to monitor examinees' test preparation and test behaviors along with instructors' attention to their course, program, or curriculum; the assessment program; and the ongoing interpretations and uses of specific tests. The California Community Colleges has for a number of years monitored the interplay and utility of course placement tests, based primarily on content- or criterion-related validity evidence, then, after an extended period of use, shifting to relying on consequential-related evidence gathered from course graduates and course instructors to gauge success and satisfaction with the initial course placement measure (Poggio & Glasnapp, 2001).

The accumulation, blending, and combination of the different sources of evidence provide an overall and convincing argument for the uses, interpretations, justification, and thus reliance on a test, its subtests, or a test battery. Although not all sources of evidence are necessary, typically more evidence will bolster the validity argument. In their development of indirect assessments for the quality enhancement plan required for SACSCOC reaccreditation, which was built to internationalize the undergraduate learning experience, Miller and colleagues (2014) reported having three indirect assessments. The Student Experience in the Research University (SERU) survey was an existing multiuniversity scale developed at the University of California–Berkeley Center for Studies in Higher Education. Two additional surveys were developed that measured attitudes and behaviors related to the international critical thinking and international communication SLOs. An international task force collected evidence via a content review and rulled on previous evidence supporting the validity of the SERU. In contrast, the two surveys developed for the university-wide program, IntCRIT and IntCOMM, collected substantially more evidence for the validity argument as no other evidence was available. The overall validity argument was informed by the following process of instrument development and collecting data for validity and reliability:

- Develop item specifications based on the SLOs and a literature review of how critical thinking and communication are operationalized in assessments with a focus on internationalization.
- Write items based on the test specifications (approximately 70 items for each SLO).
- Review of items by the international task force, the assessment committee, and other experts in assessment (i.e., content evidence).
- Revise items based on feedback from review; revisions were mostly minor changes in wording; a few items were dropped based on review.
- Pilot test items with undergraduate students at UF and eliminate those items with poor item discriminations. The initial piloting was completed with four forms to minimize the testing burden for students. Forms A and B contained overlapping sets of IntCRIT items (instrument to measure critical thinking in internationalization). Forms C and D contained overlapping sets of IntCOMM items (instrument to measure

communication in internationalization). The overlap consisted of 10 items that expert review showed helped to define the construct so that the same construct was being assessed on each form. Each form was pilot tested with 70 to 100 undergraduates.

- Item analysis of pilot data. Data were analyzed to examine the psychometric properties of the items and the scales. The scale reliabilities exceeded .95 for all four forms. Items were retained that had an item discrimination (i.e., correlation between the items and the total scale) of .25 or higher. The only trend in the data was that IntCRIT items that were phrased in terms of comparisons across cultures (e.g., one culture being better or worse than other cultures) had uniformly lower item discriminations and were eliminated (i.e., internal structure evidence and reliability).

- Second pilot test of the remaining items on a single form for each SLO. Each of the assessments was administered to approximately 70 undergraduates.

- Item analysis of second round of pilot data. Recommendations were developed to retain items with the highest item discriminations that would result in a scale with a reliability of at least .90. For IntCRIT, the recommendation was to retain 12 items. For IntCOMM, the recommendation was to retain 14 items (i.e., internal structure evidence and reliability).

- Present revised items to the international task force and assessment experts with recommendations for final review. The final review included consideration of the overall length of the assessment and the content of specific items (i.e., content evidence).

Note that validation did not include evidence on the test response process as the response process was standard and straightforward (students responding to Likert-scaled items). In addition, no relationships to other variables were included, although later studies were planned that could address the relationship between the indirect and the direct assessments. Finally, consequences were not initially an issue but may become important over time as the program results become high stakes. With the passage of time, more distinct and diverse sources and means of validation evidence become possible. The combination of different types of and designs for validity evidence helps to build a stronger argument for the many resulting uses and interpretations.

The types of validity evidence accumulated will vary in different contexts and uses of the tests. That is, the types of validity evidence that may be most important will depend on the types of tests and the uses and interpretations of the tests. For example, Patz (2016) argued that achievement testing and the associated SLOs are based on an educational system that tries to affect and measure observable behavioral changes. The key validity evidence with achievement tests built to measure SLOs is based on the alignment of assessments with the expected behavioral changes. Thus, Patz (2016) argued that content evidence would be the primary form of validity evidence needed, and in some cases, the only evidence needed, which might be the case with direct assessments. Yet as we alluded to earlier, this argument is more convincing at early periods/stages/years of use. With continued use, compelling and more relevant validation designs should be put in place for judgment and possible refinements.

Continuing this line of thought and application, as indirect assessments are not intended or, indeed, designed to measure the specific SLOs directly, the same argument would not necessarily be advanced for indirect assessments, where evidence of relationships with other variables, internal structure, and other forms of evidence may be as important as content depending on the particular constructs being measured and the specified uses and interpretations. For example, a measure of attitudes, values, or beliefs (e.g., indirect assessments) is useful in educational assessments because we assume that learning is more likely to occur if students have a positive attitude toward their learning and can reflect on the meaning or importance. Thus, the relationship between attitudes and the measures of learning may be one of the primary pieces of validity evidence for using the attitude assessment.

As a result, the selection or development of a strategy for examining validity evidence needs to be based on a solid validity argument developed for the interpretations and uses of the test (Cronbach, 1988; Kane, 2006). Kane's validity argument includes evidence to support uses and interpretations of the test as well as examining evidence that would argue against the uses and interpretations. According to Kane (2006),

> The validity argument provides an overall evaluation of the intended interpretations and uses of test scores. The goal is to provide a coherent analysis of all of the evidence for and against proposed interpretations/uses, and to the extent possible, the evidence relevant to plausible competing interpretations. An interpretive argument provides a framework for developing a validity argument. (p. 2)

Kane (2006) viewed this as the following four-step process:

1. Specify proposed uses and interpretations in terms of an interpretive argument including inferences and assumptions
2. Develop a preliminary version of the validity argument based on all available evidence relevant to the interpretive argument

3. Evaluate any problematic assumptions
4. Repeat steps 1–3 until all inferences and assumptions from the interpretive argument are acceptable. (p. 3)

We return to our position that the diversity of evidence, although complex and interactive with stakeholders, merits deliberate and thoughtful construct consideration as we work toward and potentially achieve strong inferences from indirect and direct measures of capacity and behavior. Although validity evidence is the most important evidence for the use or interpretation of test scores, consistency and fairness are also important foundations to testing.

Reliability Evidence

Reliability, or precision, is defined as the "consistency of the scores across instances of the testing procedure" (AERA, APA, & NCME, 2014, p. 33). Whereas validity examines the consistent errors or biases that result in misinterpretations or misuses of test scores, reliability examines the inconsistent or random errors that result in misinterpretations or misuses of a test that directly impact the individual.

Reliability of a test can be assessed in many ways. Different indices are calculated using different theoretical approaches. CTT (Crocker & Algina, 1986) and generalizability theory (Brennan, 2001) provide indices that examine the reliability or consistency of observed scores. In contrast, IRT (de Ayala, 2008) and factor analysis (McDonald, 1999) approaches report the reliability or consistency of latent scores. There are several other differences between indices based on different theoretical approaches as well as differences among indices using the same theoretical approach (e.g., internal consistency, split-half, and test-retest reliability). As with validity, the particular approaches and indices used to examine reliability vary depending on the types of assessments, the nature of the trait being measured, the scales of measurement, and the interpretations and uses of the assessment.

Classical Test Theory

CTT provides some of the earliest work on reliability, dating back to the seminal work of Spearman (1907, 1913). Elaborations of CTT are contained in Lord and Novick (1968) and Crocker and Algina (1986). CTT is based on a simple model that states that an observed score is the sum of a true score and error that is random (i.e., $X = T + E$). With the assumptions of random errors and the relationship between forms (e.g., parallel or tau equivalence), multiple indices have been developed. Some of the reliability coefficients are test-retest reliability, alternate or parallel forms reliability, interrater reliability, split-half reliability, and internal consistency estimates including Cronbach's alpha. Each can be meaningful within a given context. For example, when measuring change over time, test-retest reliability should be reported; when scoring, an open-ended assessment is subjective in its scoring, and, therefore, interrater reliability should be reported; when indirect assessments include more than one item, internal consistency or split-half reliability should be reported, or if the measure uses indirect questions that are to receive different points, weights, or values, the total score (referred to as the composite) may need reliability estimated via a split-half procedure. Each of the types of reliability used in CTT are based on different assumptions about the types of random error that are relevant to the testing situation. Thus, selecting the type of reliability should be guided by and align with the uses and interpretations of the test. Multiple types of reliability would be reported when multiple sources of error are expected. For example, an assessment measured over time and with subjective scoring would necessitate test-retest reliability and interrater reliability. Table 6.1 shows the types of reliability that might be relevant for different indirect assessments and sources of error under which each type of reliability would be used.

There are several advantages to using reliability measures from CTT. First, observed scores, or their transformations (e.g., standard or normalized scores), are simple to use, readily computed by software, and common to such reporting. The corollary index often reported along with it is the standard error of measurement and is also easier to understand as it is in the metric of the observed scores. Second, computing reliability coefficients and standard errors based on variances and correlations is simpler than computing estimates based on generalizability theory or theories using latent scores, particularly since most statistical software can be used to estimate reliability coefficients and standard errors. Third, when the tested group is relatively small ($n < 75$), the CTT procedures are safe, acceptable, and sound to use. Finally, the interpretation of reliability coefficients and standard errors is relatively easy, with reliability coefficients ranging from a minimum reliability of 0 to a maximum of 1, and the standard errors being in the metric of the observed scores (larger = more error; smaller = more reliable).

Although CTT is widely used, alternative approaches address the limitations and shortcomings of CTT. The limitations of CTT are the following: (a) estimates assume the scales are interval or ratio levels of measurement (i.e., continuous); (b) estimates are based on correlations that consider consistency of the rankings of scores and not the consistency of point estimates;

TABLE 6.1
Reliability Coefficient Types

Reliability Coefficient	Source of Error	Features of the Indirect Assessment
Test-Retest or Stability	Stability due to random differences in test scores over time	Measurement of growth or change in a longitudinal design, or only one form of the measure exists
Alternate or Parallel Forms	Equivalence due to random differences between different forms of a test	Measurement using two or more forms of a test due to security issues, or a very short time interval between testing and retesting
Interrater	Random inconsistencies among raters	Measurement with different raters because of the subjective scoring
Split-Half	Lack of item equivalence due to random differences among items on a test	Single administration of a test with multiple items (see note)
Internal Consistency (Cronbach's alpha, Kuder-Richardson, etc.)	Lack of item homogeneity due to random differences in statistical and construct properties among items	Single administration of a test with multiple items (see note)

Note. Split-half reliability would be used when items are heterogeneous or speeded by creating equivalent halves based on test specifications. Internal consistency reliability estimates could be used in all other single-administration situations.

(c) the correlational methods assume a simple crossed design for data collection (e.g., persons by raters or persons by items); and (d) a single estimate of the standard error of measurement is traditionally computed rather than the recognition that error can be impacted based on the score's level—that is, typically, higher and lower scores tend to be less reliable, thus resulting in greater standard errors at these score points, but this condition is ordinarily not considered or taken into consideration.

The first limitation is that CTT reliability coefficients assume that the data have continuous properties. That is, a single point difference between scores represents the same impact or separation anywhere on the scale. For example, if one examinee has a pre–post gain going from 10 to 20 and another examinee moves from 30 to 40, each examinee is assumed to have changed the same amount. In contrast, standards-based scores, are commonly used in accountability (e.g., exceeds standards, meets standards, does not meet standards), and the interval between scores is not considered or treated as equal. The amount of learning to move from "does not meet standards" to "meets standards" may be substantially larger than the learning required to move from "meets standards" to "exceeds standards." However, the same amount of change at the lower end of the scale may be harder or easier than the same amount of change at another place on the scale even though the measured rate of change is the same. Similarly, indirect assessments, such as measures of effort, may use rubrics or other tools that lead to categorical or ordinal data rather than interval data. Thus, estimates of reliability would be biased when the data are categorical or ordinal since the estimates assume the data are interval. Reliability estimates for categorical data could be estimated through decision consistency methods (Hambleton & Novick, 1973), which include percent agreement or percent agreement adjusted for chance agreement (i.e., Cohen's kappa). Sources of error would remain similar to those reported in chapter 4, but the estimate would be based on likely consistency within a category over time, form, and so on, rather than a correlation.

The second limitation of CTT is that the correlation-based estimates of reliability are best used with norm-referenced tests as they measure consistency for relative ordering. For example, suppose two raters score a set of open-ended essays. The scores of the first rater are equal to the score of the second rater minus two points. Thus, an essay with a score of 2 for rater 1 would have a 4 for rater 2. Similarly, a 3 for rater 1 would have a score of 5 for rater 2. This pattern of consistent two-point differences would lead to a perfect correlation ($r = 1$) and a conclusion that the scores of the two raters are perfectly reliable. When using the test for norm-referenced purposes, the relative ordering of scores by either rater is exactly equal. However, if considering the actual values (point estimates) of the scores, the raters are not consistent, as rater 1 always scores essays two points higher than rater 2. Generalizability theory makes a distinction between reliability for norm-referenced testing (relative error) and criterion-referenced testing (absolute error) whereas CTT is limited to the relative error use and interpretation. Estimation with generalizability theory (see discussion later in this chapter) also shows that the error variance for absolute measurement is greater than or equal to the error variance for relative measurement. This also implies that the generalizability coefficient (similar to reliability coefficient for relative error) is greater than or equal to the dependability index (similar to reliability coefficient for absolute error). Thus, using CTT when reporting criterion-referenced scores tends to underestimate the standard error of measurement and thus overestimates the reliability coefficient.

The third limitation of CTT is the limited designs that are needed for data collection. Some of the limitations of CTT data collection designs include the consideration of one source of error at a time (unless the sources of error are confounded as in the alternate form test-retest design), the use of fully crossed designs (person by source of error), and the limitation of correlating only two levels of a source of error (except in the case of internal consistency). In some situations, the latter limitations (crossed designs with two levels of a source of error) may be reasonable when piloting a new assessment as one has the flexibility to design the data collection and analysis. However, when examining reliability of an existing assessment, the existing testing may not fit the CTT data collection design. That is, in an academic, accreditation environment, there may be more than two raters for a constructed response (open-ended) assessment and the data collection may include more complex designs such as nesting (e.g., different raters rating different items). Even with these considerations, a major issue in design is that CTT limits estimates to a single source of error. Often the testing situation requires more than one source of error be considered. For example, and this is very common practice, an indirect assessment that uses multiple open-ended questions and the subjective scoring includes both rater consistency and item homogeneity as sources of error that may not be independent. Whereas CTT methods would necessitate estimating the two sources of error separately (different questions and different scorers), the multiple sources of error and their combined effects on reliability can be examined through generalizability theory and IRT. Estimation methods for generalizability theory and IRT also do not require completely crossed designs nor the use of only two levels for a source of error.

The fourth limitation of CTT, is the reliance on a single estimate of the standard error of measurement. This bears reflection. Recall the following CTT test theory model given previously: $X = T + E$. When the E components are estimated, the standard deviation of the Es is referred to as the standard error of measurement. This important measurement statistic can be shown to be equal to the standard deviation of the raw scores times the square root of 1 minus the reliability. Thus, CTT assumes that the standard error is the same at any score point in the distribution. We hasten to note that generalizability theory makes similar assumptions, but IRT uses a conditional standard error of measurement that allows the error distribution for latent abilities to vary. That is, IRT asks the following question: Given the examinee's specific score, what is the standard error? So, with IRT there is a specific standard error for each score—very precise, indeed.

Generalizability Theory

Generalizability theory (Brennan, 2001), an extension of CTT, was developed by Cronbach, Gleser, Nanda, and Rajaratnam (1972). As with CTT, generalizability theory provides estimates of reliability coefficients and standard errors based on observed scores. However, generalizability theory provides a broader range of definitions of *consistency* than CTT. One of the advantages of generalizability theory is that it estimates reliability coefficients for norm-referenced scores based on relative error (scores relative to each other) and for criterion-referenced scores based on absolute errors (scores in relation to a fixed point). The two reliability coefficients produced are called a generalizability coefficient (relative error) and the dependability index (absolute error). Each reliability estimate also has an associated standard error for confidence intervals and the interpretation of individual scores. For indirect assessments, the selection of absolute or relative error will depend upon the uses and interpretations of the assessment. For example, a criterion-referenced interpretation (absolute error) would be whether students had a certain level of beliefs or attitudes. In contrast, a norm-referenced interpretation (relative error) would be whether students in different programs had higher or lower levels of beliefs or attitudes. Thus, the dependability index would be used when estimating specific levels of performance, beliefs, or attitudes, whereas the generalizability coefficient would be used when estimating which group or individuals scored higher than others. Selecting the correct coefficient is critical to avoiding biased estimation since the absolute error variance is greater than or equal to the relative error variance, and the generalizability coefficient is greater than or equal to the dependability index. Equality is only present when the variance components for the main effects of each source of error and the interactions of the sources of error are zero. Consequently, using relative error will usually provide an underestimate of the error variance and an overestimate of the dependability index for absolute interpretations and uses.

A second advantage of generalizability theory is that multiple sources of error can be considered simultaneously. Thus, consistency could be examined when subjective measures (rater effects) of items at different times (stability) could be examined simultaneously. This would allow us to examine the main effects of each source of error as well as the interactions; that is, the unique effect of raters at a particular time point. Because the estimation of variance components is based on a random effects repeated measures analysis of variance (ANOVA), any ANOVA design that can be estimated could provide the model for the generalizability analyses (i.e., the universe of generalization). The limitation of generalizability analyses is based on the repeated measures ANOVA, which defines *consistency* much broader than CTT. The ANOVA model allows (a) multiple sources of error; (b) crossed, nested, or ill-structured designs; and (c) two or more levels for each source of error. The complexity of generalizability theory allows a wide range of measurement designs and can be understood in more depth through the texts cited in the previous paragraph.

Although generalizability theory has fewer limitations than CTT, one important and notable shortcoming is the lack of a local standard error, implying that measurement error is the same at each score. Similar to CTT, it is assumed that the magnitude of the error variance does not differ by score level. IRT will make this allowance with more precise error for each (different) score.

Item Response Theory

CTT and generalizability theory provide methods of estimating consistency for observed scores. In contrast, IRT provides a model for estimating reliability or consistency for latent scores. To be clear, a latent score represents the standing on a variable that is not directly observable, thus, indirectly observed. Components of cognition such as abstract reasoning and problem-solving are latent variables that are then carefully defined by researchers and users. Noncognitive behaviors, such as grit, conscientiousness, and self-control, likewise are indirectly measured by researchers and practitioners as well. The use of latent scores provides many advantages, particularly those associated with being able to measure people on a common scale with different sets of items, and linking the items with people on a common scale (Yen & Fitzpatrick, 2006). IRT allows us to produce "a wide range of detailed predictions, both unconditional (for groups of examinees) and conditional (for examinees at one particular ability level)" (Yen & Fitzpatrick, 2006, p. 111). Thus, unlike observed score models (e.g., CTT), IRT emphasizes conditional standard errors rather than a fixed test standard error or reliability coefficient for the total group. This advantage allows interpretations of scores with confidence intervals that vary in size due to conditional standard errors.

The main limitations of IRT are due to the mathematical complexity of the models used. The more complex models require more complex estimation procedures (e.g., maximum likelihood or Bayesian estimation) and stronger assumptions of the model that need to be met (i.e., local independence and the structure of the model). Another limitation of IRT methods is the need for relatively large sample sizes to compute their assorted psychometric estimates. Whereas CTT procedures can justifiably be used with samples of fewer than 100 cases, indeed as low as 50 to 60 cases, most IRT methods need to be carried out on minimum sample sizes of 900 to 1,200 examinees.

Fairness Evidence

Fairness is important in assessment, as it is a "fundamental issue in protecting test takers and test users in all aspects of testing. The term *fairness* has no single technical meaning and is used in many different ways in public discourse" (AERA, APA, & NCME, 2014, p. 49). Fairness can be conceived of as a portion of the validity issue that ensures the scores of every examinee are afforded the same uses and interpretations. Thus, fairness often is treated as ensuring that there are no differences in the validity arguments nor the validity evidence for different subpopulations. Other terms used in combination and equivalence with fairness are *insensitivity, offensiveness,* and *bias.*

Consequently, with indirect assessments, fairness would be analyzed by examining the validity argument and evidence that were described earlier in the validity section for differences across subpopulations. For example, suppose the indirect assessment was a measure of attitudes or beliefs. Then the validity evidence reported for content, response process, internal structure, external relations, or consequences should be the same for each gender, ethnicity, or other subpopulation (e.g., disabilities, language). Camilli (2006) provides an overview of many of the methods used in examining fairness. Two of the more widely used methods in program assessment are content review by members of the impacted group(s) and internal structure, with some referring to this attention as methods for logical review. However, differential quantitative analyses by group could be used with any validity evidence that is central to the validity argument including analyzing differences in empirical relations with other variables (i.e., Are the regression models for predicting achievement from admissions scores equivalent for different subpopulations?) or differences in consequences (i.e., Is growth on the construct over time equal for different subpopulations?).

Content reviews for fairness have been called *sensitivity reviews.* In lieu of questions about the alignment of content with SLOs, sensitivity reviews ask experts to review items in regard to their (a) sensitivity to diversity or cultural issues and (b) offensiveness or insensitivity to subpopulations, including specific sexist, cultural, or ethnic stereotypes. For indirect assessments, these content reviews would typically be conducted by faculty or past students representing the impacted groups from the program area as a part of test adoption or development.

Internal structure or empirical review explores the relationship between the items, subtests, or components and the total score (observed or latent). As a validity concern, the primary issue is whether the item or component is related to the total score, which is a measure of the construct of interest. For fairness, the question is whether the relationship between the total score (observed or latent) has the same relationship for different subpopulations.

For IRT, this relationship is modeled as the relationship between the probability of getting an item right and the ability of the examinees. Thus, fairness occurs when the probability of getting a question correct at each ability level remains the same for each subpopulation. Analysis of this relationship is referred to as differential item functioning (DIF). Some of the more common methods for assessing DIF with observed scores are the Mantel-Haenszel statistic (Holland & Thayer, 1988) or logistic regression (Swaminathan & Rogers, 1990). IRT uses tests for differences in item parameters (Lord, 1980), tests for the area between item response curves (Raju, 1988), and the likelihood ratio test (Thissen, Steinberg, & Wainer, 1993). It is not uncommon—indeed, it is common practice—to find or expect these analyses (both logical and empirical methods used on the same test) conducted on tests and assessments used in higher education evaluation. The quality enhancement plan for SACSCOC at UF included two sources of evidence for fairness. First, the international task force reviewed the items for content sensitivity to different subpopulations. Second, the more complex internal structure analyses were conducted in a doctoral dissertation using DIF analyses with IRT (Wilson, 2014).

Standardization

We have presented the key and central tenets of indirect assessment: validity, reliability, and fairness. We would nonetheless be shortsighted if we omitted from consideration a feature of assessments that often gets discussed under the rubric of reducing interpretation errors. With attention to validity and fairness, we address limiting constant errors; with reliability, we address controlling variable errors. Interpretation errors are distinct and surface when the test or assessment is thought to be systematic to all examinees, yet in the administration or scoring of the test, different procedures are followed for different examinees. For example, if the test is to be administered under conditions allowing 30 minutes for administration, but some students are given more time, or some receive less time, then the examination was not the same experience for all; if scoring allows for spelling errors for some examinees but not for others, then again, there is a lack of a common scoring experience leading to uncommon scores being attained.

To achieve equivalence of the test scoring and the testing itself, we rely on following exact, fixed, and known procedures of a test. This criterion is termed *standardization*. The descriptor or label of a *standardized test* is the very thing we have been pointing to—that the test is given and scored the same way at all times to all examinees. Let us be direct and not equivocate. We need to build or have the test be standardized (i.e., common) with the following four considerations in mind: content, administration, directions, and scoring. To begin, is it necessary for all examinees to be administered the very same test questions for a test to be standardized? No. We should state that all examinees taking the test should receive a common set of questions. Unless all examinees are exposed to the same items or a set that has demonstrated their equivalence, examinees' performance to each other or to a common standard cannot be compared. This is consideration of standardization referencing content.

Next is standardization with respect to administration. Results from assessments cannot provide meaningful information for purposes of comparability (either relative or absolute) unless the assessment is administered under the same conditions. So, we standardized by structuring and using identical test administration directions and exact time limits. Continuing, it is imperative that the examiner give directions to examinees exactly as provided in the test instructions or test administration manual. It is common for written instructions to provide a statement of the test's purpose, how and where to respond, and how the examinee is to mark her or his responses. When an examiner fails to provide all information or attempts to supplement or alter instruction directions, standardization is forfeited: It is no longer a standardized test affording comparability.

Now, considering time limits, again the standardization criterion rule is to afford exactly the same amount of time to all examinees. Time limits are not to be shortened or extended beyond the time stated by the examiner. For some examinees with learning or attention difficulties, provisions are available as defined in the test manual for more, parsed, or extended time. Read and follow precisely the test manual instructions for administration or for such allowance or accommodation.

In closing, we would be remiss if we did not mention test equating (Haertel & Linn, 1996). Many commonly used higher education tests (SATs, ACTs, GREs, MCATs, LSATs, plus many others) have multiple forms (e.g., Form A, B, C), each form containing comparable if not identical numbers of questions, in the same format, and setting out to measure exactly the same and precise skills in the same order. Refer to preceding paragraphs discussing the comparability of test content to achieve test standardization and thus test equivalence for comparison. Although test standardization gets attention, the matter of the extent of test equivalence also deserves attention. Seen by way of a simple illustration, if a test publisher had two equivalent forms, then taking one would yield the same performance had the other been taken. If this was the outcome, wonderful. This is what is desired. How can a publisher achieve this standard? The methods for determining the extent of test form equivalence are termed *test equating*. Both CTT and IRT methods are available for documenting the extent of equating equivalence. Test technical manuals should be read to learn of the test-equating designs and methods used and extent of equivalence achieved. Research and evaluation in higher education needs to be aware of such equating designs especially if tests will be used as pre- and postmeasures over long periods of time (e.g., years), or perhaps in addition to change, if skills are expected to grow into other related but different facets of a domain (moving from basic and core understandings to complex problem-solving, creativity, syntheses, product evaluation, etc.).

Conclusion

Indirect assessments can take many forms and the uses and interpretations of the assessments can vary widely. Nevertheless, all assessments (direct or indirect) should provide evidence that the uses and interpretations of the assessments are well founded in a validity argument, assessments are reliable (minimal random error), and uses and interpretations are fair and equitable across subpopulations.

For each of the foundations of the *Standards*—validity, reliability, and fairness—there is a wide range of alternative methods that can be applied in different contexts. The selection of different methods depends on the uses or interpretations of the assessment and the scale of measurement. Selecting psychometric methods is based on clear specification of the construct being measured and the purposes of the assessment within a specific context. The psychometric evidence examined will depend on the specific uses and interpretations of the assessments and is always a matter of professional judgment. Ordinarily, more information is preferred.

References

American Educational Research Association, American Psychological Association, & National Council on Measurement in Education. (2014). *Standards for educational and psychological testing*. Washington, DC: Author.

Brennan, R. L. (2001). *Generalizability theory*. New York, NY: Springer.

Camilli, G. (2006). Test fairness. In R. L. Brennan (Ed.), *Educational measurement* (4th ed., pp. 221–256). Westport, CT: American Council on Education and Praeger.

Campbell, D. T., & Fiske, D. W. (1959). Convergent and discriminant validation by the multi-trait multimethod matrix. *Psychological Bulletin, 56*(2), 81–105.

Crocker, L., & Algina, J. (1986). *Introduction to classical and modern test theory*. Fort Worth, TX: Harcourt Brace Jovanovich.

Cronbach, L. J. (1988). Five perspectives on validity argument. In H. Wainer & H. Braun (Eds.), *Test validity* (pp. 3–17). Hillsdale, NJ: Lawrence Erlbaum Associates.

Cronbach, L. J., Gleser, G. C., Nanda, H., & Rajaratnam, N. (1972). *The dependability of behavioral measurements: Theory of generalizability for scores and profiles.* New York, NY: John Wiley & Sons.

de Ayala, R. J. (2008). *The theory and practice of item response theory.* New York, NY: Guilford Press.

Haertel, E. H., & Linn, R. L. (1996). Comparability. In *Technical issues in large-scale performance assessment* (Report No. NCES 96-802, pp. 59–78). Washington, DC: U.S. Department of Education.

Hambleton, R. K., & Novick, M. R. (1973). Toward an integration of theory and method for criterion-referenced tests. *Journal of Educational Measurement, 10,* 159–170.

Holland, P. W., & Thayer, D. T. (1988). Differential item performance and the Mantel-Haenszel procedure. In H. Wainer & H. I. Braun (Eds.), *Test validity* (pp. 129–145). Hillsdale, NJ: Lawrence Erlbaum Associates.

Kane, M. T. (2006). Validity. In R. L. Brennan (Ed.), *Educational measurement* (4th ed., pp. 17–64). Westport, CT: American Council on Education and Praeger.

Lord, F. M. (1980). *Applications of item response theory to practical testing applications.* New York, NY: Routledge.

Lord, F. M., & Novick, M. R. (1968). *Statistical theories of mental test scores.* Reading, MA: Addison-Wesley.

McDonald, R. P. (1999). *Test theory: A unified treatment.* Mahwah, NJ: Lawrence Erlbaum Associates.

Messick, S. (1989). Validity. In R. L. Linn (Ed.), *Educational measurement* (3rd ed., pp. 13–103). New York, NY: American Council on Education and Macmillan.

Miller, M. D., Linn, R. L., & Gronlund, N. E. (2013). *Measurement and assessment in teaching* (11th ed.). Upper Saddle River, NJ: Prentice-Hall.

Miller, M. D., Villalon, L. A., & Brophy, T. S. (2014). *Learning without borders: Internationalizing the Gator Nation: The University of Florida quality enhancement plan.* Retrieved from http://qep.aa.ufl.edu/Data/Sites/23/media/qep/1-21-14-final-qep-with-cover-for-the-web-rev2.pdf

Patz, R. (2016). *Education and the measurement of behavioral change.* Paper presented at the annual meeting of the National Council on Measurement in Education, Washington, DC.

Poggio, J. P., & Glasnapp, D. R. (2001). *Standards, policies and procedures for the evaluation of assessment instruments used in the California Community Colleges* (4th ed.). Sacramento, CA: California Community Colleges.

Raju, N. S. (1988). The area between two item characteristic curves. *Psychometrika* 53(4), 495–502.

Rogers, G. (2006). *Assessment 101: Assessment tips with Gloria Rogers, Ph.D., direct and indirect assessment.* Retrieved from http://www.abet.org/wp-content/uploads/2015/04/direct-and-indirect-assessment.pdf

Schmeiser, C. B., & Welch, C. J. (2006). Test development. In R. L. Brennan (Ed.), *Educational measurement* (4th ed., pp. 307–353). Westport, CT: American Council on Education and Praeger.

Spearman, C. (1907). Demonstration of formulae for true measurement of correlation. *American Journal of Psychology, 18*, 161–169.

Spearman, C. (1913). Correlations of sums and differences. *British Journal of Psychology, 5*, 417–426.

Swaminathan, H., & Rogers, H. J. (1990). Detecting differential item functioning using logistic regression procedures. *Journal of Educational Measurement, 27*, 361–370.

Thissen, D., Steinberg, L., & Wainer, H. (1993). Use of item response theory in the study of group differences in trace lines. In P. W. Holland & H. I. Braun (Eds.), *Differential item functioning* (pp. 67–113). Hillsdale, NJ: Lawrence Erlbaum Associates.

Wilson, T. J. (2014). Assessing internationalization efforts: Utilizing item response theory to validate intercultural competency and global awareness in postsecondary undergraduate students (Doctoral dissertation). University of Florida, Gainesville.

Yen, W. M., & Fitzpatrick, A. R. (2006). Item response theory. In R. L. Brennan (Ed.), *Educational measurement* (4th ed., pp. 111–154). Westport, CT: American Council on Education and Praeger.

PART THREE

CASE STUDY APPLICATIONS

7

CASE STUDY: THE NEW YORK CITY COLLEGE OF TECHNOLOGY APPROACH TO GENERAL EDUCATION ASSESSMENT

Tammie Cumming, City University of New York–New York City College of Technology

L. Jay Deiner, City University of New York–New York City College of Technology

Bonne August, City University of New York–New York City College of Technology

The New York City College of Technology (City Tech) is one of the 24 colleges of the City University of New York (CUNY), a public system serving 540,000 students. City Tech itself serves over 17,000 degree-seeking students and 15,000 nondegree students. Although the college began as a community college offering associate in applied science (AAS), associate in science (AS), and associate in arts (AA) degrees, it has grown rapidly in the past 10 years, and the school now offers 24 bachelor's degrees and 27 associate degrees. Admission to most of the associate programs follows an open enrollment model, but direct admission to the bachelor's degree programs is contingent on meeting specific requirements. Nonetheless, the college has a very high acceptance rate. The low selectivity requires the institution to ensure that all students, including those who struggle with college-level work, meet rigorous expectations upon graduation. The high enrollment and rapid rate of programmatic change further demand that the institution ensure excellence across courses, which may have many sections, and across new and established programs. Assessment is therefore an important tool, enabling faculty to help students learn and thrive in this large, dynamic institution.

The goal of assessment at City Tech is to improve student learning through collection and interpretation of valid and reliable data. The goal is simple, but attempts to achieve it generate the following questions: What measurements should be used? How can psychometric principles ensure valid and reliable data? Who should be involved in the assessment and who constructs meaning from the data? Answers to our questions have emerged through engagement in the assessment process. In this chapter, we present City Tech's general education assessment process as a pattern for competency-based assessment. We then provide a case study of City Tech's assessment of the general education competency of reading.

History of Assessment at City Tech

In collecting documentation for our 2008 Middle States reaccreditation review, we faced the reality that although individual faculty, degree programs, and departments did assess student learning, our college lacked a coordinated assessment program. Creation of such a program was crucial as students graduate having taken courses across a range of disciplines and departments. We needed a holistic understanding of the capacities of our graduates, not snapshots of what they have learned in one department or course. In response to the need for a coordinated, college-wide assessment program, we created an assessment structure within the Office of Assessment and Institutional Research and formed faculty assessment committees (Figure 7.1). At City Tech, the Office of Assessment and Institutional Research is composed of one director of assessment and one full-time staff member. The role of the Office of Assessment and Institutional Research is to provide technical support and guide faculty assessment efforts, as well as fulfill institutional reporting requirements and responsibilities. As City Tech offers degree programs through its schools of arts and sciences, professional studies, and technology and design, each school has its own school assessment committee. The school assessment committees have at least one representative from each department within the school and meet on a regular basis during the semester. To coordinate the assessment efforts across schools, each school dean, the dean of continuing education, the director of the Office of Assessment and Institutional Research, the associate provost of academic affairs, and the provost comprise a college Academic Assessment Committee. This committee serves as the steering committee and prescribes the annual agenda for each of the

Figure 7.1. Organizational structure of academic assessment at City Tech.

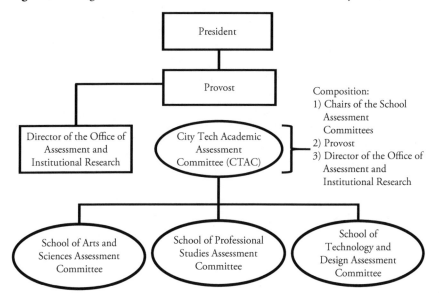

Note. The functions listed in rectangles are full-time administrative positions. The functions listed in ovals are committees composed of teaching faculty members.

three school assessment committees. The school assessment committees meet on a regular basis throughout the academic year. The three school assessment committees also meet as a unified group each semester in order to maintain a comprehensive assessment system that promotes dialogue across the college. The college recognizes faculty membership on the assessment committees, and participation in related assessment activities, as a valuable service contribution but does not provide compensation or release time for the work. Rather, assessment is considered a critical part of the teaching and learning process at City Tech.

To create the college-wide assessment program, the faculty on the school and college assessment committees and the director of the Office of Assessment and Institutional Research defined the scope of our college assessment efforts. We decided to maintain formative, discipline-specific efforts through "critical course" assessments—measures of key learning outcomes in courses that are central to individual programs and departments. We also resolved to maintain the program-level assessment required for all degree programs offered at City Tech and for the accreditation of degree programs in our engineering and professional schools. To these two initiatives, we added a college-wide assessment of our general education curriculum, the foundation of knowledge, skills, and attitudes shared by all of our students. From 2009 to 2011, we linked the college general education assessment effort to the CUNY proficiency exam (CPE), a three-hour test focused on analytical reading, writing, and other general education outcomes. All CUNY baccalaureate-seeking students took this exam after completion of associate-level work or the completion of 60 credit hours. In 2011, the university discontinued administration of the proficiency exam. Concomitantly, the university and the college began the process of reimagining the general education curriculum. To properly assess the evolving general education curriculum, City Tech became a partner institution in the Association of American Colleges & Universities (AAC&U) Liberal Education and America's Promise (LEAP) initiative. Accordingly, we adopted the AAC&U Valid Assessment of Learning in Undergraduate Education (VALUE) rubrics as our baseline instruments to assess our new general education learning outcomes.

Concurrent with the creation of a new organizational structure for assessment was a conscious attempt to foster a positive assessment culture at City Tech. Our goal was that faculty would come to value assessment as a useful tool for developing their teaching methods and constructing curricula to improve student outcomes. To build such an assessment culture, we focused on the following aspects: educating the faculty about best practices in assessment, and celebrating faculty achievements in assessment. To educate faculty, the Office of Assessment and Institutional Research invited faculty to workshops focused on the assessment process—for example, rubric development or curriculum modification in response to assessment data. Since 2009, workshops at the Office of Assessment and Institutional Research have served more than 350 faculty and administrators, with some faculty members attending more than one workshop. To celebrate faculty achievements in assessment, we invited faculty who were actively using assessment data to present their results in college-wide meetings and, in some cases, in meetings to the broader university (CUNY). We also invited faculty members to attend the annual Middle States Commission on Higher Education Conference. By the spring of 2013, after 4 years of workshops, conferences, and faculty involvement in the assessment process, 76.2% of surveyed full-time faculty and 71.5% of surveyed part-time faculty indicated that they understood the purpose of assessment at City Tech.

General Education at City Tech

Beginning in 2013, City Tech embraced a new competency-based general education curriculum. The new curriculum consisted of a small number of common required courses, and a range of student-selected courses from prescribed categories. Irrespective of the courses that an individual student chooses, we expected that he or she will emerge with competencies in the following 14 areas:

1. Civic engagement
2. Creative thinking
3. Critical thinking
4. Ethical reasoning
5. Foundations and skills for lifelong learning
6. Information literacy
7. Inquiry and analysis
8. Integrative learning
9. Intercultural knowledge and competence
10. Oral communication
11. Quantitative literacy
12. Reading
13. Teamwork
14. Writing

Because our general education expectations were competency based, it was clear that our assessment of general education should also be focused on competencies rather than individual courses or departments. Also clear was that the large number of competencies would require careful organization of the schedule for assessment. To achieve this organization, the assessment committee produced a calendar mapping assessment of each competency to a three-year cycle, and staggering the cycles for the competencies in blocks of four or five (Figure 7.2). Then, for each competency, the subtasks associated with the assessment process were further mapped onto calendar months (Figure 7.3).

The remainder of this chapter focuses on the details of enacting the subtasks listed in Figure 7.3 of a case study of applying this process to assess the general education competency of reading and a selection of lessons learned through the assessment process.

The activities listed in Figure 7.3 were derived by applying psychometric standards of fairness, validity, and reliability to a traditional assessment cycle (AERA, APA, NCME, 2014). The application of these standards has resulted in an enhanced assessment cycle (see Figure 7.4). The traditional assessment cycle comprises planning, data collection and reporting, analysis and evaluation, and improvement planning and implementation; the enhanced assessment explicitly considers the psychometric principles guiding each step. This model recognizes the necessity of psychometrics to ensure the quality of the data and the utility of the assessment cycle as a whole.

Figure 7.2. Scheduling of three-year assessment cycles for 14 general education competencies.

General education learning outcome	Three-year assessment cycles for 14 general education competencies							
	Year 1	Year 2	Year 3	Year 4	Year 5	Year 6	Year 7	Year 8
	Spring Fall							
Oral communication Writing Information literacy Reading Quantitative literacy	Cycle 1 (competencies 1–5)			Cycle 2 (competencies 1–5)				
Critical thinking Teamwork Ethical reasoning Civic engagement			Cycle 1 (competencies 6–9)			Cycle 2 (competencies 6–9)		
Foundations and skills for lifelong learning Creative thinking Inquiry and analysis Integrative learning Intercultural knowledge and competence				Cycle 1 (competencies 10–14)			Cycle 2 (competencies 10–14)	

Note. Through this schedule, all of the general education competencies will have undergone two full cycles of assessment every eight years.

Subtasks Involved in Competency-Based Assessment of General Education

The following sections describe the assessment process at City Tech for one complete assessment cycle. This includes course selection for sampling, instrument development, establishing psychometric properties, data analysis, reporting results, and utilizing the data to improve student outcomes.

Course and Department Selection

The first step of our assessment cycle was to select the departments and courses in which the competency was measured. As the chief academic officer of the college, the provost ultimately oversaw academic assessment and was in charge of selecting departments to participate in the assessment of a given competency (see Figure 7.1). Departments were selected with careful consideration of the curricula and student learning outcomes of the programs, and to ensure a broad range of participants.

Once the departments were selected, the department chairs were advised of the department's participation and asked to select appropriate courses for

Figure 7.3. Assessment subtasks mapped onto three academic years.

Assessment Subtask	Year 1										Year 2										Year 3									
	Feb	Mar	Apr	May	Summer	Sep	Oct	Nov	Dec	Jan	Feb	Mar	Apr	May	Summer	Sep	Oct	Nov	Dec	Jan	Feb	Mar	Apr	May	Summer	Sep	Oct	Nov	Dec	Jan
Assignment of department and course	■																													
Communication with course coordinator and faculty; distribution of rubric		■																												
Development or selection of assignment for assessment		■	■																											
Content validity activity			■																											
First data collection (pilot)				■																										
Interrater reliability activity					■	■																								
Analysis and reporting of data to faculty and chairs						■																								
Full-scale data collection								■	■																					
Interrater reliability activity											■																			
Analysis and reporting of data to faculty and chairs											■																			
Evaluate report											■																			
Draft improvement plan													■	■																
Implementation of improvement plan																■	■	■	■		■	■	■	■		■	■	■	■	

Note. At City Tech, faculty work on nine-month appointments. Accordingly, no assessment activities are scheduled for the summer break months of June, July, and August. Due to holidays and winter recess, no assessment activities are scheduled for January.

Figure 7.4. Application of psychometric standards of fairness, validity, and reliability to a traditional assessment cycle.

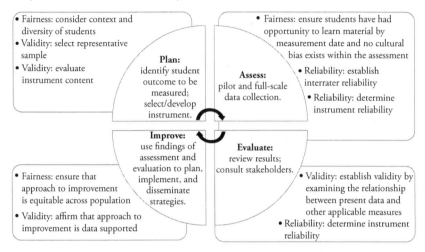

participation in the general education assessment. Thus, although selection of the participating departments is a central administrative function, selection of the particular courses is a local department function. Ideally, the department chairs make their course selections based on their curriculum maps or an evaluation of the learning outcomes listed on the course outlines of the departmental courses. An ideal course for our general education assessment is usually considered to be a second-semester freshman- or sophomore-level course with high enrollment and the chosen competency explicitly listed as a learning outcome. These considerations when selecting courses are a fundamental step in adhering to the standard of establishing validity (Crocker & Algina, 1986).

Communication of Course Selection and Designation of Course Assessment Leader

Once the department chairs selected the courses for the assessment, they informed the course coordinators of the courses identified for data collection. The course coordinator then worked with the department assessment liaison (the department's representative to the school assessment committee) to organize the assessment process within the department. In particular, the course coordinator and assessment liaison ensured timely instrument development, data collection, selection and submission of student exemplar samples, and communication of the results to their department chairs and faculty.

Instrument Development by Faculty Members

The course coordinator invited all faculty who taught the selected courses to participate in an instrument development activity—in essence, coming together to create a rubric that could be used to measure the general education competency. At City Tech, this process was initiated at the department level with faculty working together to review and discuss the VALUE rubric for the competency being evaluated. Then, the Office of Assessment and Institutional Research organized meetings in which faculty participating in the competency assessment met in small cross-departmental groups to work together to optimize the VALUE rubric for use at City Tech. In these meetings, cross-departmental groups discussed and analyzed the VALUE rubric to determine whether and how it should be modified for meaningful work at City Tech. Then, on a common computer whose desktop was projected onto a wall-mounted screen, the small groups of faculty worked together to modify the rubric in real time during the meeting. After these meetings, the Office of Assessment and Institutional Research circulated a draft of the edited rubric to all participants for subsequent editing in a virtual environment.

Once the faculty approved the collaboratively edited rubric, the course coordinator within each department circulated the rubric to faculty who would be teaching the course selected for the general education competency assessment. At the same time, the course coordinator asked faculty teaching the course for suggestions for the assignment that was used to assess the students. For all assessment activities at City Tech, we included at least one measure of direct assessment for each learning outcome. We defined *direct measures* to include locally developed exams (accompanied by a test blueprint), performance appraisals, and standardized exams. Because the assessments of all City Tech general education competencies are conducted across multiple departments, we pursued an assessment model where the assignments were the same for all sections of a particular course within a department but may vary from department to department. The goal was one shared assignment per selected course. During the process of assignment development, many of the course coordinators received multiple assignment suggestions and then worked with faculty to synthesize a single assignment.

Content-Based Evidence of Validity and Fairness

Important validity evidence can be established by evaluating the relationship between the instrument content and the student learning outcome (AERA, APA, & NCME, 2014). Does the assignment actually measure the desired general education competency? This question is best answered by the subject

Figure 7.5. Schematic of the transformation of a standard rubric to a content validity worksheet for self-auditing.

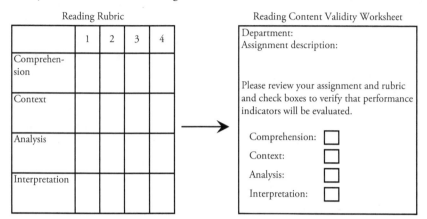

Note. In this rubric, evaluative criteria comprehension, context, analysis, and interpretation are listed in the first column. Quality standards 1, 2, 3, and 4 would be defined in the subsequent columns. To transform the rubric to a content validity sheet for self-auditing, the faculty would describe the assignment and state how it allows for measurement of evaluative criteria.

matter experts, the faculty. The individual departments proceeded with the first step in establishing content-related validity evidence by filling out content validity worksheets for their proposed assignments (Figure 7.5). The worksheets translated the rubric elements into a tool that enabled faculty to review the assignment and document alignment with the selected rubric. The worksheets provide a tool to engage in a self-auditing process.

After all departments completed the content validity worksheets and submitted their selected assignments to the Office of Assessment and Institutional Research, the office organized and conducted a two-hour meeting where departments came together to provide constructive feedback on one another's assignments. The review of assignments occurred in interdepartmental groups of approximately six faculty members. Feedback from the review process was summarized in the reviewers' version of the content validity sheet (Figure 7.6). This activity served as an external audit, providing a fresh perspective as to whether the selected assignment could be a valid measure of the general education competency. While establishing content-related evidence of validity, faculty also reviewed the assessment for content-related sources of bias or fairness. Faculty considered whether the assignment measured the general education competency equitably given the diversity of student experiences and identities. Taken together, the content review and fairness activities served as opportunities for faculty to gain a deeper

Figure 7.6. Reading content validity worksheet used for faculty to review one another's assignments.

Content Validity for Reading

Reviewer name: _____ Reviewer department: _____

Department assignment sample: _____

Instruction: Please review the assignment carefully and familiarize yourself with the City Tech Reading Rubric. Please document how the assignment (and instructions) will cover each of the following performance indicators:

Comprehension

_____
_____
_____

Context

_____
_____
_____

Analysis

_____
_____
_____

Interpretation

_____
_____
_____

understanding of the assessment process. Anecdotally, we have found that this enhanced understanding is a critical step to helping faculty see value in assessment.

Pilot-Scale Assessment

During the pilot-scale assessment, we collected data involving a small number of the total sections of the courses that would later be included in the full-scale data collection. This pilot-scale data collection tested the utility of the assignment and rubric and provided exemplars of student work that were used to examine the consistency among raters (interrater reliability).

To perform the pilot-scale assessment, department chairs chose the participating section(s) of the course and notified the Office of Assessment and Institutional Research of their selection. The Office of Assessment and Institutional Research then prepopulated scannable rubrics with student names from the class rosters of the participating sections. Then, at the beginning of the semester, the Office of Assessment and Institutional Research distributed the scannable and prepopulated forms to piloting faculty. In accordance with the standards of fairness, faculty conducted the assessment after the students had the opportunity to learn the material covered on the assessment.

Faculty then scored student work using the rubric. Then, faculty sent the scored and scannable rubrics to the Office of Assessment and Institutional Research for processing. In addition to the scored rubrics for all students, faculty sent copies of exemplars of student work, providing samples for each of the levels of student performance in the rubric. For example, if the levels of student performance corresponded to appraisals of "does not meet criterion," "approaching criterion," "meets criterion," and "surpasses criterion," then exemplars for each of these levels would be provided.

We noted that the purpose of the scannable rubrics was to decrease faculty workload associated with the data collection process. As of fall 2016, scannable rubrics were replaced with a fully automated assessment software system, again with the idea that data collection, data entry, and data archiving should not be onerous processes for the faculty.

Interrater Reliability

At the beginning of the semester following the pilot data collection, the Office of Assessment and Institutional Research convened faculty to assess interrater reliability. All faculty who participated in the pilot and who were likely to participate in the full-scale data collection were invited, and RSVPs were requested. To prepare for the meeting, the Office of Assessment and Institutional Research blind coded the student exemplars submitted from the pilot administration (i.e., removed student names from work). When faculty arrived at the meeting, they were assigned to tables of four to five people. Each participant received a packet containing four examples of student work for one assignment. Faculty members then read each student exemplar, one at a time. After reading each assignment, the faculty member scored the assignment using the rubric. When all participants at a table had assigned their individual scores to an assignment, the group of four to five faculty members discussed their scoring rationale with one another, and they discussed any difficulty they may have had using the rubrics. After all assignments were scored, faculty made suggestions for modification to the rubric or the assignment. The rubrics were then edited and finalized to incorporate suggestions from the faculty. In our interrater reliability working groups, we found that interrater reliability coefficients varied from moderate to high (0.5 to 0.9 for the local instruments). Although these interrater reliability coefficients did not meet the threshold expected for high-stakes appraisals, for our pilot phase of the assessment, the interrater reliability coefficients were useful benchmarks and an important part of the process of learning how the rubric and assignments could be improved. We recognized that improvements in the rubric led to increased interrater reliability. As such we believe that the value of the interrater reliability working group meetings was primarily that they allowed faculty to finalize the rubric and their assignments for the full-scale data collection. We also found that these meetings provided an excellent forum for in-depth conversation among the faculty about the students' achievement throughout the college.

Full-Scale Data Collection

Once we established the content-based evidence for validity and improved the rubric and assignment in accordance with faculty suggestions from the interrater reliability meeting, we pursued the full-scale data collection involving enough sections to have adequate representation of the population of students—for small programs, this may be all sections of a particular course. To facilitate full-scale data collection, course coordinators contacted faculty to offer support in using the rubric and the assignment. Department chairs also notified the Office of Assessment and Institutional Research of the courses and their associated student rosters. This enabled the Office of Assessment and Institutional Research to prepare scannable rubrics containing prepopulated names for each student in the course. Faculty received these forms mid-semester, but they were typically administered toward the end of the semester to provide the most insight into student achievement. Even though the faculty decided how to incorporate the assignment into their syllabi, we strongly encouraged that some stakes be attached to the assignment as students tend to take such assignments more seriously. After administering the assessment, faculty scored student work using the rubric and then sent the scored rubrics and student exemplars of different levels of proficiency to the Office of Assessment and Institutional Research. Again, the scannable rubrics and organizational assistance from the Office of Assessment and Institutional Research were provided to minimize faculty workload related to data collection, entry, and archival. In fall 2016, some of these work-saving functions were performed by a fully automated assessment software package.

Data Analysis

The goal of data analysis was to take the raw data set and transform it into a meaningful and representative picture of student achievement—to move from data to quality information that could be used to improve student learning outcomes. The chapters on direct and indirect assessment methods provide a thorough discussion of the mathematical and logical constructs for analysis of educational data. Each institution, and each data collection effort, will likely generate a data set with its own particular challenges. In City Tech's competency-based general education data sets, we sometimes encountered the challenge of how to properly weight the data generated from courses with unequal numbers of sections and students and with achieving representation from throughout the entire college. For example, if we measured a competency in 15 sections of biology and 7 sections of physics, we needed to weight the results so that our understanding of student learning did not disproportionately reflect student learning in biology. Irrespective of the particular challenges of the data set, we believe that the most robust and impartial analysis of the data comes from collaborative work between individuals directly involved in design and execution of the assessment and those who may first encounter the data after they are collected. During the first full-scale data collection at City Tech, the local Office of Assessment and Institutional Research analyzed the assessment data in consultation with CUNY's central Office of Institutional Research and Assessment's director of assessment. Other institutions may wish to consider the expertise of faculty members in the mathematics or social science research departments to assist with statistical concerns.

Data Reporting

After analyzing the data, the Office of Assessment and Institutional Research drafted reports for each course section and then aggregated the data appropriately for the course (aggregating across sections), program, department, school, and college as a whole. The Office of Assessment and Institutional Research then shared these reports with the instructors, department chairs, and administration. The chairs distributed the aggregated results during a department meeting designated to discuss the assessment activities. The goal of publicizing the reports in department meetings was that all faculty, not just those involved in executing the assessment, were aware of and could benefit from the results. In our reports, only course aggregate results were shared; no section- or instructor-specific data were shared. We provided reports with only aggregated data because we believe it is the best way to ensure that assessment is used for college-wide improvement. This was crucial because one of the reasons that faculty were sometimes reluctant to participate in assessment was the concern that the results of the assessment would be used to target or shame them. Aggregated data helped to remove this concern. At City Tech, the senior administrators strongly supported this philosophy and clearly stated that the assessment process must be conducted to improve student learning, and not to evaluate individual faculty.

Evaluation

Once we disseminated the assessment reports, we initiated a conversation about how to contextualize, interpret, and respond to the data. At the administrative level, the discussion of the reports focused on their utility for meeting documentation requirements of accreditation, and on possible improvements and financial support that is required to support improvement strategies. At the department level, the chair, course coordinator, and faculty conducted discussions of the reports to gain an understanding of students' skills in the measured competency. This understanding could be used to tailor syllabi and to determine possible support resources.

Fundamental to the evaluation was consideration of psychometric properties of reliability, validity, and fairness. One method appropriate to establishing the reliability in our context was to compute a measure of internal consistency, for example, Cronbach's alpha. In some cases, it was possible to establish concurrent validity by examining the relationship between the present data and other measures of the same learning outcome. Various professional accreditation bodies, such as ABET (formerly known as Accreditation Board for Engineering and Technology) and the Council for the Accreditation of Educator Preparation, have been advocating this practice in their best practices assessment training.

Improvement Planning

The improvement plan is the set of steps or changes that were identified in order to support student achievement in the measured competency. The improvement plan takes into consideration the standards of fairness and validity that have guided the entire process. We considered fairness by ensuring that the improvement plan was equitable across the population. When the data revealed similar trends across departments, we implemented a college-wide improvement plan. In cases where there was less interdepartmental homogeneity, the improvement plan was drafted within the department to address specific needs, but still keeping in mind that the full population's needs must be addressed. We considered validity in affirming that our approach to improvement was data supported. The key to ensuring a successful assessment cycle was following through with the improvement plans and implementing the improvement strategies in a timely manner.

Reassessment

Our assessment cycle called for reassessment of each general education competency every three years. The reassessment provided us with our new baseline and allowed us to determine whether our improvement plans did, indeed, enhance students' mastery of the general education competencies.

Reading Assessment at City Tech

In spring 2012, City Tech began assessment of the general education competency of reading. Together with writing and information literacy, reading was one of the first general education competencies we assessed as we transitioned from the CUNY proficiency exam method of assessment to a model based on the VALUE paradigm. We included reading in this first group for the central role it plays in college-level learning, as well as faculty members' long-standing concern that many students either weren't reading the assigned texts or weren't able to make use of the texts they had read. The faculty needed to have a measure of this competency to assist our students. For the pilot-scale data collection, the provost chose departments from each of our three schools: arts and sciences, professional studies, and technology and design. In turn, the chairs of these departments selected courses for participation in pilot-scale data collection. In total, 143 students distributed across eight courses were selected through stratified sampling to participate in the pilot-scale data collection.

The faculty in the selected courses participated in adapting the VALUE rubric for reading assessment. Through the collaborative rubric construction process, City Tech faculty agreed on a rubric with the following four performance indicators to measure reading competency: comprehension, context, analysis, and interpretation (Table 7.1). These performance indicators were similar to, but distinct from, the original VALUE performance indicators, which included comprehension, genres, relationship to text, analysis, interpretation, and reader's voice. The City Tech reading rubric provided faculty with an instrument to score student work on a scale that included "does not meet criterion," "approaching criterion," "meets criterion," and "surpasses criterion." The VALUE rubric scale includes "benchmark," "milestones," and "capstone."

Once faculty finalized and approved the rubric, and course coordinators shared the rubric and pilot-scale assessment expectations, faculty within each of the selected courses worked with their course coordinators to propose an assignment. The faculty worked together to establish validity through content-based evidence, performed the pilot-scale data collection, and determined interrater reliability for a set of student exemplars that represented the range of student performance. The pilot-scale data collection and related activities were important to our understanding of assessment of reading at City Tech. First, through the validity and interrater reliability processes, a number of faculty noticed that the level or phrasing of their assignments should be modified. Second, even discounting the data from assignments that may have exceeded college-level reading, the data from the pilot-scale assessment of reading supported faculty members' impressions that reading

TABLE 7.1
City Tech Rubric for Reading

Performance Indicator	Does Not Meet Criterion	Approaching Criterion	Meets Criterion	Surpasses Criterion
Comprehension	Is unable to comprehend technical information.	Evaluates how textual features (e.g., sentence and paragraph structure or tone) contribute to the author's message; draws basic inferences about context and purpose of text.	Uses the text and background knowledge from within the discipline in order to draw inferences from the material.	Uses the text, background knowledge from within and outside of the discipline to draw sophisticated inferences from the material.
Context	Is unable to apply information from the reading to broader context either within or outside of discipline.	Struggles to apply information toward a broader context, but aware that it is useful and important.	Is able to apply information from the reading within the discipline.	Is able to proficiently apply information to broader contexts, both within and outside of discipline.
Analysis	Fails to identify the incremental steps of an argument. Unable to evaluate or compare facts, positions, and procedures among various texts.	Identifies at least one idea or argument but may not evaluate it. Struggles at comparing or contrasting information between different sources.	Identifies ideas or arguments but may not always be able to evaluate them. Shows increasing ability to compare or contrast information between different sources.	Correctly identifies and evaluates ideas or arguments. Is able to compare or contrast information competently between different sources.
Interpretation	Makes little or no interpretation of the text.	Uses information from the text to make simplistic interpretations of the text without using significant concepts or by making only limited connections to other situations or contexts.	Uses information from the text to interpret significant concepts or make connections to other situations or contexts logically through analysis, evaluation, inference, or comparison/contrast.	Uses information from the text to make sophisticated interpretations of the text while making connections to other situations.

Note. This rubric is based on the AAC&U rubric but was adapted by City Tech faculty.

was a challenge for many students. This created motivation for the full-scale data collection and engendered a college-wide conversation about what we could do to improve mastery of this crucial general education competency.

As a result of this conversation, the provost; associate provost; director of the Office of Assessment and Institutional Research; and faculty from the departments of English, biology, business, and computer engineering technology wrote a university grant proposal, funded in fall 2013, to support redesigning three high-enrollment gateway courses so that explicit and effective reading instruction was embedded. These courses all had high failure and withdrawal rates, and it was hypothesized that students' weakness in reading could be a contributing factor to the low pass rates. It should be noted that the pilot data results were so compelling that the college opted to move forward with the grant application for Reading Effectively Across the Disciplines (READ) prior to completing the full-scale data collection (fall 2013, n = 529) rather than waiting an additional year for the full-scale results to become available. Once the full-scale data collection was completed, the reliability coefficient, internal consistency of the full-scale data collection, was indeed high (α = .78), and the results were consistent with the pilot findings.

The funded initiative, READ, included two aspects of course redesign for enhanced reading instruction. The first was professional development of faculty. Seventy-five percent of faculty teaching in the selected courses would receive coaching from City Tech faculty considered to be reading specialists. The coaches would present best practices for gauging the difficulty level of reading assignments, designing appropriate assignments, growing students' discipline-specific vocabulary, and helping students become attentive readers. The second aspect of course redesign was incorporation of peer-assisted learning into the high-enrollment, low-pass-rate courses. Student peer leaders would receive training for enhancement of reading through a one-credit independent study course. The trained leaders would facilitate group work in and out of class and participate in online discussions.

Prior to the fall 2013 full-scale data collection, in spring 2013 we collected additional baseline data in order to prepare for the grant application (149 students). The results of this additional baseline data confirmed the results of the spring 2012 pilot study, again indicating that college-level reading was a struggle across the disciplines at City Tech. Consistency between the spring 2012 and spring 2013 results was high (r = .92), which provided evidence that our assessment results were reliable within our context. No performance indicator showed more than 80% of students met or exceeded the college-level expectation of proficiency. For the performance indicator of "analysis," slightly more than 50% of the students met or exceeded the expected college-level proficiency (Figure 7.7).

Figure 7.7. Percentage of students who met or exceeded criteria for the four reading performance indicators assessed in spring 2013.

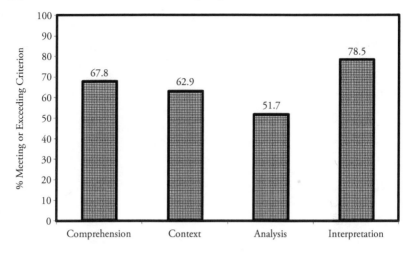

In spring 2014, after the READ program had been in place for two semesters, we collected data using multiple measures to monitor the progress of the READ initiative. It is important to note that the spring 2014 data, collected specifically to monitor the effectiveness of the READ program, was in addition to the data collected as part of the City Tech general education assessment cycle (see Table 7.2).

In contrast to the spring 2013 data collection effort, the spring 2014 data collection effort focused solely on students who were in courses receiving READ support. Thus, even on similar measures, it was not possible to directly compare the spring 2013 data to the spring 2014 data because it was not possible to separate the effect of READ from the possible differences between the spring 2013 cohort (students from a range of courses) and the spring 2014 cohort (students from only READ-supported courses). However, the faculty leading the READ initiative utilized the full range of data collected in spring 2014 to assess students' performance on key learning outcomes and to further enhance the READ program. Upon completion of the two-year, grant-funded initiative, City Tech determined that the READ program was successful in supporting its students in their attainment of college-level learning outcomes in reading and subsequently decided to sustain the program with alternate funding sources.

At City Tech, we consistently emphasize that assessment is a means to produce meaningful instructional strategies, not just an exercise to meet accreditation requirements. The general education assessment of reading and the resulting READ program is a clear example of data driving an educational

TABLE 7.2

Data Collected for the General Education Assessment of Reading and for Assessment of the READ Intervention Program

General Education Assessment	Assessment of READ Program	Reliability	Validity and Fairness
Spring 2012 (*n* = 143); general education pilot data alerted us to necessity for intervention		Compared spring 2012 and spring 2013, provided a reliability coefficient of stability (*r* = .92)	Content validity worksheets and discussion preceded each data collection; review of fairness occured concurrently with content validity; the college was in the process of examining the predictive validity of reading assessment instrument
	Spring 2013 (*n* = 149); established baseline for READ program		
Fall 2013 (*n* = 529); full-scale general education data collected		Computed reliability coefficient of internal consistency (α = .78)	
	Spring 2014 (*n* = 271); monitored effectiveness of READ program for grant reporting		
Fall 2016 (in progress); full-scale general education data collected			

Note. Activities to ensure reliability, validity, and fairness are described in parallel.

initiative that ultimately leads to enhanced student learning. Having such initiatives improves education at City Tech and serves to communicate the value of assessment to faculty and administrators. We believe it is part of our ongoing work to promote a positive assessment culture at the college and recognize its importance as a part of the curriculum and not a secondary activity.

Lessons Learned Through the Assessment Process

A consistent theme that has emerged since the beginning of our college-wide assessment effort in 2009 is that the people are the process. It is not possible to design a data collection effort, collect and evaluate data, and then make meaningful instructional improvement without the participation, support, and credence of faculty, staff, and administrators. Therefore, in closing this chapter, we highlight a few practices that we believe favor these factors.

- *Respect people's time.* Colleges and universities are busy places where everyone is balancing multiple competing priorities; time is the greatest commodity. Faculty, staff, and administrators will quickly come to resent anything that requires a large time investment for little payoff. Therefore, it is critical to examine the assessment process to make sure that busywork and time burdens are minimized. This suggests that automation of certain parts of the assessment process (e.g., data entry) is a useful investment. Similarly, requests that disrupt a carefully constructed schedule can also be met with resistance. As a result, advance planning and early communication of assessment efforts is necessary. Although three months may seem like an adequate amount of time to request participation, from the perspective of a chairperson, this may represent the need to rearrange staffing during a given semester. As such, a year of advance notice is preferable.
- *Enhance faculty and administrator engagement by including psychometric principles in the assessment process.* Faculty and administrators generally have academic research backgrounds, but they may not have significant experience in education research, in particular educational measurement and psychometrics. We have found that one of the best ways to empower faculty to drive a sustainable assessment program is through on-the-job training. By involving faculty in content review and interrater reliability activities, data collection, and report evaluation, they learn how to conduct the assessment process, and even more importantly, they gain confidence in the quality of the data and their utility. Even though there is a commitment of time involved in the processes described, the benefit to faculty and the college makes the investment of time worthwhile.
- *Enhance faculty and administrator engagement by publicizing improvement strategies resulting from assessment.* When faculty know that their data collection efforts result in real improvement strategies, like READ, they are more likely to see assessment as a driver of change, capable of impacting student learning outcomes.
- *Create a positive assessment culture.* In this context, we define a *positive assessment culture* as one that celebrates the achievements of faculty participating in assessment. For example, if data collection and an improvement plan result in enhanced student learning, we make sure to recognize the involved faculty and promote their work through conference participation and publication.

- *Remember, compliance is not the goal; the work is the goal.* Sometimes a department or faculty member misses a deadline or otherwise neglects to participate in an initiative. Instead of focusing on bringing the department or faculty member into compliance, we focus on collaborating with the faculty member to determine what we can do to get the work done. What are the current impediments to this faculty member's participation in the process? Does the faculty member need support in writing an assignment or interpreting a rubric?
- *Provide a supportive structure.* Ensuring that faculty have the support they need to develop and conduct their assessments is considered a valuable resource at City Tech. Various services are available, including psychometric assistance, assessment planning, data analysis and reporting, and referrals for planning improvement strategies.

As the assessment cycles have continued, and an increasing number of faculty have had direct experience with the assessment process, they have come to recognize the value that a thoughtfully constructed assessment offers them in achieving their own most important goals for student learning. Instructors can use data to detect more precisely the obstacles to learning, as well as to hone the strategies they devise to improve learning. When data analysis is a tool in their own hands rather than an evaluation instrument imposed upon them, faculty members are able to discover the broad range of its usefulness in supporting their own best work. City Tech faculty are offered assistance both in improving instruction in their own disciplines and in helping to strengthen the integration across the college curriculum of general education, the groundwork on which disciplinary knowledge is established, and the context for its application. The resulting professional partnerships—across disciplines and between faculty and administration—hold the promise that both the students and the institution will benefit.

References

American Educational Research Association, American Psychological Association, & National Council on Measurement in Education. (2014). *Standards for Educational and Psychological Testing.* Washington, DC: Author.

Crocker, L., & Algina, J. (1986). *Introduction to classical modern test theory.* Orlando, FL: Harcourt Brace Jovanovich.

8

CASE STUDY: TEXAS CHRISTIAN UNIVERSITY ASSESSMENT SYSTEM

Catherine M. Wehlburg, Texas Christian University

Texas Christian University (TCU) is a private, coeducational, largely residential liberal arts university located in Fort Worth, Texas. In 2015, TCU enrolled approximately 8,500 undergraduate students and 1,500 graduate students. TCU was founded in 1873 as the AddRan Male and Female College, in honor of the founding brothers Addison and Randolph Clark, leaders of the Restoration Movement and the Disciplines of Christ church. The Clark brothers were strong advocates for education of all people. In part because of the educational philosophies of the Clark brothers, TCU has always been focused on its mission as a residential liberal arts institution.

History of Assessment at TCU

Assessment of student learning has long been a part of teaching and learning practice at TCU, but it was not until 2001 that the Office for Assessment and Quality Enhancement, now called the Office for Institutional Effectiveness, was created. The creation of a central office was, in large part, due to an upcoming visit of TCU's regional accreditor, the Southern Association of Colleges and Schools Commission on Colleges (SACSCOC). The SACSCOC visit in 2003 identified several issues in assessment of student learning, and TCU was required to submit SACSCOC monitoring reports to show that the institution was, indeed, measuring student learning and using that information to improve and enhance the educational practices at TCU. Through faculty efforts and leadership from the Office for Assessment and Quality Enhancement, the SACSCOC's final report indicated no issues with assessment. During their subsequent visit in 2013, the SASCOC again reported no issues with assessment, demonstrating that TCU maintained its improvements in assessment.

Philosophy of Assessment at TCU

While the creation of TCU's Office for Institutional Effectiveness was based on accreditation requirements, staff in the office believe accreditation is not the primary reason for assessment. Rather, assessment is a part of teaching and learning and, therefore, must be a formative process with the goal of continuously improving student learning through meaningful curriculum modifications and improvements and enhancements in pedagogy. This philosophy is clearly and publicly articulated by the office:

> Good assessment can promote quality enhancement at all levels of the university by providing us with the necessary evidence to guide effective decision making in many areas: including programmatic changes, classroom teaching modifications, support service adjustments, policy or procedure revisions, campus climate improvements, and structural reorganizations. Simply put, we need to know how we are doing before we can do better. In addition to these internal purposes, we will use assessment to respond to external requests for accountability. (TCU Office for Assessment and Quality Enhancement, 2016, p. 5)

In accord with this philosophy, academic departments are encouraged (and sometimes pushed) to make sure that they are not just measuring the student learning that will show that they are "good." Rather, they are encouraged to ask the questions that will lead them to answers pointing to areas in need of improvement. In order to keep a focus on assessment for learning, the Office for Institutional Effectiveness provides several different venues for faculty to learn about and participate in the process. This reflects the underlying notion that if faculty are fully aware of the utility of assessment and the process of educational measurement they will be more likely to consider these activities as a regular part of their teaching responsibilities.

Structure of Assessment and Institutional Effectiveness at TCU

Per its mission statement, the function of the Office for Institutional Effectiveness is to "enhance student learning and institutional effectiveness at TCU by providing leadership and assistance to the campus community in assessment activities" (Texas Christian University, n.d.a). As part of the process of providing services to TCU, the office aims

- to coordinate and support an ongoing, systematic program of institutional evaluation and assessment of student achievement, and facilitate the incorporation of the findings into the planning and accreditation processes;
- to support a broad based, comprehensive, program of institutional planning;
- to publish assessment research and maintain an active role in professional organizations; [and]
- to engage in community outreach activities that promote the institutional mission (Texas Christian University, n.d.b.).

The mission and articulated activities imply that assessment at TCU is largely decentralized, with faculty deeply involved in identifying, creating, and managing assessment activities. The Office for Institutional Effectiveness follows up with each department on an annual basis, submits reports for the institution for accreditation, and ensures that the assessment process is ongoing and functioning in ways that allow for both the improvement of learning and the sharing of information for accountability. The provost requires most departments (through their academic dean) to complete assessment reports in a timely manner.

To complement the decentralized assessment activities, there are a select number of centralized assessments focused on measuring university-wide programs. One such program is the general education curriculum, also known as the TCU Core Curriculum. The director of the TCU Core Curriculum sets a calendar of required activities, and assessment is performed by the faculty learning communities (FLCs; see Wehlburg & McNertney, 2009, for a more complete description of the FLC program). Similarly, the assessment of undergraduate research goals is spearheaded by the Office for Institutional Effectiveness and based on information provided by academic deans.

As is evident from the previous discussion, most assessment activities are owned by the faculty and are formative in nature. Similarly, much of the Office for Institutional Effectiveness's assessment planning is focused on the use of educational data for improvement of student learning. Nonetheless, the reality exists that some assessment results must be summative in nature and used to demonstrate accountability. As assessment for improvement and assessment for accountability are distinct uses, they imply different considerations for ensuring validity, reliability, and fairness. This dichotomy is quite clear in departments and programs that have specialized accreditation and must demonstrate that they meet that accreditor's standards. In these cases, both end uses of data must be considered in constructing the assessment activities.

Process of Assessment at TCU: Evidence of Best Practices

TCU has a wide variety of categories of best practices. Many of these are shared on the TCU assessment website and more are provided through the series of workshops conducted each year. TCU's best practices in each area of assessment are described in the following sections.

Engaging Faculty With the Process of Assessment

Much of the work done by the Office for Institutional Effectiveness is to build relationships with faculty and create an atmosphere of inquiry about learning. A basic three-step process is emphasized:

1. *Identify* what the faculty/staff/program is trying to do. What should students know and be able to do if the course/degree program is successful?
2. *Discover* how well the faculty/staff/program is doing in accomplishing the learning goals.
3. *Use* the information collected in the discover process to enhance and improve the course/program.

The initial step in enacting these processes is identifying faculty partners in each department. Toward this aim, at the start of each academic year, the Office for Institutional Effectiveness asks department chairs to provide the name of a faculty member who will be assigned the title of assessment liaison. This provides the Office for Institutional Effectiveness with a contact within the department. Some department chairs choose to name themselves as liaison, while others identify a faculty member. The Office for Institutional Effectiveness suggests that the assessment liaison be a tenured faculty member, but the ultimate choice resides with the chair. The position of assessment liaison does not include additional salary or course release time, but it does allow the faculty member to claim credit for service activities as this title is now recognized across campus.

Beyond identification of the assessment liaison, achieving broad faculty participation in assessment can be very challenging. Faculty have a multitude of responsibilities and may ignore a request to participate in assessment if it is viewed as extraneous to their core work. While the associate provost works through each college's academic dean for the authority to require faculty involvement in the assessment process, it is far preferable when faculty participate voluntarily. The Office for Institutional Effectiveness, with the support of the provost and chancellor, serves a critical role in ensuring faculty understand the importance of engaging in the assessment activities by educating faculty about the benefits to students and programs. In support of this aim, the Office for Institutional Effectiveness reaches out to faculty to participate in assessment workshops and to FLCs whose function includes assessing general education.

Assessment Workshop Offerings
Faculty are surveyed periodically to determine what types of assessment workshops may be of interest, and the Office for Institutional Effectiveness facilitates these workshops. As a result of the survey, the workshops provided included the following:

- "Developing Basic Assessment Skills": "How-to" workshops providing information on writing student learning outcomes
- "Understanding Data Integrity": Providing information on creating or establishing valid and reliable measures
- "Closing the Loop": Using assessment for improvement in the development of action plans for the following academic year
- "Using TCU's Online Assessment Database": Training faculty to use a third-party system to track and organize assessment reports
- "Advanced Assessment Workshops": Engaging in advanced topics related to national issues (e.g., the Higher Education Reauthorization Act) or providing in-depth information about assessment processes (e.g., advanced topics in validity and reliability)

FLCs for Assessing General Education
The faculty at TCU adopted a general education sequence based on learning outcomes. Concomitantly, six FLCs were created through a collaborative effort among the Office for Institutional Effectiveness, the Office for the Core Curriculum, and the Center for Teaching Excellence. Each FLC had a focus on a different area within TCU's general education program. Each FLC had two faculty facilitators whose responsibilities included convening each meeting, developing an initial assessment plan for that particular category and outcome, and submitting an assessment report. The elements of the TCU Core Curriculum are assessed on a seven-year cycle, and faculty are the primary creators of the assessment process and of deliberating on the findings in order to make recommendations for improvement.

The Office for Institutional Effectiveness supports FLCs' work in assessing the general education curriculum. Departments are encouraged to set high standards for their students' learning; therefore, not all departments meet all of their stated outcomes each year. When departments identify areas of concern, there is a focus on that particular area for the next year (or longer). As a result, assessment is often seen as a way to find areas that are weaker so that these areas can be strengthened. To emphasize this constructive quality of assessment, faculty are encouraged to attend professional development conferences to understand the core issues in the alignment among teaching, assessing, and learning. Depending on the year and the interests of the faculty, some have attended the Association of American Colleges & Universities (AAC&U) Assessment and General Education conference, regional assessment conferences, or the SACSCOC annual conference. The attendance at these conferences is fully funded by the Office for Institutional Effectiveness.

Identifying the Learning Goals and Outcomes for Departmental Programs

Faculty are often very experienced in assessing student learning within their individual courses. They regularly create tests and assignments for students in order to demonstrate what students know. However, the process of constructing and assessing program-level or college-wide learning outcomes may be less familiar. One way TCU helps faculty identify what students need to learn in their program or major is to use the "Ideal Graduate" exercise. Asking a department to think of an "ideal graduate" from their program is an excellent way to get faculty thinking about the outcomes that are most important within their specific discipline or area. Often when faculty begin to think about this "ideal" student, they start to consider the skills, knowledge, behaviors, and beliefs that they want to see in their graduates. Unfortunately, many departmental assessment plans were created by looking at what data the department had available rather than thinking about what they really wanted their graduates to gain. Using the "Ideal Graduate" exercise can help faculty move back to the beginning of the process and focus on what they want to foster in their students so that resulting measures will give them information that can be transformative. At TCU, the following prompt and follow-ups are used to help faculty identify learning goals:

- If you were to meet a student five years after that student successfully completed your program/major/degree:
  - What would that student tell you that he or she remembered in terms of facts or ideas?

o What would that student tell you that she or he does within the
field or discipline?

o What attitudes or beliefs would that student express?

Following these prompts, faculty are asked to share how they responded, and these ideas are written on a board. Faculty can then see all of the areas that they believe are important. Of course, not all faculty agree with all elements that get listed, so some responses must be culled. Faculty identify areas that they believe are crucial, and any areas that don't have near-unanimous agreement are not included. Sometimes this means that there are only one or two major learning goals listed on the board after the culling. But this allows the faculty to have the final say on what their students need to know. Assessment goals can be written from this listing. Specific student learning outcomes can then be created for each goal. This often results in having assessment plans with only a few learning outcomes. At TCU, however, it is believed that having a few learning outcomes supported by all (or most) faculty within the department is more important than a longer listing of outcomes that may not have the support across the program.

Faculty are encouraged to use a version of "SMART" outcomes (adapted from Drucker, 1954). These outcomes describe behaviors, attitudes, and abilities that a student will be able to demonstrate as a result of the program. SMART is an acronym that stands for

- *Specific:* Student learning outcomes are specific to the program and stated in clear and definitive terms.
- *Measurable:* Outcomes must be clearly measurable (quantitatively or qualitatively). Therefore, faculty are encouraged to use action verbs to help ensure that the outcomes are measurable. Verbs such as *understanding* or *appreciate* are discouraged.
- *Attainable:* TCU helps faculty within departments to think carefully about what they hope for their students to achieve. Outcomes should be a reasonable statement of what a program can actually teach so that students can demonstrate their learning.
- *Results oriented:* Good learning outcomes should focus on the end result for student learning.
- *Time bound:* TCU encourages faculty to frame their student learning outcomes in ways that identify the time of the semester or particular point in an academic program. For example, will an outcome focus on what students can do at their senior year? Or perhaps after completing a capstone course?

Psychometric Considerations in Performing Educational Measurements

The field of educational measurement and psychometrics provides a vast literature that can be applied to higher education assessment. These principles ensure that measurements are valid, reliable, and fair. TCU is in the beginning stages of utilizing psychometric principles in its assessments, but the university is firmly committed to moving forward in this direction. Part of the reason for this shift is the hope that the use of psychometrics will inspire confidence, and faculty and administrators will readily use assessment results to make institution- and program-level decisions.

Validity

As new programs are developed, the faculty involved in designing the curriculum must create an assessment plan that includes the following:

- Mission statement for the new program
- List of student learning outcomes
- Measures for each of the learning outcomes
- Timeline or schedule to indicate how these measures will be implemented

This assessment plan is forwarded to the Office for Institutional Effectiveness following approval at the department level. If the assessment plan appears reasonable, the department receives a letter indicating that its assessment plan has been approved. The department then forwards this letter along with the curriculum and the rationale to the appropriate college-level curriculum committee for approval. Departments are encouraged to provide validity evidence for the measures selected to assess student learning.

Many of the assessment techniques used to measure student learning are embedded into courses. This provides faculty with an opportunity to be involved in validation through content analysis of their own assessments and through analysis of their assessments' alignments with the program-level goals. Specific assignments (typically drawn from capstone or other advanced courses) and assessments that have been used to assign student grades can also be used to measure program effectiveness. These embedded assessment tools have some level of validity, as indicated by the department review and approval process, which can be considered a step in providing content-based evidence of validity.

Reliability

At this point in time, TCU does not require numerical estimates of reliability of its assessments. However, TCU incorporates educational measurement practices within its assessment model, and many of these practices can be used to establish sufficient reliability. For example, TCU employs rubrics in its assessments, and rubrics allow for a standardized scoring system that could be used to establish interrater reliability. Of course, the interrater reliability can be measured only when more than one faculty member scores the assessment, and TCU has not yet performed assessments in which multiple faculty score the same student artifacts. Moving forward at TCU, the assessment improvement plan calls for the involvement of multiple raters as instruments are developed and pilot tested. This will be used to determine interrater reliability. Reliability estimates from the pilot study may indicate that a single rater can be used in subsequent scoring. Once reliability is established, it needs to be reestablished on a cyclical basis (e.g., every three years), thus keeping the workload for assessing reliability manageable.

Fairness

Fairness, as Deborah J. Harris describes more fully in chapter 2, is certainly an issue that is carefully considered throughout the assessment process. This is an area that is still being considered and vetted at TCU.

Assessing the Assessment Process

TCU uses an assessment rubric to help departments improve their assessment planning and evaluate the mission, goals, measures, findings, and action plans. The rubric is used with each program every two to three years. A blank copy of the rubric is sent to the department chair and assessment liaison to fill out in advance of a meeting. Next, the associate provost meets with the chair and the assessment liaison after completing her or his own rubric for that department. The resulting discussion is often rich and far reaching and is an opportunity to ensure agreement when looking at the validity of the assessment plan for the program. The plan includes a thorough review of the assessments including the alignment between the content and assessment uses and interpretations.

Path Forward and Concluding Thoughts

TCU has implemented a program review process for those departments or programs that do not have specialized accreditation. The academic program review is designed to be a collaborative process that will enhance TCU's overall mission through the work done by departments and programs by providing opportunities for these programs to assess, share, and improve their educational impact. Each program review provides an opportunity for the department and the institution to take a comprehensive look at the unit, evaluate its strengths and weaknesses, and plan for its future. Such a process allows TCU to engage with exciting new paths of educational inquiry and discovery, while also supporting quality and distinction in each academic area. The basic principles guiding the program review process are as follows:

- Provide a portrait of program strengths and limitations that will result in program improvement.
- Engage broad participation of stakeholders.
- Facilitate planning in areas such as assessment planning, curricular development, scholarship activities, and resource allocation.

Two external program evaluators are selected by the department in collaboration with the department's academic dean. The two reviewers receive the departmental self-study and then visit the campus for three days to interview and observe faculty and students. The resulting report from the external reviewers is then discussed by the department, the academic dean, and the provost to create a set of recommendations to use as the department or program moves into the next academic year. These program reviews are done every six years for those departments without specialized accreditation. Programs that have specialized accreditation do not go through the TCU program review process. Instead, the report that is generated from the department and the response of the specialized accreditor is used in lieu of the external reviewer report.

Overall, the assessment process at TCU has been reasonably successful. Certainly by the measure of the report from its regional accreditor, assessment at TCU meets the accreditation standards. In general, faculty participate in the assessment process, and the reports that are created by departments demonstrate that assessment is providing opportunities for departments to modify their curriculum and course sequencing and to improve the types of pedagogy used. Faculty and departments routinely request assessment data concerning their alumni and the levels of student preparation as indicated by the National Survey of Student Engagement and some of the freshman surveys that students take as they enter TCU.

Despite these successes, there is still much that needs to be done. A number of academic departments and programs continue to view the assessment reporting process as a bureaucratic process and do not understand its utility. As new faculty are hired and the assessment system at TCU has evolved, more faculty embrace assessment and assessment practices as part of their teaching responsibilities. At the same time, if it is expected that faculty are to participate in assessment and make program- and institution-level decisions based on the empirical evidence they generate, it is important that the integrity of the data is carefully considered. As assessment in higher education is evolving, faculty need to be supported as they work toward understanding the importance of psychometric considerations within their work and establishing the validity and reliability of the measures used for assessment. Some progress has been made at TCU in moving forward in a new direction with respect to assessment; however, there is more work that needs to be done to better integrate the methodologies of assessing student learning with the consideration of psychometric principles of validity, reliability, and fairness.

References

Drucker, P. F. (1954). *The practice of management.* New York, NY: HarperBusiness.

Texas Christian University. (n.d.a). Institutional effectiveness: About: Our history and mission. Retrieved from https://assessment.tcu.edu/about/history-mission/175

Texas Christian University. (n.d.b). Institutional effectiveness: Goals for the Office of Institutional Effectiveness. Retrieved from https://assessment.tcu.edu/about/

Texas Christian University Office for Assessment and Quality Enhancement. (2016). *Assessment and quality enhancement for institutional effectiveness at TCU.* Fort Worth: Texas Christian University.

Wehlburg, C., & McNertney, M. (2009). Faculty learning communities as an assessment technique for measuring general education outcomes. In T. W. Banta, E. A. Jones, & K. E. Black (Eds.). *Designing effective assessment: Principles and profiles of good practice* (pp. 114–118). San Francisco, CA: Jossey-Bass.

9

CASE STUDY: THE UNIVERSITY OF FLORIDA ASSESSMENT SYSTEM

Timothy S. Brophy, University of Florida

The University of Florida (UF) is a land-, space-, and sea-grant public Association of American Universities (AAU) institution with more than 50,000 students; approximately 5,700 full-time, part-time, and adjunct faculty; and 13,000 full- and part-time staff employees (University of Florida Office of Institutional Planning and Research, 2015). The university administrative units comprise 16 colleges, 10 vice presidential units, 4 senior vice presidential units, the Florida Museum of Natural History, the Graduate School, and a comprehensive library system (University of Florida Office of Institutional Planning and Research, 2016).

The purpose of this chapter is to describe the institutional assessment and effectiveness practices and procedures that comprise the UF assessment system. The assessment system is a coordinated and carefully designed set of processes and tools used by university accreditation coordinators, administrators, and faculty to submit, review, and store academic program assessment plans, institutional effectiveness plans, and data reports.

Initially driven by accreditation requirements, a recent internal study of the processes and practices of the university's assessment and accreditation coordinators has shown that the institutionalization of these processes has advanced the enculturation of assessment and effectiveness across the campus as faculty and administrators familiarize themselves with assessment processes and their value in program improvement (Das & Gater, 2015). This chapter begins with a description of the institutional context. Then, it describes the academic assessment and institutional effectiveness processes for planning and reporting goals and outcomes for each unit, our communication strategies, and our ongoing evaluation and improvement of internal processes.

UF's assessment system was developed to collect, manage, and monitor academic assessment and institutional effectiveness plans and data reports as evidence of the university's compliance with institutional effectiveness standards established by the Southern Association of Colleges and Schools Commission on Colleges (SACSCOC). SACSCOC defines *institutional effectiveness* as "the systematic, explicit, and documented process of measuring performance against mission in all aspects of an institution" (SACSCOC, 2012, p. 115).

Several factors incentivize institutional assessment and effectiveness and frame our processes for measuring these components. We address the internal structures that drive these processes and how these have shaped the assessment system. Internally, the university's mission and goals are the focus of our institutional assessments. Externally, the State University System of Florida Board of Governors' regulations on academic assessment set forth undergraduate assessment requirements for all universities within the system, and accreditation standards require that all educational programs establish student learning outcomes (SLOs), measure them, and use the results for improvement. These influences are described here.

Philosophy of Assessment: Mission Alignment for Academic and Administrative Unit Assessment

In order to consider the validity of the entire assessment process, UF begins by examining the institutional mission and its alignment with department, unit, and program missions. Mission fulfillment grounds all institutional assessment activity at UF. The academic and unit missions are the frameworks within which faculty and staff establish goals and outcomes for their respective departments or units. The interlocking academic, unit, and institutional missions ensure that all outcomes and goals align with and support the university's mission and its concomitant goals. The unit missions are entered into the assessment system annually and form the basis for curriculum programming and SLO assessment.

Process of Assessment

The assessment system at UF includes an evaluation of the academic learning, as well as the administrative support units throughout the university.

Academic Assessment

UF created an Academic Assessment Committee to provide faculty oversight of the academic assessment process. The committee consists of eight faculty and one student member as well as liaisons from the university's general education committee, the Office of Undergraduate Affairs, and the undergraduate catalog editor. Because this is a joint senate-presidential committee, four members are elected by the senate, and four are appointed by the president. The chair of the committee is the director of institutional assessment, and the cochair is elected from the senate members.

The Academic Assessment Committee is charged with reviewing SLOs across the institution. The committee is also tasked with providing recommendations to the provost regarding appropriate measurement tools for the assessment; developing methods to assess the implementation of curricular recommendations; developing long-term assessment plans for the undergraduate program at an institutional level; and providing an annual report of its work, findings, and recommendations to the senate and the president (University of Florida, 2016b).

Online Faculty Support

The assessment system is facilitated by two online tools. The first is the Academic Approval System, which was designed to track the approval of curriculum and assessment actions, starting at the department level and moving through all stages of approval (University of Florida, 2016a). This tracking system manages the large number of curriculum and assessment actions that are endemic to a comprehensive research university. When a new program is approved and a new assessment plan is developed or a substantial modification is made to an existing assessment plan, faculty enter a request into the Academic Approval System, which routes the request through the various stages of the process until it arrives at the Academic Assessment Committee level for review and an approval decision. This process is detailed further in the next section.

The second tool is our commercially licensed accreditation software platform, which houses the academic assessment and institutional effectiveness plans for each unit, as well as the data reports that each unit submits annually. Faculty enter their Academic Assessment Plans and assessment data reports annually into the accreditation software program.

Assessment Planning and Instrument Development and Selection

Academic Assessment Plans are an essential component of the assessment process for measuring student learning in the academic programs. The Academic Assessment Plans are an important part of the formal review and validation of the SLOs and their associated assessments that faculty have developed or selected for their programs. Faculty in all academic programs—undergraduate, graduate, professional, and certificate—annually develop or update an Academic Assessment Plan. These plans, including the instruments developed or identified for the purposes of the assessments, are submitted for review and approval by the Academic Assessment Committee. The faculty who develop and revise the Academic Assessment Plans are identified at the department level; the Office of Institutional Assessment does not oversee this selection process. Faculty members address specific components of their assessment processes within these Academic Assessment Plans as explained in the following sections.

Mission alignment   Institutional mission fulfillment is hierarchically structured. Program missions align with the department, college, and institutional missions. In this section, faculty state the program mission and describe how it aligns with and supports the college and university missions.

Program goals and SLOs   All programs are required to develop or review their respective program goals and SLOs and must adhere to the university's guidelines. The SLOs are statements of what students should know and be able to do at the conclusion of their program. Goals must be specific, measurable, attainable, relevant, and time bound (SMART), and outcomes must describe observable, measurable behaviors using active verbs.

Criterion for success for each SLO   The criterion for success is the percentage of students who successfully demonstrate outcome achievement in the program. The level of performance defining success is determined by the faculty. Faculty establish the criteria for success based on factors they consider important indicators of program effectiveness. While the Office of Institutional Assessment does not determine any program's criteria for success, the Academic Assessment Committee has established a minimum criterion for success of 70% for all programs. If faculty wish to establish a criterion for success less than 70%, they must provide a rationale to the Academic Assessment Committee and receive its approval.

Curriculum map (for undergraduate programs)   Undergraduate programs are generally sequential, and students follow a preestablished curriculum sequence. The curriculum map for undergraduate programs (Table 9.1) lists the program outcomes in the left column, and the top row lists the courses in which the program outcomes are introduced (I), reinforced (R), and assessed (A). The cells are populated with these labels at the points in the program where the outcomes are addressed.

Assessment timeline (for graduate and professional programs)   The assessment timeline is the mapping tool for graduate and professional programs. While graduate and professional programs share common programmatic

TABLE 9.1

UF Undergraduate Curriculum Map Template

Curriculum Map for [enter program name]

Key: Introduced   Reinforced   Assessed

SLOs	Course 1	Course 2	Course 3	Course 4	Course 5	Course 6	Course 7	Additional Assessments
Content Knowledge								
#1								
#2								
Critical Thinking								
#3								
#4								
Communi-cation								
#5								
#6								

benchmarks (theses, dissertations, professional examinations, etc.), graduate and professional students often individualize their pathways through the courses in their programs. The timeline provides a tool for faculty to indicate where program assessments occur in the program. The blank template is shown in Table 9.2.

Assessment cycle   The assessment cycle maps the frequency of SLO assessments over a period of one to three years. This is a grid that lists the SLOs in the left column and six academic years across the top row and column headers. Faculty are expected to measure one or more SLOs each year and indicate the year the SLO is planned for assessment and reporting with an "X" in the corresponding cell (Table 9.3).

Methods and procedures   In this section, faculty provide a description of the assessment methods and procedures they plan to use and include at least one rubric that is used to measure an SLO if appropriate. Faculty who are using other direct assessment methods, such as an examination, submit a description of the measurement instrument. Faculty are also expected to include a balance of direct and indirect measures and consider the educational

TABLE 9.2
UF Graduate and Professional Program Assessment Timeline Template

Assessment Timeline for [enter program name]

SLOs	Assessment 1	Assessment 2	Assessment 3	[Enter more as needed]
Knowledge				
#1				
#2				
Skills				
#3				
#4				
Professional Behavior				
#5				
#6				

TABLE 9.3
UF Graduate and Professional Program Assessment Cycle Template

Assessment Cycle

Analysis and Interpretation: From _____ to _____

Improvement Actions: Completed by _____

Dissemination: Completed by _____

SLOs	Year					
	2014–2015	2015–2016	2016–2017	2017–2018	2018–2019	2019–2020
Content Knowledge						
#1						
#2						
Skills						
#3						
#4						
Professional Behavior						
#5						
#6						

measurement properties of the instrument (e.g., instrument reliability, validity considerations).

Research (for graduate and professional programs)   Graduate research programs require faculty to identify the research expectations for students. If the graduate degree is not a research degree, faculty include a brief description of any research-related activities that students complete in the program.

Assessment oversight   In this section, faculty list the names and contact information of those individuals who are responsible for the assessment processes in the programs.

The criteria for reviewing the plans are shown in Table 9.4. The review of the assessment within the academic context provides content-based validity evidence through the alignment of the assessment with program goals and SLOs. Once these plans are approved, only substantive changes to the plan need to be reviewed by the Academic Assessment Committee for approval.

Academic Assessment Data Reporting

Each academic program reports progress on the achievement of its goals and outcomes annually. The report data are entered and stored in the online accreditation software program. The report components are described as follows:

- *Assessment results: SLOs.* In this section the faculty summarize the student learning data for the academic year being reported, which they have reviewed and analyzed for each outcome assessment activity; determine the percentage of students who successfully demonstrated outcome achievement; and indicate whether or not this percentage meets the criterion for success established in the Academic Assessment Plan.
- *Results: Program goals.* In this section, faculty summarize the data they have collected for each goal and present their analysis and the results of their analysis.
- *Use of results for program improvement.* In this section, faculty state who reviewed the results, and they describe how the results have been used to determine improvements or modifications to the program.

The director of institutional assessment and select staff review the data reports for their adherence to university guidelines regarding reporting assessment data and SLOs (University of Florida Office of Institutional Assessment, 2016b, 2016c). If the data reports are incomplete or unclear, especially pertaining to the use of results for modification and improvement of the program, the report is returned for revision until the guidelines are met.

TABLE 9.4

UF Criteria for Developing and Reviewing Academic Assessment Plans

Plan Component	Criteria
Mission statement (all programs)	The mission statement is articulated clearly.
	The unit mission supports the university mission.
SLOs (all programs)	SLOs are stated clearly.
	SLOs focus on demonstration of student learning, using active verbs that describe specific observable behaviors.
	SLOs are measurable.
Curriculum map (undergraduate)	The curriculum map links SLOs to program courses.
	The curriculum map identifies where SLOs are introduced, reinforced, and assessed.
	The curriculum map identifies the assessments used for each SLO.
Assessment map (graduate and professional)	The assessment map indicates the times in the program where the SLOs are assessed and measured.
	The assessment map identifies the assessments used for each SLO.
Assessment cycle (all programs)	The assessment cycle is clear.
	All SLOs are measured.
	Data are collected at least once in the cycle.
	The cycle includes a time for data analysis and interpretation.
	The cycle includes time for planning improvement actions based on the data analysis.
	The cycle includes time for dissemination of results to the appropriate stakeholders.
Methods and procedures (undergraduate)	Methods and procedures are clear.
	Measurements occur at appropriate times in the program.
	Measurements are appropriate for the SLOs.
	Methods and procedures reflect an appropriate balance of direct and indirect methods.
	The report presents examples of course and program assessment tools.

(*Continues*)

TABLE 9.4 (*Continued*)

Measurement tools (graduate and professional)	Measurement tools are described clearly and concisely.
	Measurements are appropriate for the SLOs.
	Methods and procedures reflect an appropriate balance of direct and indirect methods.
	The report presents examples of at least one measurement tool.
Research (graduate and professional)	Research expectations for the program are clear, concise, and appropriate for the discipline.
Assessment oversight (all programs)	Appropriate personnel (coordinator, committee, etc.) charged with assessment responsibilities are identified.

Quality Assurance for Academic Assessment

Using the university's online Academic Approval Tracking System, program faculty submit their Academic Assessment Plans into a specific approval sequence for the type of submission entered. The tracking path for these plans mirrors the path for all university curriculum approvals. This forms a solid basis for examining the validity of the assessments through a series of internal (within program) and external (outside of program) reviewers.

The process begins with the faculty entering the assessment plan using the online accreditation software system. The Academic Assessment Plan is reviewed at the college level and then sent to the Office of Institutional Assessment for review. Once the plan is approved by the director of the Office of Institutional Assessment, subsequent approvals are required by the Academic Assessment Committee, the University Curriculum Committee, and Student Academic Support System personnel.

Throughout this process, the committees are charged with reviewing the assessment instruments (e.g., rubrics, locally developed exams) with the consideration of educational measurement principles of reliability, validity, and fairness as outlined in chapter 2.

Once the plan is finalized, it goes to the university catalog editor. Figure 9.1 presents a graphic of the approval process.

Assessment of Administrative Units

As a large and diverse public institution, UF has multiple units dedicated to providing service and operational support for institutional administration,

Figure 9.1. UF Assessment System assessment plan approval process.

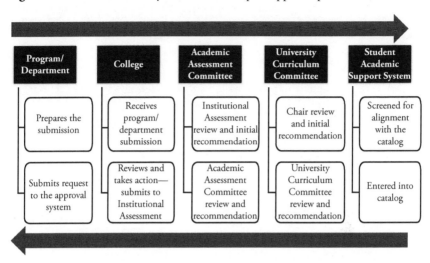

academic and student support, research, and community and public service to ensure efficient and effective fulfillment of the university's mission. These units include the 16 colleges, 10 vice presidential and 4 senior vice presidential units/divisions, the Graduate School, and the libraries (University of Florida Office of Institutional Planning and Research, 2016). Similar to the academic units, administrative units (a) establish goals for their programs and services, (b) plan actions to meet these goals, (c) systematically assess the extent to which they are attained, and (d) use the results of those assessments to improve services and internal operations. The assessment of administrative unit goals and outcomes is an ongoing process that is carried out within the units and overseen by the Office of Institutional Assessment. The ultimate responsibility for this process lies with the senior leadership within each unit. The institutional effectiveness process varies slightly from the assessment process engaged by the academic units.

Staff develop their plans using the guidelines and criteria shown in Table 9.5. These plans are entered into the university's accreditation software program on an annual basis. Unlike the Academic Assessment Plans, these are not entered in the academic approval system because that system is specifically designed to manage curriculum and academic assessment actions, not administrative unit actions. Because these are not academic unit actions, the plans are not under the charge or purview of the Academic Assessment Committee and are reviewed only by the director of institutional assessment. Similar to the Academic Assessment Plan review process, plans are returned for modifications if the director's review warrants this action. The plans are stored in the university's online accreditation software program.

TABLE 9.5

UF Criteria for Developing and Reviewing Institutional Effectiveness Plans

Component	Criteria
Mission statement	Mission statement is articulated clearly.
	The program mission clearly supports the university's mission and includes specific statements describing how it supports the mission.
Unit goals	Goals are stated clearly.
	Goals focus on areas of strategic importance to the unit.
	Goals are measurable.
	Measurements are appropriate for the goals.
	Goals modification process is clear.
Service delivery goals	Goals are stated clearly.
	Goals are measureable.
	Measurements are appropriate for the goals.
	Goal modification process is clear.
Administrative support services	Administrative support services are described clearly.
	Services are monitored regularly.
	Services are measured appropriately.
	The services modification process is clear.
Academic and student support services	Academic and student support services are described clearly.
	Services are monitored regularly.
	Services are measured appropriately.
	The services modification process is clear.
Research support services	Research support services are described clearly.
	Services are monitored regularly.
	Services are measured appropriately.
	The services modification process is clear.
Community and public service activities	Community and public service activities are described clearly.
	Activities are monitored regularly.
	Activities are measured appropriately.
	The activities modification process is clear.
Effectiveness oversight	Appropriate personnel (coordinator, committee, etc.) charged with assessment responsibilities are identified.

Administrative Unit Reporting

Similar to the academic units, the administrative units collect data annually, review and analyze the data, and use their results to modify and improve the unit's operations and internal functions. The institutional effectiveness data reports address the following components:

- *Annual progress on goals.* In this section, unit personnel briefly summarize their results and include or attach the data collected in summary form.
- *Evaluation.* Units state the measurement methods used, identify who reviewed the results, and briefly summarize their evaluation of the data they reviewed.
- *Actions for improvement.* In this section, units report on the actions taken as a result of their evaluation.

Administrative units use data from national assessments that have reported validity, reliability, and fairness indices. For example, UF uses the National Survey of Student Engagement (NSSE) and the Student Experiences in a Research University (SERU) survey. The SERU was used as an additional validation criterion in the international assessments described in chapter 4. Administrative units have used social media and rewards such as football tickets to increase return rates on surveys and thus improve the generalizability of the results.

Data reports are submitted annually. These data reports are reviewed only by the director of institutional assessment, and they are returned for modification if the reports do not meet the university's guidelines (University of Florida Office of Institutional Assessment, 2016d).

Best Practices in Assessment

The UF assessment system is based on the established best practices in the literature, as well as the *Standards for Educational and Psychological Testing* (AERA, APA, & NCME, 2014). Best practices include consideration of the technical or psychometric characteristics of the assessments as well as the process of managing the assessment system.

Psychometrics to Improve Assessment

Assessment has a long history as a requirement for accreditation. UF's administration recognized the value of enhancing the traditional assessment model with the principles of educational measurement and psychometrics. During the most recent regional accreditation quality enhancement initiative, educational measurement faculty were selected for their expertise and charged to lead the effort. Capitalizing on the credibility of these faculty was crucial in ensuring faculty and staff throughout the university were aware of the systematic and deliberate consideration of the *Standards* (AERA, APA, & NCME, 2014) and the concepts of validity, reliability, and fairness. The transition to a psychometrically supported assessment model was possible at UF because assessment had been part of the institutional culture for many years. Thus, it was natural that UF serve as a pioneer in the emerging fields of psychometrics and higher education assessment.

Validity   When faculty and administrators select measures of student learning or program goals, we expect that they have determined that the inferences from the scores or data obtained from these measures are appropriate for their intended use, and that they represent SLO and goal achievement. However, validity issues do arise, and the Academic Assessment Committee and Institutional Assessment Administration have set several requirements and processes in place at the institutional level that are designed to address validity concerns.

In most cases, locally developed instruments are used to measure program SLOs. When external assessment methods are used, faculty must provide evidence that the intended use of the external exam scores comports with the inferences made regarding the degree of SLO achievement claimed. For example, a program requested that a state licensure exam for teachers be used as a program SLO measure. In this case, the examination is a graduation requirement for state teaching licensure, and faculty provided evidence of content-based validity within the course and program. Because faculty provided evidence that the scores on the external measure were appropriate for this intended use, validity was established for this purpose.

Faculty most often select course-level measures as program measures. When a course measure is used as a program SLO measure, we expect that the faculty have reviewed and determined that evidence exists that inferences from the course assessments are appropriate for their new intended use as program SLO measures. In addition, during the assessment review process, we examine the plans to confirm that SLO and program goal measures produce data pertinent to the SLO or goal. When this review raises a concern about validity, program faculty are contacted and the concern is resolved. For example, one program developed a goal pertaining to the improvement of recruitment strategies but planned to measure this goal by tracking admissions. In this case, the admissions data would not provide direct evidence of recruitment efficacy, so we contacted the program, and leaders modified the measure accordingly. In another case, a professional program chose to use the professional licensure exam as a program SLO measure. The intended use of the scores for this professional exam is to determine licensure for the

profession and not student learning in the program. It was also not a requirement for graduation. In this case (and similar cases) validity could not be
established, and program leaders were asked to select assessments that were
developed and administered by the faculty during the program, prior to the
licensure exam, as program SLO measures. The licensure exam scores are
now used as a program goal measure, and the faculty have established the
appropriate use of the inferences made from the professional exam scores to
measure their program goal.

All Academic Assessment Plans must present an example of a rubric used
to assess an approved SLO measure. The Academic Assessment Committee also reviews these rubrics for evidence of their validity. In cases where
the rubric criteria raise validity questions, the committee requests additional
information as needed.

Reliability   Because of the size and scope of our institution, we place
the primary responsibility of reliability and fairness at the program level; we
do not monitor this at the institutional level, except for some institution-
wide programs developed since 2011 (these are discussed in the next section).
Faculty are expected to establish the reliability of their measures.

At the time of this writing, UF uses an online learning management
system (LMS), and many faculty teach courses within this LMS and assess
student learning through online assignments. The LMS has several built-in
reliability features. Item analyses and reliability coefficients are automatically
calculated for examinations, and faculty can access this information easily to
check the degree of measurement error and adjust their examinations accordingly. For rubric-scored assignments, the LMS information is more limited.
For example, when a course-level assignment has been selected as a program
SLO measure, faculty may associate a program SLO with an assignment
rubric and electronically collect SLO mastery information for the SLO.

However, the rubrics in the LMS capture SLO achievement in mastery
categories, not scores; this is an inherent component of the LMS software.
In 2014, as a direct requirement of our reaffirmation of accreditation, the
university instituted a Quality Enhancement Initiative for undergraduates.
This initiative, Learning Without Borders: Internationalizing the Gator
Nation (University of Florida Internationalization Task Force, 2014), is a
program that offers students the opportunity to become an international
scholar through a set of requirements that leads to this designation (students
also receive a medallion at graduation). Three institutional SLOs were established for this program related to content knowledge, communication, and
critical thinking. Institutional measures were developed for communication
and critical thinking; these measures were piloted, analyzed, and revised and
repiloted until item discriminations were acceptable. Because this project is

longitudinal, statistical analyses are calculated annually to ensure that reliability and item discriminations remain acceptable.

Fairness   UF has a diverse population of students and has subsequently emphasized accessibility and fairness as fundamental issues in assessment. This is a very important consideration for faculty, staff, and students, and it enables the university to ensure adherence to the recommended best practice emphasized in the *Standards* (AERA, APA, & NCME, 2014).

As an institution, we are working to strengthen our oversight of validity, reliability, and fairness in the academic programs. All institution-wide programs developed since 2011 (the year the Office of Institutional Assessment was established) are now designed from the beginning with validity, reliability, and fairness at the forefront of discussions. For example, the redesign of the general education program (the UF Core) includes new measures that will be monitored institutionally (University of Florida, 2013). We continue to work on the improvement of this component of the assessment system, balancing the rights of academic freedom and responsibilities of faculty to report assessment information with concomitant expectations for institutional improvement and the requirements of institutional accreditation.

Programs are provided with psychometric measures through the LMS software. While these data are not included in formal reporting, faculty use this information to examine their assessment practices within their courses and at the program level. Obtaining the reliability coefficients and item analyses statistics through the LMS is an important foundational step in faculty using psychometric data for planning program assessments. Providing faculty with these psychometric tools has been helpful in improving their active engagement in the process and creating a sustainable, faculty-driven effort. Overall, this inclusion lends more credibility to the assessment process.

Managing and improving the assessment system   Both the academic and institutional effectiveness processes described in this chapter undergo ongoing review for their effectiveness and efficiency. Like all units at UF, the Office of Institutional Assessment sets forth goals, collects and reviews data, and modifies and improves the assessment system as warranted by these reviews. We conduct internal research on the methods and operations of the units and use these results to modify and improve institutional processes. We have also established a communication system to disseminate important institutional assessment information to the campus.

Internal communication   One of the challenges of maintaining and effectively sustaining any large-scale institutional reporting process is consistent internal communication with each unit so they are able to meet university requests and requirements successfully. We have addressed this by assigning accreditation coordinators in each of the administrative and academic units on campus. The coordinators are selected by the deans of the academic units and the vice presidents of the administrative units. These individuals are the contact points for the Office of Institutional Assessment as well as for the faculty and staff within their units, and their primary duty is to ensure that all plans and data reports are reviewed at the college or unit level and submitted into the assessment system. The accreditation coordinator is a critical component of the communication system. When staff at the Office of Institutional Assessment need to distribute information or contact the units with inquiries, the accreditation coordinator is the primary contact. The coordinators are responsible for responding directly to requests from, or sharing information with, appropriate faculty and staff. If the faculty or staff have a question or query about assessment or institutional effectiveness, they contact their accreditation coordinator, who answers the question or contacts the director of institutional assessment. The director also meets with the coordinators twice yearly to share new information and review institutional processes.

Enhancing the assessment system   In the interest of improving institutional processes, the Office of Institutional Assessment engages in internal research projects designed to gauge the operationalization of institutional assessment and effectiveness in the units. Das and Gater (2015) completed an internal study of the college accreditation coordinators to collect data on how the colleges use the assessment system as a tool for planning and data reporting and manage assessment and effectiveness operations at the college level. Office of Institutional Assessment staff distributed a survey and followed up with interviews with each accreditation coordinator.

Results revealed that the colleges engaged in institutional assessment and effectiveness work in diverse ways. The coordinators reported that defining and collecting data for program goals and SLOs were highly beneficial to some programs, and all agreed that assessing program goals and SLOs is an integral element to any college- or department-specific accreditation criteria. Several key themes and practices emerged, which led to the following set of recommendations that comprise a set of best practices for success:

- Hierarchical networks of support and communication are critical to facilitate these processes.
- A clear distribution system for information is important so that faculty report data and close the assessment loop in a timely manner.
- A variety of training and professional development is needed. Options should fit faculty schedules; be flexible; and include a variety of

training options such as written guides, online guides, video tutorials, and in-person meetings.

- Regular engagement with campus leaders is important to build relationships, lines of communication, support, and trust.
- Messaging and marketing should emphasize the value of assessment efforts to improving academic programs (Das & Gater, 2015).

These results have led to some modifications of the Office of Institutional Assessment's strategies. The office has increased engagement with campus leaders through personal meetings with these individuals for the purpose of sharing information and updates that are customized for the unit on an as-needed basis. We have also developed online "how-to" modules for planning and reporting and the accreditation software system. Our faculty professional development materials include guides for the development of program goals and SLOs, templates for Academic Assessment Plan components, guidelines for data reporting, a guide for rubric development, and other relevant information (University of Florida Office of Institutional Assessment, 2016a, 2016b, 2016c, 2016d, 2016e, 2016f).

Our future research is guided by ongoing needs and the interests of the Academic Assessment Committee. Our immediate research projects are focused on faculty engagement with institutional assessment, the feasibility and utility of institutional SLOs (distinguished from those that are in the programs), and ways to further develop the campus assessment culture. At the time of this writing, a campus-wide study of faculty attitudes was approved by the Institutional Review Board for implementation by the Academic Assessment Committee and a focus group was designed to provide evidence of how faculty and administrative staff engage in the assessment process.

Conclusion

UF is exploring new assessment processes to engage faculty in assessment practices to inform teaching and learning while also serving the goals of accreditation. Thus, the psychometric properties of assessments have shifted from an emphasis solely on accreditation to an emphasis on student learning.

UF is committed to meeting the university's mission by supporting the ongoing, comprehensive, and integrated processes through which it plans, allocates resources, and documents success in its academic programs and administrative units. These processes are well established and synergistic, and they include multiple steps for quality review. The ongoing assessment of academic programs and administrative effectiveness reflects a shared responsibility for the success of the university and its long-standing culture of academic excellence, research, and service. The university's assessment processes synergize the responsible units to advance goal attainment and fulfill the university's mission. Through continuous improvement of its units, the university moves closer to reaching its overall goals and realizing the president's aim for UF to be "a premier university that the state, nation, and world look to for leadership" (University of Florida Goal-Setting Task Force, 2015, p. 4).

References

American Educational Research Association, American Psychological Association, & National Council on Measurement in Education. (2014). *Standards for educational and psychological testing.* Washington, DC: Author.

Das, R., & Gater, C. (2015). *Assessing assessment: Fostering new energy to maintain momentum for institutional effectiveness.* Presentation for the 2015 SACSCOC annual conference, Houston, TX.

Southern Association of Colleges and Schools Commission on Colleges. (2012). *Resource manual for the Principles of Accreditation: Foundations for quality enhancement* (2012 ed.). Decatur, GA: Author.

University of Florida. (2013). *The UF Core: Transforming UF's general education.* Retrieved from http://gened.aa.ufl.edu/uf-core.aspx

University of Florida. (2016a). *Academic approval tracking.* Retrieved from http://approval.ufl.edu/

University of Florida. (2016b). *Academic Assessment Committee.* Retrieved from http://fora.aa.ufl.edu/University/JointCommittees/Academic-Assessment-Committee

University of Florida Goal-Setting Task Force. (2015). *Office of the President Goal-Setting Task Force.* Retrieved from http://president.ufl.edu/media/presidentufledu/documents/Goal-Setting-Task-Force-Final-Report---The-Decade-Ahead.pdf

University of Florida Internationalization Task Force. (2014). *Learning without borders: Internationalizing the Gator Nation.* Retrieved from http://sacs.aa.ufl.edu/media/sacsaaufledu/files/UF-QEP-2014.pdf

University of Florida Office of Institutional Assessment. (2016a). *Academic assessment: Assessment planning resources.* Retrieved from http://assessment.aa.ufl.edu/Data/Sites/22/media/2015-16/2015-16-university-of-florida-guide-for-developing-program-goals-and-student-learning-outcomes.pdf

University of Florida Office of Institutional Assessment. (2016b). *Data entry guide for* Compliance Assist! *Reporting academic program goals data.* Retrieved from http://assessment.aa.ufl.edu/Data/Sites/22/media/datareportingtemplates/data-entry-guide-for-compliance-assist---academic-program-goals-data.pdf

University of Florida Office of Institutional Assessment. (2016c). *Data entry guide for* Compliance Assist! *Reporting SLO data.* Retrieved from http://assessment

.aa.ufl.edu/Data/Sites/22/media/datareportingtemplates/data-entry-guide-for-compliance-assist---slo-data.pdf

University of Florida Office of Institutional Assessment. (2016d). *Data entry guide for division/unit goals.* Retrieved from http://assessment.aa.ufl.edu/Data/Sites/22/media/datareportingtemplates/data-entry-guide-for-compliance-assist---division-unit-goals-data.pdf

University of Florida Office of Institutional Assessment. (2016e). *Developing program goals and student learning outcomes.* Retrieved from http://assessment.aa.ufl.edu/Data/Sites/22/media/2015-16/2015-16-university-of-florida-guide-for-developing-program-goals-and-student-learning-outcomes.pdf

University of Florida Office of Institutional Assessment. (2016f). *Institutional effectiveness planning and data reporting resources.* Retrieved from http://assessment.aa.ufl.edu/institutional-effectiveness-plans

University of Florida Office of Institutional Planning and Research. (2015). *Workforce, Fall 2015.* Retrieved from http://ir.aa.ufl.edu/workforce

University of Florida Office of Institutional Planning and Research. (2016). *University of Florida administrative officers.* Retrieved from http://ir.aa.ufl.edu/uf-org-charts#Administration Officers

CONCLUSION

M. David Miller, University of Florida

Tammie Cumming, City University of New York–New York City College of Technology

In this book, we have attempted to make the case for the importance of psychometrics, particularly validity, reliability, and fairness, when using assessments in higher education. Indeed, assessment has a long history in higher education that has not yet focused enough on issues of the technical quality of the assessments. As pointed out in chapter 1, there were clear national movements in the 1980s to examine the use of assessments in higher education both within the academy (e.g., the First National Conference on Assessment in Higher Education in 1985) and outside the academy (e.g., *A Nation at Risk*; U.S. Department of Education, National Commission on Excellence in Education, 1983). Currently, the Council for Higher Education Accreditation and the regional accrediting agencies hold rigorous assessment standards that result in rigorous practices and reporting from all degree-granting institutions. However, the emphasis in assessment in higher education has been on the uses and interpretations of assessments, but not the documented quality through psychometric evidence. We also acknowledge that current assessment practices may have psychometrically sound assessments, yet procedures have not been clearly defined to provide documentation regarding the validity, reliability, and fairness.

The field of psychometrics and educational measurement also has a long history that includes professional standards dating back to the 1950s. The rigor in the field of psychometrics has had a strong impact on K–12 assessment and other areas. However, this link has not been as firmly established in higher education. As discussed in chapter 2, the current version of the *Standards for Educational and Psychological Testing* (2014) identifies three foundations of assessment practice—validity, reliability, and fairness—and provides guidance for best practices in those areas of assessment. Each of these foundational areas of assessment should be viewed as a property of the particular use of the assessment rather than a global property of the assessment. For example, we provide evidence for a particular use or interpretation of an assessment rather than evidence that we have a "valid assessment." Thus, it is incumbent upon the user to consider the context of the particular use or interpretation and whether the validity, reliability, and/or fairness evidence is applicable.

As the particular use or interpretation of the assessment is the key to considering the quality of the assessment, chapters 3 and 5 of this book examined the types of assessments that are commonly used in higher education. Chapter 3 discussed direct assessments, or assessments that measure the student learning outcomes (SLOs) for a program. Chapter 5 considered indirect assessments that measure other aspects of a program such as perceptions, attitudes, achievements, skills, or behaviors not specified in the SLOs. Chapters 3 and 5 pointed to a broad range of assessments that include multiple methods (e.g., open- or closed-ended items). The broad range of assessments will, no doubt, continue to grow and change over time and will be crucial to understand the types of psychometric evidence that should be collected for any use or interpretation.

Chapters 4 and 6 outlined some of the methods used to establish validity, reliability, and fairness evidence within the context of direct and indirect assessments, respectively. As discussed in those chapters, the methods of establishing evidence for validity, reliability, and fairness have evolved over time and will continue to evolve. Thus, it will be important for those involved in assessment in higher education to continue to evaluate new and developing methods for examining their psychometric properties of their assessments as well as using current methods.

Finally, chapters 7, 8, and 9 provided three case studies of assessment practices in three colleges or universities. Each case study is based on recognition of the importance of considering psychometric properties of assessments at the institutions. However, psychometric methods have certainly not been universally adopted in higher education. The concepts are new to many faculty, and providing evidence of validity, reliability, and fairness is a cutting-edge practice that currently exists only in a few universities and colleges. Thus, each case study provides examples of the use of specific methods (e.g., content review) particularly for assessments in the context of larger populations of students. Each case study provides examples of the use of psychometric methods that can be considered models of assessment practices in higher education. Nevertheless, each case study model also recognizes room for growth and improvement in establishing evidence of validity, reliability, and fairness.

Implications

Establishing evidence of validity, reliability, and fairness is crucial to guaranteeing the efficient and fair use of assessments in higher education. No one would argue the importance of ensuring that assessment results are based on the correct uses and interpretations, that assessment measures consistently while minimizing measurement errors, and that assessment results are fair across all subpopulations (e.g., race, ethnicity, gender). Thus, it is imperative that we establish these qualities exist for an assessment that we are using for accountability, to measure student learning, to measure changes in student behaviors, or for any other program outcomes.

Assessments are broadly used within and across disciplines in higher education especially with the accountability requirements of accrediting agencies. Nevertheless, evidence of validity, reliability, and fairness is not widespread. Providing evidence establishes a firmer basis for efficient and fair test use and interpretation. However, we should also be clear that lack of evidence does not mean that the assessments are not valid, reliable, or fair for the intended uses or interpretations. Lack of evidence simply suggests that we cannot be sure that an assessment has the desired properties of validity, reliability, and fairness for any specific use or interpretation.

Although few would argue the importance of the psychometric properties for using assessments, it is also clear that collecting this type of evidence requires a certain level of expertise and support. Consequently, this would not be adopted as a standard practice without support to understand what methods are needed or should be considered and how to implement psychometric studies. Furthermore, personnel time and financial support (e.g., personnel, software, computing) may be required even with the necessary knowledge and skills to implement psychometric studies.

The amount of support and expertise will vary with the context and the types of evidence being collected. For example, psychometrics may be more essential when using assessments to make important decisions about programs or students in the context of large-scale use of an assessment. The international assessment described in chapter 6, which describes a more comprehensive approach to validity, reliability, and fairness, is a program for an undergraduate program at a large research institution (more than 30,000 students) that had financial and personnel support combined with expertise. A small program that enrolls 20 or fewer students annually would likely receive less support and in most cases have less expertise to seriously examine the psychometric quality of required assessments. Thus, we suggest the following recommendations for examining validity, reliability, and fairness for higher education assessments.

Validity

As discussed in the chapters of this book, validation can take many forms and the methods can range from fairly simple to very complex. Luckily, the simpler methods provide one of the key forms of validity evidence that would support the use and interpretations of assessment in higher education: content-related evidence. Content-related evidence is based on expert judgment about the content of an assessment and its relationship to the use or interpretation. For direct assessments, it may simply ask questions of content experts such as the following: Is the assessment based on content that measures the SLOs? Are the items of the assessment consistent with the interpretations of the assessment? We would suggest that most assessments in higher education are developed or selected by faculty who provide the necessary expertise to make these judgments. In addition, those faculty typically are already examining the content of their assessments without formalizing the process for validity purposes. It becomes content-related evidence of validity when data are systematically collected so that we can establish statements such as the following:

- A committee of the faculty met and carefully reviewed the assessment to determine that the content of the assessment did provide a representative sample of items that measured the following SLO. . . . (Evidence collected in a meeting of faculty that allows discussion and consensus.)
- Each of the faculty reviewed the items of the assessment and rated its concordance with the SLO. Each of the items had at least 80% agreement that they measured the SLO. Faculty also found that no key elements of the SLO were absent in the assessment. (Evidence collected through faculty surveys about the assessment with ratings for each item.)

We believe that content-related evidence should always be collected when using assessments in higher education. It is simple to collect and document, and it may already be a part of the assessment practices without formal documentation. As the *Standards* states, validity is the most important characteristic of an assessment. On the basis of this, we believe that all assessments should go through a careful review process to establish content-related evidence of validity.

Some other forms of validation are more complex, requiring student assessments or other forms of data that are then analyzed (e.g., factor analysis, correlations with other assessments, evidence of consequences) to provide evidence of validity. These may not be standard practice for all higher education programs but might be useful in situations where the assessment results are more high stakes and for larger groups of students, or where the primary argument for use or interpretation is based on evidence other than content.

Reliability

Reliability includes a broad range of methods also described in this book. Methods for determining reliability require expertise, support, time, and statistical software. Estimating reliability also requires the administration of the assessment and the analysis of student data. If an assessment is adopted from another user, the reliability estimates would be useful as long as the population that it was established on is similar to the population being tested and the testing situation is similar. If the assessment is locally developed, reliability would be estimated based on administration(s) of the assessment and data analyses that range from percent agreement in scoring to correlational methods to more complex modeling using item response theory (IRT). Each of the methods would require some expertise in statistical methods. However, the statistical procedures can be as simple as estimating percent agreement or correlations in Excel, or estimating internal consistency estimates in SPSS or other software.

Fairness

Fairness includes faculty review of assessments to determine that they are not insensitive to affected subpopulations as well as statistical analyses to determine differences in performance related to subpopulations. The reviews for sensitivity could be included in the review for content-related validity evidence with simple questions for each item, including whether the item contains any content that is offensive or insensitive to specific subpopulations (e.g., ethnicities, gender). This could be reported as an aggregate of faculty ratings or as a committee consensus. Empirical evidence of subpopulation differences on the assessments would require greater expertise to complete but would be essential in a high-stakes environment where subpopulation differences would occur.

Psychometrics and Accountability

With the increased demands for assessment and accountability by regional and professional accreditation organizations, there has been substantial growth in assessment methods in higher education. We believe it is important that the increased focus on assessment encourage the consideration of the data quality. In this book, we have introduced the principles of educational measurement and psychometrics as tools to ensure the soundness of accountability and accreditation decisions.

Because accreditation actions are made by the accreditation authorities based on the results, it is important to ensure the sound basis for the development and use of the assessments. The 2014 *Standards for Educational and Psychological Testing* provides a useful resource for considering assessment decisions at various levels; that is, the educational measurement and psychometric literature provides a wealth of knowledge that can be used by faculty and assessment specialists in higher education.

References

American Educational Research Association, American Psychological Association, & National Council on Measurement in Education. (2014). *Standards for educational and psychological testing*. Washington, DC: Author.

U.S. Department of Education, National Commission on Excellence in Education. (1983). *A nation at risk: The imperative for educational reform*. Washington, DC: U.S. Government Printing Office.

Accountability is a relationship where one party is responsible to another party for achieving and assessing agreed-upon goals.

Assessment is a term that is sometimes distinct from testing but can be broader. It is a process that integrates test information with information from other sources, but it can be as narrow as a single test (AERA, APA, & NCME, 2014).

Construct validity is the broadest form of validity; it refers to the "concept or characteristic that an assessment is designed to measure" (AERA, APA, & NCME, 2014, p. 11).

Direct assessment is the measurement of student knowledge, behaviors, and learning and is linked to specified student learning outcomes.

Evaluation is the process of assessing the value, worth, or effectiveness of an educational program, process, or curriculum; it includes evidence-gathering processes that are designed to examine program or institution-level effectiveness.

Goals are the general aims or purposes of an educational system, often at the program level, that are broadly defined and include intended outcomes.

Indirect assessment is the measurement of student learning experiences often linked to direct assessments but not measuring student learning outcomes. Consequently, indirect assessments can include opinions or thoughts about student knowledge, values, beliefs, and attitudes about educational programs, processes, and curriculum. They may also include measures of student outcomes such as retention rate, course grades, or grade point averages that are not direct assessments of the student learning outcomes.

Objectives are brief, clear statements of the expected learning outcomes of instruction, typically at the course or program level.

Outcomes are the student results of programs including behaviors, knowledge, skills, and level of functioning. They are usually measured as a test or assessment.

Outputs are the results of program participation that specify types, levels, and targets of service. They are often measured as a count (e.g., number of students participating in a program).

Reliability is the consistency of scores across replications of a testing procedure (AERA, APA, & NCME, 2014).

Student learning outcomes (SLOs) are behavioral statements that specify what students will learn or can do as a result of a learning program, process, or curriculum.

Tests are devices or procedures in which a sample of an examinee's behavior in a specified domain is obtained and subsequently evaluated and scored using a standardized process (AERA, APA, & NCME, 2014).

Validity is the degree to which evidence and theory support the interpretations of test scores or assessment results for proposed uses (AERA, APA, & NCME, 2014). There are many types of validity and sources of evidence discussed.

Reference

American Educational Research Association, American Psychological Association, & National Council on Measurement in Education. (2014). *Standards for educational and psychological testing.* Washington, DC: American Educational Research Association.

CONTRIBUTORS

Bonne August is provost and vice president for academic affairs at the New York City College of Technology/City University of New York (CUNY). Previously, she was chair of the English department and professor of English at Kingsborough Community College/CUNY. August has served as principal investigator for two institutional projects funded by the National Science Foundation. ADVANCE IT-Catalyst (2008–2011) addressed issues facing women faculty in STEM. A National Science Foundation I^3 grant, The City Tech Incubator: Interdisciplinary Partnerships for Laboratory Integration, sought to generate both external and internal partnerships to strengthen students' hands-on experiences and research. August holds a PhD in English and American literature from New York University. Her professional interests and publications include work on poetry, women writers, writing assessment, portfolio assessment, articulation between high school and college, and faculty development.

Jennifer Bergeron is the director of educational research and assessment at Harvard University where she is working to establish the Bok Center's new legacy of assessment and evaluation work, which seeks to integrate systematic and thoughtful self-reflection into the practice of teaching, curriculum building, and strategic planning. Bergeron hopes to assist the university move forward as it navigates new territory, helping faculty redefine how they teach and discover what and how students learn from the use of new technologies and teaching approaches being developed at the Bok Center and by faculty on the Harvard campus. She is a trained psychometrician with a research focus in educational psychology. She has over 10 years of experience working in higher education. Before coming to Harvard, she was the manager of assessment and evaluation at Stanford University. Bergeron has also served as an evaluator both nationally and internationally on projects for the National Science Foundation, the Western Association of Schools and Colleges (WASC), for state and for not-for-profit organizations.

Allison BrckaLorenz is a research analyst and project manager for the National Survey of Student Engagement and Faculty Survey of Student Engagement. In these roles she is involved in planning, administration, reporting, and client support for these large-scale national surveys of four-year college and university students and faculty. BrckaLorenz regularly assists participating institutions with the use of their data and results by consulting with a variety of audiences and participating in such activities as conducting workshops and training sessions. Assistance can range from the development of a research or assessment plan before the administration of surveys to the analysis of the resulting data and interpretation of reports to providing guidance in creating a culture of assessment. Her personal research has focused on the engagement of underserved minorities such as LGBTQ students, multiracial and biracial students, or transgender and gender-variant students, and the professional development and effective teaching practices of faculty and graduate students. She earned her PhD in higher education from the University of Iowa.

Timothy S. Brophy is director of institutional assessment at the University of Florida and professor of music education. Brophy joined the University of Florida in 2000, became assistant dean for research and technology in the College of the Arts in 2009, and assumed his institutional assessment role in the office of the provost in 2011. He holds a doctorate in music education from the University of Kentucky, a master's in music from the University of Memphis, and a bachelor's in music education from the Cincinnati College–Conservatory of Music. Brophy has published more than 40 articles and 8 books and has presented widely throughout the United States and abroad. He holds national and international leadership roles in assessment, served as a past national chair of the assessment special research interest group of the National Association for Music Education, and is the founding and organizing chair of the International Symposia on Assessment in Music Education (ISAME). He cofounded the first assessment, measurement, and evaluation special interest group for the International Society for Music Education. Brophy is the University of Florida's liaison to the Southern Association of Colleges and Schools Commission on Colleges (SACSCOC) and has served on the SACSCOC board of trustees as a chair of compliance and reports.

Tammie Cumming directs the Office of Assessment and Institutional Research for the City University of New York (CUNY)–New York City College of Technology and is an adjunct professor for graduate programs at the City University of New York Graduate Center and Hunter College. Cumming has provided educational research and assessment support services in higher education and at ACT, Inc. for more than 25 years and has been an invited speaker on educational assessment and accreditation on an international level, including Brazil, France, Lebanon, Qatar, Russia, United Arab Emirates, and the United Kingdom. She currently serves as an international program assessment workshop facilitator for ABET (formerly Accreditation Board for Engineering and Technology) and has recently served as a U.S. delegate for the Organization for Economic Cooperation and Development's assessment of higher education learning outcomes task force. She also holds an adjunct appointment at the CUNY Graduate Center and Hunter College. Cumming earned her PhD in applied statistics and psychometrics from the University of Iowa.

L. Jay Deiner is an associate professor of chemistry at the New York City College of Technology of the City University of New York (City Tech, CUNY). Since arriving at City Tech, Deiner has taught general chemistry and instrumental methods of analysis and has led development of a new bachelor's program in applied chemistry. He maintains an active chemistry research program in electrocatalytic materials and device fabrication. Deiner also pursues pedagogical research in application-based service-learning and the development of methods to teach scientific writing. His interest in assessment began with using assessment as a tool to better understand his own classes. Deiner's involvement with assessment has grown as his work in pedagogical methods development has progressed. He earned his PhD in chemistry from Harvard University and performed postdoctoral work at Harvard's Derek Bok Center for Teaching and Learning and at the Chemical Institute of São Carlos of the University of São Paulo, Brazil.

Peter T. Ewell is president emeritus of the National Center for Higher Education Management Systems (NCHEMS). A member of the staff since 1981, Ewell focuses his work on assessing institutional and higher education system effectiveness and the outcomes of college and involves both research and direct consulting with institutions and state systems on collecting and using assessment information in planning, evaluation, and budgeting. He has directed many projects on this topic, including initiatives funded by the W.K. Kellogg Foundation, the National Institute for Education, the Consortium for the Advancement of Private Higher Education, the Lumina Foundation, the Bill & Melinda Gates Foundation, the Spencer Foundation, and the Pew Charitable Trusts. In addition, he has consulted with more than 425 colleges and universities and 24 state systems of higher education on topics related to performance indicators and the assessment of student learning. He has authored or coauthored eight books and numerous articles on the topic of improving undergraduate instruction through the assessment of student outcomes. In addition, he has prepared commissioned papers for many state agencies and national organizations. A graduate of Haverford College, he received his PhD in political science from Yale University in 1976 and was on the faculty of the University of Chicago.

Deborah J. Harris, vice president of measurement research at ACT, Inc., is a nationally recognized scholar in the field of measurement. She is responsible for providing psychometric consultation and support for resident and contract programs and ensuring the effective delivery and communication of measurement and reporting services to external and internal customers. Harris has more than 30 years of experience in equating, scaling, and issues related to large-scale, high-stakes testing, such as context effects, domain scoring, and forensics research/cheating detection. She is also an adjunct at the University of Iowa and is the author or coauthor of more than 140 publications and presentations.

Thomas F. Nelson Laird teaches in the higher education and student affairs program at Indiana University Bloomington and directs the Center for Postsecondary Research. Nelson Laird's work focuses on improving teaching and learning at colleges and universities, with a special emphasis on the design, delivery, and effects of curricular experiences with diversity. He is principal investigator for the Faculty Survey of Student Engagement, a companion project to the National Survey of Student Engagement. Nelson Laird is author of dozens of articles and reports, and his work has appeared in key scholarly and practitioner publications. He also consults with institutions of higher education and related organizations on topics ranging from effective assessment practices to the inclusion of diversity in the curriculum.

M. David Miller is a research methodologist interested in psychometrics and large-scale assessment. Miller also serves as the director of Collaborative Assessment and Program Evaluation Services (CAPES) at the University of Florida. CAPES was established to support grant funding in the social sciences by providing expertise in evaluation, assessment, and research design. In addition, Miller has directed the development of the university's quality enhancement plan (QEP). The QEP is a required part of the Southern Association of Colleges and Schools accreditation. The QEP has developed a campus-wide initiative to enhance the learning environment for undergraduate students around the theme of internationalization. This initiative, Learning Without Borders: Internationalizing the Gator Nation, includes curricular enhancement, faculty training, a speaker program, cocurricular enhancements, and a new international scholar program. Miller has numerous publications and is a recognized measurement expert, authoring the 11th edition of *Measurement and Assessment in Teaching* (Pearson, 2012), a widely used textbook in teacher education programs. Miller is also the recipient of numerous National Science Foundation and U.S. Department of Education research grants.

Kimberly J. O'Malley is currently the senior vice president of education and workforce development at RTI International. Prior to this position and during the time she contributed to this book, she was senior vice president of school research at Pearson. She has more than 20 years of experience in psychometrics, research, and statistics and has built research teams in health and education. O'Malley has global experience in measurement, the use of technology to improve learning and assessments, predictive analytics, and research on system-level improvements in education. She has served as a member of various boards, committees, and service organizations in the United States, including the National Council on Measurement in Education (NCME), Council of Chief State School Officers (CCSSO), and the National Center for Education Research and Technology (NCERT). She has advised ministries of education in Brazil, China, India, Japan, and Singapore.

John P. Poggio is a professor of educational psychology and research at the University of Kansas teaching courses in measurement, evaluation, and statistical analysis. Poggio works with a research team on grants and contracts in areas involving human assessment in learning contexts, higher education admissions, course placement decisions, planning and conducting educational program evaluations, assessment needs for special populations and nontraditional audiences, and monitoring education improvement for education agencies. Central to this work has been the development and evaluation of testing systems that meet professional standards of validity, reliability, freedom from bias, test form equating, creation and evaluation of performance assessments, and establishing test performance standards. Poggio has worked to ensure links and vital connections among assessments, curriculum, and instructional approaches to create assessments that support and advance teaching and student learning. His work is breaking new ground, moving from traditional paper and pencil formatted/offered tests to a variety and array of computerized assessment systems. Poggio has served as an adviser on student testing and school accountability nationally and internationally. He has authored more than 200 papers, articles, technical reports, book chapters and tests, and a text on topics relating to testing, assessment, evaluation, and statistical analysis.

Terrel Rhodes is vice president of the Office of Quality, Curriculum, and Assessment and executive director of the Valid Assessment of Learning in Undergraduate Education (VALUE) at the Association of American Colleges & Universities (AAC&U), where he focuses on the quality of undergraduate education, access, general education, and assessment of student learning. He is also codirector of the annual AAC&U General Education Institute. Rhodes received his BA from Indiana University at Bloomington and his MA and PhD in political science from the University of North Carolina at Chapel Hill. Before moving into national higher education work, he was a faculty member for 25 years. Rhodes is a recognized expert in leading undergraduate curriculum development efforts, teaching public policy at the graduate and undergraduate levels, developing learning outcomes assessment plans, and forging interinstitutional collaborations with community colleges and high schools. Prior to joining AAC&U, he was vice provost for curriculum and dean of undergraduate programs at Portland State University and professor of public administration. He has received grant support from the Fund for the Improvement of Postsecondary Education (FIPSE); the State Farm Companies Foundation; the National Science Foundation, under the Louis Stokes Alliances for Minority Participation program of the National Science Foundation; the Bill & Melinda Gates Foundation; and the Lumina Foundation. Rhodes has published extensively on undergraduate education reform issues, public policy, and administration. His books and articles cover such issues as integrative learning, assessment, ePortfolios, high school–college connections, and public policies affecting urban American Indian communities.

Jon S. Twing is the senior vice president of psychometrics and testing services in the school assessment group at Pearson. He has more than 35 years of experience in psychometrics, research, and assessment development. Twing is focused on the development, validity, and efficacy of learning systems that integrate measurement and instruction. He is a member of the school assessment executive leadership team, focusing on improved student learning through better measurement. Twing has served as a member of various boards, committees, and service organizations, including the College Board Psychometric Panel, American Educational Research Association, National Council on Measurement in Education, Council of Chief State School Officers, Association of Test Publishers, and American Psychological Association. Twing is a member of the University of Iowa College education advisory board and sits on the board of directors for ACT Aspire LLC. Twing is also an honorary Oxford research fellow. He is Pearson's voice regarding assessment, research, measurement best practices, and legal defensibility of assessment.

Catherine M. Wehlburg is the associate provost for institutional effectiveness at Texas Christian University. She has taught psychology and educational psychology courses for more than a decade; she served as department chair for some of that time and then branched into faculty development and assessment. Wehlburg has worked with both the Higher Learning Commission of the North Central Association and the Commission on Colleges with the Southern Association of Colleges and Schools as an outside evaluator. In addition, she has served as editor of *To Improve the Academy* and is currently the editor in chief for the *New Directions in Teaching and Learning* series. Wehlburg regularly presents workshops on assessment, academic transformation, and the teaching/learning process. Her books include *Promoting Integrated and Transformative Assessment: A Deeper Focus on Student Learning* (Wiley, 2008) and *Meaningful Course Revision: Enhancing Academic Engagement Using Student Learning Data* (Wiley, 2006). She earned her PhD in educational psychology from the University of Florida.